25—

CHILDREN'S FILMS

CHILDREN'S LITERATURE AND CULTURE
VOLUME 12
GARLAND REFERENCE LIBRARY OF THE HUMANITIES
VOLUME 2165

Children's Literature and Culture

Jack Zipes, *Series Editor*

Children's Literature Comes of Age
Toward a New Aesthetic
By Maria Nikolajeva

Rediscoveries in Children's Literature
by Suzanne Rahn

Regendering the School Story
Sassy Sissies and Tattling Tomboys
by Beverly Lyon Clark

White Supremacy in Children's Literature
Characterizations of African Americans, 1830–1900
by Donnarae MacCann

Retelling Stories, Framing Culture
Traditional Story and Metanarratives in Children's Literature
by John Stephens and Robyn McCallum

The Case of Peter Rabbit
Changing Conditions of Literature for Children
by Margaret Mackey

Little Women and The Feminist Imagination
Criticism, Controversy, Personal Essays
edited by Janice M. Alberghene and Beverly Lyon Clark

Ideologies of Identity in Adolescent Fiction
by Robyn McCallum

Narrative Africa
George Henty and The Fiction of Empire
by Mawuena Kossi Logan

Transcending Boundaries
Writing for a Dual Audience of Children and Adults
edited by Sandra L. Beckett

Children's Films
History, Ideology, Pedagogy, Theory
by Ian Wojcik-Andrews

Russell Hoban/Forty Years
Essays on His Writings for Children
by Alida Allison

Translating for Children
by Riitta Oittinen

Children's Films

History, Ideology, Pedagogy, Theory

Ian Wojcik-Andrews

Garland Publishing, Inc.
A member of the Taylor & Francis Group
New York & London
2000

Published in 2000 by
Garland Publishing, Inc.
A member of the Taylor & Francis Group
29 West 35th Street
New York, NY 10001

10 9 8 7 6 5 4 3 2 1

Library of Congress Cataloging-in-Publication Data

Wojcik-Andrews, Ian, 1952–
Children films : history, ideology, pedagogy, theory / Ian Wojcik-Andrews.
p. cm.—(Garland reference library of the humanities ; v. 2165.
Children's literature and culture ; v. 12)
Filmography; p.
Includes bibliographical references and index.
ISBN 0-8153-3074-x (alk. paper)—ISBN 0-8153-3794-9 (pbk. : alk. paper)
1. Children's films—History and criticism. I. Title. II. Garland reference library of the humanities ; vol. 2165 III. Garland reference library of the humanities. Children's literature and culture ; v. 12

PN1995.9.C45 W59 2000
791.43'75'083—dc21

99-047804

Between the time Website information is gathered and the date of publication, individual sites may have moved or may no longer be active. Therefore, the publisher cannot guarantee that the Websites listed herein are still accessible at the URL provided.

Printed on acid-free, 250-year-life paper.
Manufactured in the United States of America

To Roberta, Eric, Ryan

Contents

Series Editor's Foreword

Dedicated to furthering original research in children's literature and culture, the Children's Literature and Culture series includes monographs on individual authors and illustrators, historical examinations of different periods, literary analyses of genres, and comparative studies on literature and the mass media. The series is international in scope and is intended to encourage innovative research in children's literature with a focus on interdisciplinary methodology.

Children's literature and culture are understood in the broadest sense of the term *children* to encompass the period of childhood up through late adolescence. Owing to the fact that the notion of childhood has changed so much since the origination of children's literature, this Garland series is particularly concerned with transformations in children's culture and how they have affected the representation and socialization of children. While the emphasis of the series is on children's literature, all types of studies that deal with children's radio, film, television, and art are included in an endeavor to grasp the aesthetics and values of children's culture. Not only have there been momentous changes in children's culture in the last fifty years, but there have been radical shifts in the scholarship that deals with these changes. In this regard, the goal of the Children's Literature and Culture series is to enhance research in this field and, at the same time, point to new directions that bring together the best scholarly work throughout the world.

Jack Zipes

Series Editor's Foreword

Acknowledgments

Many people at Eastern Michigan University helped me with the preparation of this book. Thanks go to Professor Henry Aldridge at the Collegium for Advanced Study for allowing me to present my research in its early stages. Professor Marcia Dalbey at the Department of Language and Literature granted me a sabbatical leave (1996–97). Colleagues such as Audrey Beisel, Ledia Dittberner, Gina Stough, Akosua Slough, Jennifer Szabo, Geoffrey Kroepel, Kenneth Kidd, and Craig Dionne lent me articles, made suggestions, nodded approvingly as I talked endlessly about children's films, and generally helped me in various ways. Many of the ideas in this book first saw the light of day in Eng 450 and Lit 207, two of the children's literature classes I teach at Eastern Michigan University.

Beyond Eastern, the various editors at Garland Press—Marie Ellen Larcada, Kristi Long, James Morgan, Maria Zamora, and series editor Jack Zipes—were most helpful. My thanks go to Johns Hopkins University for permisssion to reprint "Telling Tales to Children: The Pedagogy of Empire in MGM's *Kim* and Disney's *Aladdin*" from *The Lion and the Unicorn*. The essay was coauthored with friend and colleague Professor Jerry Phillips.

I would also like to thank Mary Corliss at the Film Stills Archive in the Museum of Modern Art for the photographs reproduced in this book, for being kind, patient, and helpful, and for answering my questions about film stills and permissions with promptness.

Not all academic work is done in academia. Accordingly, thanks must also go to Vera, Dee, John, Sheryl, Edith, Vicky, and Bill for their encouragement, enthusiasm, and patience. Thanks also to the folks at Dom's.

List of Figures

PART ONE

Introduction

What Is a Children's Film?

> *[First], we explore the idea of cinema for children. This term can mean simply the exhibition of films for a general audience containing some children; it can also mean the dedicated production of films for children. By "children" we mean people under the age of about twelve.*
>
> —BAZALGETTE AND STAPLES, 92

The above quote about the idea of children's cinema and film comes from a 1995 essay entitled "Unshrinking the Kids: Children's Cinema and the Family Film." The essay is in an anthology called *In Front of the Children: Screen Entertainment and Young Audiences.* The quote prompted me to explore the "idea of cinema for children" from several perspectives. Accordingly, the following six areas of discussion—personal, pedagogical, critical, textual, institutional, and cultural—are intended merely as forays into the "idea of cinema for children," signposts indicating the direction in which future research might travel.

PERSONAL

My own understanding of children's films grew out of various personal experiences. One day my then eight- and five-year-old boys Eric and Ryan came home from school declaring they had outgrown *Barney, Sesame Street, Lamb Chop, Reading Rainbow, The Land Before Time, Ferngully, Fantasia, Home Alone* and *Home Alone 2: Lost in New York,* and were now old enough to watch instead cartoons such as *The Power Rangers, The Centurions, Captain Planet, Dragon Ball Z, Swat Cat, Beavis and Butthead,* and *South Park,* and films such as *Free Willy, Batman, Batman Forever, The Mask, Ace Ventura: Pet Detective, Terminator 2: Judgment Day,* and *Starship Troopers.* For Eric and Ryan, appropriate viewing no longer meant children's shows such as *Sesame Street,* but films for older viewers such as *Scream.* For Eric and Ryan, the idea of children's films included some decidedly adult movies.

With this transition from *Barney* to *Beavis and Butthead* and from *Sesame Street* to *Starship Troopers,* my home became a domestic war zone! Fiery questions about how repeated exposure to scenes involving killing, maiming, shooting, punching, kicking, cursing, and ridiculing produces violent children exploded around the house. For a time, the war being fought on the ideological battleground of ideas otherwise known as children's media was also being fought in our living room! At times it seemed as though the Cold War had returned disguised as the Culture War!

Because of these heated exchanges, Eric and Ryan probably have seen more films in the past few years, but also have been subject to more explanations about what children's films teach than most young people. Whether or not the movies they have seen, from *The Birth of a Nation* to *The Seventh Seal, Blank Check,* and *Cinema Paradiso,* to *Last Action Hero* and *What Dreams May Come,* from *Parents* to *Matilda* and *Harriet the Spy,* and the accompanying analyses (religion, the afterlife, race, intertextuality, and class) have done them immeasurable harm or incalculable good time alone will tell: either that or the psychiatrist![1] Regardless, they know that a critical knowledge and a keen eye are everything and that to know something about a film is to know something about how society sees them and how they might in turn see society.

Sean French thinks about the "idea of cinema for children" in terms of fatherhood, violent film content, and point of view. French argues that "Fatherhood has had no effect on my political views" (8) except in one regard. French says that he can now "barely tolerate the [violent] use of children as victims in fictional films on television or in the cinema" (8). French now divides violent films starring children into "those I saw before and after becoming a father" (8). Before fatherhood, French used to think Nicolas Roeg's 1973 *Don't Look Now* (based upon a short story by Daphne du Maurier) "was a great film" (8), even though it "begins with a little girl drowning" (8). Now, however, the serious injuries inflicted upon Sally Ryan (played by child actress Thora Birch) in Philip Noyce's *Patriot Games,* for example, greatly upsets him.

French further admits that, whilst the violence committed against the young girls in *Don't Look Now* and *Patriot Games* disturbs him, from his point of view, several of his "favorite films are about children in danger" (8). French cites *The Window* (1949)—"One of the best B-films ever made" (8)—and *Night of the Hunter*—"the most frightening film ever made" (8)—as enjoyable but violent. French also adds that *Night of the Hunter, The Wizard of Oz,* and *E.T.* try to "show the world from a child's point of view" (8). These films "take children's fears and blow them up big. A child could watch all of these (in theory, I mean) and share in their mood" (9). French offers no solutions to these contradictions—violent films starring children are personally repugnant yet personally attractive—except to say that the issue of definition is a "real and important subject" (8).

One wonders what French, whose article was published in 1992, would make of films like *Lolita* (Adrian Lyne's 1996 remake of Stanley Kubrick's 1962 adaptation of Vladimir Nabokov's 1955 novel), *A Time To Kill* (1996), which begins with the rape of ten-year-old Tonya Hailey, or Vincent Ward's *What Dreams May Come* (1998). *What Dreams* begins with the death of siblings Marie (Jessica Brooks Grant) and Ian Nielsen (Josh Paddock), and also with the deaths of their devoted mother and father Annie (Annabella Sciorra) and Chris (Robin Williams).

Reading French against the grain, perhaps he is really defining a children's film not so much in terms of personal experience (fatherhood), content (levels of violence), or point of view—does *Dead Calm* or *The Wizard of Oz* present or misrepresent a child's point of view and how can you tell—but in terms of canonicity. *Night of the Hunter, The Wizard of Oz,* and *E.T.* are canonical films. *Dead Calm* and *Patriot Games* are not. The former are considered classics. The latter are considered commodities. Furthermore, most films children and young viewers see contain violence. Is the violence in *Aladdin, Salaam Bombay, Virtuosity, Ransom, A Time To Kill, Face-Off,* and *Smilla's Sense of Snow* acceptable or unacceptable? Are *Barney* and *Sesame Street* acceptable because they contain *no* violence? Perhaps the violence of film content rather than the violence of film form depends less upon personal preference and more upon generic context. As every child knows, cartoons are notoriously violent, literally death-defying, but immensely enjoyable nonetheless, and one of the few genres kids of all ages view repeatedly.

PEDAGOGICAL

In class, I suggest to my students at Eastern Michigan University that one way of reflecting upon "the idea of cinema for children" might be through Mark Crispin Miller's 1996 article in *The Nation* called "Free The Media." In this article, Miller points out that, contrary to what it may seem today, there is in fact a "contracting media cosmos" (9) in which giant corporations like General Electric, Time Warner, Westinghouse, *and* Disney/Capital Cities control most of today's news divisions and major film studios, including those that make children's films. In his article, Miller points out that General Electric owns, among other things, the National Broadcasting Company (NBC). He shows that Time Warner owns Seagrams as well as Home Box Office (HBO), Turner Pictures, and Warner Brothers and that Westinghouse owns Columbia Broadcasting System (CBS). According to Miller, Disney/Cap Cities owns Touchstone Pictures, Miramax Films, ESPN, ESPN2, the Mighty Ducks, American Broadcasting Corporation (ABC), the Disney Channel, theme parks like Disneyland, Disneyland Paris, Tokyo Disney, and Disney stores around the world.

As a result, Miller claims, we live in a National Entertainment State, whereby entertainment, including children's entertainment, is not freely given to consumers, but is in fact closely controlled, monitored, and sold to young consumers according to the demands of the corporate world. The entertainment kids see is that which the corporations deem profitable.

One way consumers might fight back, or free the media from the stranglehold put on it by big business, Miller argues, is to create "industry-specific maps [that] show [exactly] who owns each culture industry: the newspapers, the magazines, the book business and music business, cable, radio and the movie studios" (10). For Miller, maps connecting specific corporations to particular media outlets allow consumers not just to navigate the superinformation highway more efficiently but also to know who to demand better programs from, including programs for the young.

In this context, the following map shows something of the inroads Sumner Redstone's Viacom, not included in Miller's map, has made into children's entertainment, including children's films. Even this partial map shows the general direction in which Viacom is heading: the exporting of American children's entertainment around the world. As such, for Viacom, children's entertainment is clearly a product that, if packaged correctly, can be sold to young consumers in both developed and developing countries (see Figure 1).

CRITICAL

Works of children's film criticism, such as Douglas Street's *Children's Novels and the Movies* (1983), have made valuable contributions in the past to the ongoing debate about the "idea of cinema for children." Street's introduction to *Children's Novels* defines a children's film as one adapted from a classic work of children's literature. For Street, there are three kinds of canonical children's fiction: those conceived for a child audience, those written for an adult audience, and those seminal works

Figure 1. Viacom Map, Facts and Figures[2]

---

*1998 revenues of $12.1 billion
*an operating budget of $1.7 billion
*a global reach of over one hundred countries
*over five hundred thousand copyrights
*Viacom owns Blockbuster, Paramount Pictures, MTV, Nickelodeon, Wonderland, Nick. Jr., VH1, www.SimonSaysKids.com, Comedy Central, and so forth, all of which connect to children's entertainment at some juncture

Paramount Pictures
Harriet the Spy, The Indian in the Cupboard,
Ferris Bueller's Day Off, Rugrats
Europe Asia United States Africa Australia

Nickelodeon Television
Nickelodeon exists in over one hundred countries, including
Turkey, Australia, Latvia, Belarus, Russia, Kazakhstan, etc.
United States Japan Hungary Brazil Europe
Phillipines Middle East

Blockbuster Videos
Blockbuster operates six thousand stores in
twenty-seven countries around the world
Asia Australia New Zealand United States Europe

"energetically adopted by young readers" (xiv). Street then argues that it is "The timelessness and imaginative richness of . . . truly great literary works attracts filmmakers decades apart" (xxi). In other words, for Street, canonical works of children's literature attract filmmakers and are adapted into the movies. A children's film is so defined.

But what of *Jurassic Park,* for example? *Jurassic Park* was adapted from Michael Crichton's novel. After it became a film, it became a picturebook entitled *Welcome to Jurassic Park* (1993). The picturebook was adapted by Mike Teitelbaum from a screenplay by Michael Crichton and David Koepp that was based on the original novel by Michael Crichton!

Other examples that show how films children see are not necessarily based upon renowned works of children's literature that have stood the proverbial test of time include newspaper comic strips and comics. Bob Thomas's *Disney's Art of Animation: From Mickey Mouse to Beauty and the Beast* recounts how, back in the early days of the twentieth century, newspaper comics were the basis for the first animated drawings. Talking about the history of animation in the years prior to Walt Disney, Thomas writes that "Many of the early cartoon characters were lifted intact from newspaper comics: John Foster's *Katzenjammer Kids,* Jack King's *Happy Hooligan,* Raul Barre's *Mutt and Jeff,* Leon Searl's *Krazy Kat* and *Ignatz Mouse* (28) were all adapted to cartoon. These newspaper comics were classics of their kind but surely not classics of children's literature!

Think here also of *Skippy,* a 1930s film with child star Jackie Cooper, that was adapted from a comic strip, or *Bon Voyage, Charlie Brown (And Don't Come Back),* a 1980s adaptation of the "Peanuts" comic strip. *Skippy* (and its 1931 sequel *Sooky*) and *Bon Voyage* are obviously good children's films, but are they just as obviously good children's literature? In short, not all films young viewers in the United States see are adapted from canonical works of children's literature, so defined as those that stand the test of time. Not all canonical works of children's literature are adapted into film.

In "Toward Supreme Fictions," Peter Brooks writes: "If we begin by asking what we mean by "children's literature," the indefinition and ambiguity of our subject is immediately apparent. We probably don't mean literature by children, though this would be a rich field for investigation (as, for instance, in the case of the Bronte children). But do we mean literature read by children, or literature written for children. The two are not coterminous" (5). Similarly, Perry Nodelman in *The Pleasures of Children's Literature* discusses eleven traits that typically yet problematically define children's literature as a genre. For example, in a section of *The Pleasures* entitled the "Children's Literature Is About Childhood," Nodelman writes, "We can conclude neither that all children's literature is about children nor that all books about children are children's literature" (81).

Defining children's cinema and film is similarly difficult. Just as there is "literature written by children," "literature read by children," and "literature written for children" (Brooks 5), so there are G-films made for children (*Hansel and Gretel: An Appalachian Version*), PG 13-rated films made about children and childhood (*Radio Flyer, Stand By Me, Radio Days, Au Revoir les Enfants*), and R-rated films children see, regardless of whether or not they are children's films (*Robocop, Starship*

Troopers, Spawn, Alien Resurrection, The Relic, Mimic). To paraphrase Nodelman: Not all children's films are just about children and not all films children see are just children's films. Defining a children's film, and thus the child viewer said films presuppose, is something of an impossibility.

TEXTUAL

This is not to see children's films as devoid of any defining textual characteristics. Quite the contrary. In *Women's Pictures: Feminism and Cinema,* Annette Kuhn defines a classic realist film, generally the kind produced by Hollywood and otherwise known as mainstream or dominant, as organized according to a "classic disruption-resolution narrative structure" (258). Countercinema, on the other hand, is "Cinema which operates against, questions, and subverts dominant cinema, usually on the levels of both signification and of methods of signification and of methods of production, distribution, and exhibition" (258). Linear and teleological, mainstream films are structured according to a traditional, Aristotelian narrative pattern: There is a beginning, middle, and end. A beginning disruption or conflict forces the hero or heroine on a physical or psychological journey. Upon completion of the journey, said conflict is resolved. Like canonical fairy tales, mainstream films generally end happily ever after: One, starring Drew Barrymore, is even called *Ever After* (1998)! Unsurprisingly, mainstream films privilege the heroic actions of the individual rather than the heroic actions of the collective: Plot and setting, for example, are subordinated to character development and character development is subordinated to the requirements of the narrative, itself subordinated to the costs of film production. Mainstream films reflect the status quo, even when they least appear to support it. Produced by the dominant institutions of capitalism, they recapitulate capitalism's dominant ideologies. Countercinematic films, as the term suggests, contest the production, distribution, and exhibition values of mainstream films and the dominant society that produces them. Countercinematic films have much less rigid narrative structures. Often the narrative structure consists of cyclical or loosely structured thematic vignettes. The action of countercinematic children's films—if action is the right word—often takes place in real rather than movie time.

Borrowing from Kuhn, children's films financed by corporate Hollywood can be defined by the way that are organized according to a "classic disruption-resolution narrative structure" (258). As in children's literature, the initial disruption is often caused by the death of a family member or close friend. In *Bright Eyes* (US, 1934), for example, Shirley Temple's character, Shirley Black, loses both parents, the father in an airplane crash, the mother in a car crash. *Stand By Me* (US, 1986) begins with writer Gordie Lachance (played by Wil Wheaton as a child and Richard Dreyfuss as an adult) learning about the death of his best childhood friend, Chris Chambers (played by River Phoenix). In *The Cement Garden* (UK, 1992), both parents die, the father from a heart attack, the mother from grief at her husband's death. In *Angels in the Outfield* (US, 1994), Roger's mother and JP's father are both dead. Roger, who is eleven years old, and JP, who is slightly younger, live in a foster home. *Fly Away Home* (US, 1996) begins with a violent car accident in which thirteen-year-old Amy Alden's mother is seriously injured. After the mother dies in hospital, Amy, played by Anna Paquin from *The Piano* (New Zealand, 1993) lives with her estranged and eccentric father (Jeff Daniels).

Children literally orphaned or merely separated from their parents for whatever reason are often adopted by other friends and adults into a surrogate family. In *Bright Eyes,* Shirley is adopted by Loop Merritt (James Dunn). At the beginning of *Angels in the Outfield* (1994), Roger (Joseph Gordon-Levitt) and JP (Milton Davies, Jr.) are living in the foster care of Maggie Nelson. At the end of the movie, George Knox (Danny Glover), the manager of the ailing California Angels, adopts both Roger and JP. In *The Lion King* (US, 1994), Simba (voiced by Jonathan Taylor Thomas and Mathew Broderick) is adopted by Timon (Nathan Lane) and Pumba (Ernie Sabella). In *Salaam Bombay* (India, 1988), Krishna (Shafiq Syed) is abandoned by his family. Homeless, Krishna travels to Bombay where the members of his surrogate family include a pimp (Baba, played by Nana Patekar), a drug addict and pusher (Chillum, played by Raghubir Yadav), and a peasant girl.

Bright Eyes and *The Lion King,* like so many Hollywood films, end happily ever after. In the former, Shirley, Loop, and Adele Martin constitute a nuclear family. In the latter, Simba assumes his rightful place as king. Order, harmony, and balance are reestablished. *Salaam Bombay,* like so many non-Hollywood films, ends tragically. Krishna's surrogate family disintegrates and he is left alone, abandoned to the slums of Bombay. *The Lion King* concludes with the birth of a child. *Salaam Bombay* concludes with the death of innocence.

The disruption so characteristic a feature of the beginning of most children's and young adult films, mainstream or countercinematic, often has little to do with a parent. Consider two extremely different films, one for young viewers and the other for older viewers: *You Lucky Dog* and *Kids.* Disney's *You Lucky Dog* (1998) begins with the death of Mr. Windsor, whose $64 million fortune is subsequently inherited by his dog. Larry Clark's *Kids* (1995), produced by Disney/Capital Cities subsidary Miramax, begins with HIV-positive Telly (Leo Fitzpatrick) forcing a young girl (played by Sarah Henderson) to have sex with him. Soon thereafter, another of Telly's conquests, Jennie (played by Chloe Sevigny), discovers that she, too, is HIV-positive, because she succumbed to Telly's predatory sexual advances. In both films, as in most children's literature, parents play minor roles.

Films starring younger and/or older children characteristically begin with a disruption, a physically or emotionally violent event that propels the child forward on a journey. Journeys are indeed a further characteristic feature of films either starring children or aimed at child audiences.

Of course, whilst most children's films have child protagonists embarking upon a journey, not all of the journeys upon which the child protagonist embarks are the same: different films show different journeys. *The Bicycle Thief* (Italy, 1948) has working-class Italians Antonio (Lamberto Maggiorani) and his son Bruno (Enzo Staiola) search for their stolen bicycle in the city. Hector Babenco's searing portrait of homeless children, *Pixote* (Brazil, 1981), has Pixote (Fernando Ramos de Silva), a ten-year-old boy abandoned by his family, wander the streets of Sao Paul in search of friendship. Countercinematic, *Pixote* unflinchingly dwells on the grim details of Pixote's life: abandonment, prison, rape, drugs, theft, and eventually murder. *Pee-Wee's Big Adventure* (US, 1985) has Pee-Wee Herman (Paul Reubens) take to the road when his bicycle is stolen.[3] The similarities between these films end there, of course. Whereas *The Bicycle Thief* is a generally considered a masterpiece of Italian neorealism, *Pee-Wee's Big Adventure,* directed by ex-Disney animator Tim Burton, is generally considered a masterpiece of American postmodernism.

Playfully or seriously, mainstream and/or countercinematic children's films contain moments of self-awareness or self-discovery that lead to equally important moments of choice. Certain scenes in other words show protagonists, male or female, heterosexual or homosexual, confront what are obviously pivotal situations in which life itself appears to be held in the balance and make what they feel are appropriate decisions. In Disney's *Beauty and the Beast* (US, 1991), intelligent and attractive Belle consciously decides not to marry the arrogant and conceited

Gaston (Richard White) with whom all the other girls nonetheless flirt. And later Belle knowingly exchanges her freedom for her father's imprisonment when she learns that he is held captive deep in the Beast's castle. Despite their completely different backgrounds, schoolgirls Evie (Laurel Holloman) and Randy Dean (Nicole Parker) consciously pursue a lesbian relation in Maria Maggenti's *The Incredibly True Adventure of Two Girls in Love.* Toward the end of Mira Nair's *Salaam Bombay,* Krishna sees a pimp named Baba (Nana Patekar) violently arguing with his prostitute wife Rekha (Aneeta Kanwar). Krishna stabs Baba. Horrified, Rekha and Krishna leave the apartment only to be engulfed and ultimately separated by the swarming crowds outside attending a religious festival. Seeking refuge down a deserted alley, Krishna, abandoned by society and barely eleven, stares into the camera and weeps.

As in canonical works of children's literature such as C. S. Lewis's *The Lion, the Witch, and the Wardrobe,* a defining characteristic of children's films and children's culture in general is the presence of an alternative world. This is unsurprising given that "Childhood is often seen as another world" (Bazalgette and Buckingham 1). Thus, in children's films, child protagonists usually find themselves transported (disruption), willingly or unwillingly, to another place from whence they must ultimately escape in order to make the trip home (closure). In *The Wizard of Oz* (1939), Dorothy's dream involves being transported from drab and boring Kansas to colorful and exciting Oz. In *E.T.,* the arrival of E.T. from outer space in the opening scenes quickly establishes the presence of space as an alternative world. In *Jumanji,* adapted from Chris Van Allsburg's brilliant picturebook of the same name, and defined as an "in-your-face kiddie spectacular with plenty of noise, hectic activity, and dizzying special effects" (*Movie Guide* 337), a magical boardgame transports the kids back through time to the jungles of Jumanji. In *The Secret Kingdom,* young siblings Mark and Kelly find an alternative world beneath their kitchen sink when a lightning bolt strikes.[4]

Often the child's body *itself* is the source and scene of exploration, discovery, and transformation. Indeed, the presence of the child's body *as* the alternative world is a characteristic feature of films starring children and films aimed specifically at children, though here again there are incredible variations on a theme. Not a children's film but a film about childhood, *The Exorcist* has twelve-year-old Reagan (Linda Blair) possessed by the Devil and in desperate need of an exorcism by Father Merrin (Max von Sydow). Reagan has changed from a sweet, innocent child to a raving monster possessed by the devil. She spews vomit and curses at Father Merrin: Hence the need for the exorcism. The scenes in which Reagan's tortured and possessed body slowly and eerily rises from the bed, her blood-soaked head twisting 360° (alluded to most recently in *Toy Story*), and the scenes in which she masturbates with a crucifix, remain shocking.[5] Less controversially, in *Big* (1988), one of a number of body-switching films from the 1980s that can surely be defined as children's films, Josh Baskin (Tom Hanks), a kid, finds himself walking around in a thirty-five-year-old man's body. Francis Ford Coppola's 1996 *Jack* (PG-13) also has a boy in a man's body, ten-year-old Jack (Robin Williams), as a forty-year-old man.[6] Mulan's body, domesticated or rebellious, dressed or undressed, in male or female clothing, close-up or long shot, is obviously the focus of *Mulan.* No doubt for younger and older viewers, the charm of *Tarzan* (1999) is watching Tarzan's body physically and emotionally change, grow, and develop from feral child raised in the savage jungle to adult citizen raised in civil society.

A further way of defining a children's film is through the issue of metafilmicity. In "Metafiction, Illustration, and the Poetics of Children's Literature," Geoff Moss first distinguishes between canonical children's books such as *Charlotte's Web* and *The Wind in the Willows* that "unproblematically fit into the category" (45), and children's literature and books by Robert Cormier, Alan Garner, Jill Paton Walsh, and others that do not fit the definition of "fiction for children" (45), even though they are often taught in children's literature classes. Acknowledging the work of Roland Barthes, Moss calls these latter texts "writerly" (quoted in Moss 45). Moss then argues that writerly texts are often metafictional, defined by Patricia Waugh as writing that consistently displays its "conventionality, which explicitly lays bare its conditions of artifice, and which explores thereby the problematic relationship between life and fiction" (quoted in Moss 46).

Just as children's literature is often metafictional, children's films as different as *The Three Caballeros, Stand By Me, Life of Brian, Last Action Hero, North,* and/or *Toy Story* might be defined by their metafilmic qualities, those that suggest innovation, experimentation, and a high degree of playful self-consciousness. These and other films draw attention to themselves as artifice by playing with the various filmic conventions and extrafilmic practices that constitute cinema as a whole, including children's cinema. In the process, they contest the very definition of what constitutes a children's film. They situate themselves within a category they themselves resist and blur a debate of which they themselves are the focus. To borrow from Jameson, these and other children's films offer a "commentary [which is] at the same time a metacommentary as well" (5).

On the one hand, Rob Reiner's R-rated *Stand By Me* (US, 1986) is a successful adaptation of Stephen King's partly autobiographical short story *The Body.* Upon hearing of his friend's death, Gordie Lachance, played by Wheaton as a young boy/writer and Richard Dreyfuss as an older man/writer, thinks back to his childhood and the adventures they had together as kids. Particularly, the film looks back to when they went searching for the dead body of a local, neighborhood kid named Ray Braur. When the film was released in 1986, it was a box-office hit, earning $22 million upon release and introducing child stars such as River Phoenix, Wil Wheaton, and Corey Feldman. Reiner followed *Stand By Me* with films like *When Harry Met Sally* (1989), *North* (1994), and *Ghosts of Mississippi* (1996).

On the other hand, *Stand By Me* is as much about one man's personal story as it is the way in which stories are told and give rise to other stories. Like Cormier's *I Am the Cheese,* or any other postmodernist work of young adult fiction that contests the very category—young adult fiction—it is supposed to represent, *Stand By Me* is a story about the fictionality of film. *Stand By Me* draws attention, in other words, to its own artificiality. In the film's opening scenes we meet writer Gordie Lachance who has just learnt of the death of his friend, attorney Chris Chambers. Pensive, reflective, Gordie sits motionless in his car in a quiet country lane. By his side, a 1985 newspaper headline from *The Oregonian* reads: "Attorney Chris Chambers Fatally Stabbed in Restaurant." An off-screen narrator's voice, whom we assume is Gordie, says: "I was twelve going on thirteen the first time I saw a dead human being." With this comment, the film takes us back in time to Gordie's childhood in Castle Rock, Oregon and the summer in which he and his childhood friends, Chris, Vern, and Teddy went looking for Braur's body. This opening sequence sets viewers of in numerous directions. First, there are the opening scenes of the movie we are watching that show us Gordie thinking about his friend's death. Second, there is the newspaper article that prompts Gordie's thoughts, but that also encourages us to read about Chris's death (the disruption that begins the film). Third, the voiceover then begins another story, that of Gordie's childhood memories with Chris. In short, we are watching, reading, and listening to not one but three stories. To adapt the title of Salman Rushdie's recent book, *Stand By Me* contains a sea of stories.[7]

Once *Stand By Me* has returned us to Gordie's childhood, the film continues to concern itself with the telling of stories. For example, whilst looking for Ray Braur, Gordie, Chris, Teddy and Vern camp out one night. Gordie (an allusion to a young Stephen King), a twelve-year-old boy who wants to be a writer, tells Chris, Vern, and Teddy the story of Davy Hogan, otherwise known as "Lard-ass Hogan" or simply "Wide-load," who entered a pie-eating contest not to win but to get revenge over his audience, many of whom had spent years ridiculing his enormous weight. Hogan's revenge involves eating so many pies he throws up over the audience who, disgusted, vomit over one another. Wave after wave of regurgitated blueberry pie washes over Hogan's audience. When Gordie finishes his tale about Davy's "complete and total bafarama," Teddy, Chris, and Vern become literary critics, deconstructing Gordie's ending and thus effectively making Gordie's story "writerly" rather than "read-erly." Chris comments that the story "was the best, just the best." Teddy, rather more critical of the ending and wanting more, asks Gordie: "Then what happened . . . What kind of an ending is that . . . What happened to Lard-ass?" Gordie, ever the patient storyteller, appeases Teddy's obvious discomfit with the original ending by inventing another: "Maybe he went home and celebrated with a couple of cheeseburgers," Gordie remarks. Teddy, however, insists upon completely rewriting the ending: "Why don't you make it so that Lard-ass goes home, shoots his father . . . and joins the Texas Rangers. How about that?" Vern rewrites the beginning rather than the ending of the story, commenting: "But there's one thing I didn't understand. Did Lard-ass have to pay to get in the pie contest?" By the end of this discussion, Gordie's original story has almost been completely rewritten—which of course challenges the idea of an originating story.

That *Stand By Me* incorporates within itself an ongoing discussion about the way in which stories, including the story that is *Stand By Me,* get told, is further suggested by the fact that Gordie is not *Stand By Me*'s only storyteller. To counteract the stories of his father's abusiveness, Teddy compulsively tells the story of how his father "stormed the beaches at Normandy." Clearly, for Teddy, stories function therapeutically. Chris tearfully confesses to Gordie how he was wrongly punished for stealing the school's milk money. Chris tells Gordie that he returned the money to one of the teachers who subsequently bought new clothes. Chris's story of personal remorse and class betrayal by those whom he once respected is brilliantly told and acted by River Phoenix. At the end of the film, when they finally find the dead body of Ray Braur, it is Chris who comforts a distraught Gordie with the knowledge that there are

Figure 2. Rob Reiner's *Stand By Me,* with River Phoenix (*l*) and Wil Wheaton (*r*). Photo: Museum of Modern Art/Film Stills Archive, New York. Courtesy of Columbia Pictures.

more stories to tell: "You might even write about us guys if you get hard up for material" (see Figure 2).

Chris's prophecy comes true. In the film's closing scenes, Reiner leaves the 1950s and brings us back to the 1980s where we find the previously downcast Gordie, having returned home from the country lane where we first met him, writing on his computer the story he has just told and we have just seen.

Similarly set up as a movie within a movie, John McTiernan's PG-13/15 *Last Action Hero* (US, 1993) has cineaste Danny Madigan (played by Austin O'Brien) magically thrown into the filmic world of action hero Sergeant Jack Slater. Like Woody Allen's PG *The Purple Rose of Cairo* (US, 1985), whereby characters step out of the film into the real world of the audience, Danny crosses over from the real world into the film world of Jack. As *Last Action Hero* moves back and forth between real and fictional worlds, so Danny and Jack solve various mysteries, murders, and other drug-related crimes. Toward the end of *Last Action Hero,* Jack is shot. With the help of a magic movie ticket, Danny returns Jack to his own fictional world. Danny returns home to the real world.

Last Action Hero self-consciously draws attention to its own filmicity, its sense of itself as a filmic construction. Once inside the fictional world of action-hero Jack Slater, Danny finds he must convince Jack of his own fictionality (just as Woody in *Toy Story* must convince Buzz Lightyear of *his* own fictionality). Danny must convince Jack that he is an action-hero starring in an action-adventure movie. Midway into the movie Danny thinks of a scheme. Knowing full well that action-adventure movies are generally rated PG-13 or PG-15, Danny writes down a word (presumably a curse word) and asks Jack to say it. Inevitably, Slater refuses because excessive swearing is not allowed in action-adventure movies. In other words, through Jack's refusal (ironically, a denial of action in an action movie) the film draws attention to the fact that his adventures are part of a movie and that his words, or lack of them, are part of a movie script written according to the needs of a targeted audience. Jack cannot swear even if he wanted to because he is an actor in a film bound by the generic conventions that limit the possibilities for certain kinds of speech utterances. Certain words are permissible in action-adventure movies, others are not.

Throughout *Last Action Hero,* Danny in fact self-consciously and self-mockingly offers a metacommentary on the conventions of the action-film genre and whether or not those generic conventions are observed or ignored. The audience is invited to play along with the game. For example, corrupt police officer John Practice (played by F. Murray Abraham) insists upon talking as he prepares to kill Jack (Jack and Danny are eventually rescued by a cartoon character). What Jack sees as potentially tragic (not knowing he is in a movie he thinks they are really about to die), Danny sees as potentially comic (knowing he is in a movie, he knows they are really about to live). Danny knows that he and Jack will escape because talking before killing (speech before action) is a "classic movie mistake" made by a "typical villain."

These metafilmic issues, whereby children's films playfully and self-consciously raise the question of what kids are and are not allowed to see or say, can be found in movies as different as *North* (1994), *Jurassic Park* (1993), and *Toy Story* (1995). Winchell (Mathew McCurley), supposedly North's friend, organizes a revolution on behalf of oppressed children everywhere, whilst North travels around the world looking for new parents. As the all-powerful Winchell and North's ambulance-chasing attorney Arthur Belt (Jon Lovitz) discuss their future political strategy in a massage parlor, Winchell, playing the role of the crooked journalist/gangster surprisingly well, remarks to Belt: "And as of next

Monday no parent will be permitted to see an R-rated movie unless accompanied by a kid."

Self-conscious self-censorship exists in animated movies such as Disney/Pixar's *Toy Story.* Andy has been given Buzz Lightyear as a present. Woody, Andy's favorite toy until the arrival of Buzz, is jealous. Exacerbated by the attention directed at Buzz, at one point Woody comments: "Look, we're all very impressed with Andy's new toy." Buzz challenges the way Woody defines him as a toy. "Toy," Buzz queries. "T-O-Y, toy," Woody replies. Not giving in, Buzz says: "Excuse me. I think the word you're searching for is "Space Ranger." Woody sarcastically replies, "The word I'm searching for, I can't say, because there's preschool toys present." *Toy Story,* like *Last Action Hero,* playfully defines the kind of language permissible in a film watched by people "under the age of about twelve" (Bazalgette and Staples 92).

INSTITUTIONAL

Beyond these textual matters, corporate video stores like Hollywood Video and Blockbuster Video, the latter owned by Viacom, predetermine what constitutes a children's film or video. For example, the Kids section of my local Hollywood Video contains *Winnie-the-Pooh, Sing Along Songs, Sesame Street,* and *Mister Roger's Neighborhood,* as well as *Muppet Treasure Island, The Swan Princess: Escape from Castle Mountain* (1997), *Pippi Longstocking, Mighty Ducks the Movie: The First Face Off, The X-Men,* and *The Mighty Morphin Power Rangers.*

Less corporate, more independent companies such as Facets Video sell catalogs that contain sections on children's films. Here, one finds the usual fare such as *Beauty and the Beast, Free Willy,* and the like. However, Facets Video also lists foreign children's films, those that star children and those that are about childhood and young adulthood. Thus, alongside reviews of *Ponette* (France, 1996), one finds information about videos such as *Anne Frank Remembered* (GB/US, 1995), *Acla's Descent into Floristella* (Italy, 1987), *Flight of the Innocent* (Italy, 1993), and *Street Kid* (Germany, 1991). Whilst not all of these films are appropriate for children, the lists demonstrate how differently American and European directors view film and children. Marx says, "the educator himself needs educating" (*Theses* 12). Facets Video provides an important source of information for teachers interested in children's films.

The debate about how one might define a children's film is ongoing within Hollywood itself. In "Film Studios Find PG-13 Can Be Golden,"

Amy Wallace notes that more and more executives have recognized that movies aimed at kids are financially lucrative. Wallace cites John Cywinski, for example, who argues that "Seven, eight- and nine-year-olds are seeing more PG-13 films than ever before" (quoted in *The Ann Arbor News,* E2). Amy Pascal of Columbia Pictures argues that because kids are raised these days on Nickelodeon and the Cartoon Network, "Stuff that's more babyish doesn't appeal to them anymore" (*The Ann Arbor News* E2). As a consequence, studio executives are increasingly concerned to obtain a PG-13 rating. According to the logic of the studio chiefs, films like *Armageddon, Men in Black, Lost in Space, Godzilla, Deep Impact,* and so forth are PG-13 children's films that have in mind a specific image of the child: that of a consumer.

Peter Weir's *The Truman Show* has brought several of these issues into focus. Talking to Susan Stark of *The Detroit News,* Weir notes that "Back in 1995, when we were preparing the project, it was . . . Scott Rudin who asked me if I knew Jim Carrey, who had been mostly in children's films—ah, I should say broad comedies" (quoted in *The Detroit News* C1). According to Stark, *The Truman Show* is the film "that's going to expand Carrey's audience outside the realm of "children's films—ah, broad comedies" (C1). According to this logic, Jim Carrey's previous films, *Ace Ventura: Pet Detective, Ace Ventura: When Nature Calls, The Mask,* and *Liar, Liar,* are children's films because they contain plenty of "flatulence gags" and "wild verbal and physical outbursts" (C1)! Children's films are so defined.

CULTURAL

Culture, and the economics of culture, have affected children's cinema. Whilst exploring the "idea of cinema for children . . . under the age of about twelve" (92), Bazalgette and Staples point out that not long after the cinema emerged as an important cultural activity for adults and kids alike, "On both sides of the Atlantic the idea of a specialised cinema for children began to take firm hold . . ." (93). They quote a 1936 editorial from *Sight and Sound,* which called for the "provision of children's films and children's cinemas just as there are children's books and children's libraries" (94). However, cultural and economic factors soon came into play. In America "the notion of specialised production for such a small audience . . . was [considered] just bad business" (94). In the United States, children's cinema evolved into the family film. Children in the United States see G, PG, and PG-13 films from the "Disberg stables" (93) such as *Hook, An American Tail,* and *Beauty and the Beast.* Meanwhile, in Europe the culture of state subsidies kept a fledgling children's cinema alive. In Iran, for example, government funding in the form of state subsidies or grants and agencies such as the Institute for the Intellectual Development of Children and Young Adults produce films like *Khane—ye Doust Kodjast? (Where Is My Friend's Home?)* (1987). According to Bazalgette and Staples therefore, when thinking about the "idea of cinema for children" one must distinguish between "the family film (essentially American) and what they call 'children's films' (essentially, but no longer exclusively, European)" (95).

According to Bazalgette and Staples, a central difference between American and European children's films, between *Hook* and the Danish *Mig og Mama Mia* (*Me and Mama Mia*) (1989) begins with "casting" (95). In the United States, children who appear in family films must be perfect. They must have star appeal as well as "sexual appeal" (95). It should be added that they also must have commodity appeal: They must make money for studios such as Warner Brothers and Paramount and their owners Time Warner and Viacom. One thinks of child actors such as Shirley Temple, Jane Withers, Macaulay Culkin, Anna Paquin, Ashley Olsen, and Mary-Kate Olsen. By contrast, the "children's film movement in Europe has always held that the child protagonists in a children's film should *not* be desirable moppets" (95). Here, one thinks of Enzo Staiola in *The Bicycle Thief,* Jesus Navarro and Alma Fuentas from *Los Olvidados* (1950), and Fernando Ramos da Silva from *Pixote* (1981).

Bazalgette and Staples write, "That children's cinema—and cinema generally—should be so thoroughly dominated by American companies seems perfectly natural in the United States, as one would expect. That it also seems perfectly natural in many other countries is the outcome of a cinematic cultural imperialism that has been energetically promoted throughout the twentieth century" (97). In other words, most children's cinema around the world is synonymous with American children's cinema. American children's cinema dominates the children's cinema market: hence the term "cinematic cultural imperialism" (97). That is, with the help of perfect child stars, American children's films sell around the world: *The Little Rascals* was released in the United Kingdom, the United States, Portugal, Spain, and Sweden at the same time. *Jurassic Park* was released in the United Kingdom, the United States, France, Germany, Netherlands, Australia, Singapore, Spain, Sweden, Norway, and Finland! By comparison, striving for cultural realism and aesthetic legitimacy, these same European countries make films that, with a few noticeable exceptions, do *not* sell around the world. Even films such as *Burnt by the Sun* (Russia, 1994) or *City of Lost Children* (France, 1995) that make it to the United States, though relatively successful—they grossed $2.8 million and $1.5 million respectively—make little money compared to, say, *Star Wars Episode 1: The Phantom Menace.* This film grossed $64.81 million on its opening May weekend. Put another way, like Ford, General Motors, and Chrysler, who make globocars, transnational American corporations such as 20th Century Fox, Time Warner, Disney/Capital Cities, Viacom, DreamWorks SKG, and Pixar make globo children's films.[8] Stated differently, owned by Viacom, Paramount Pictures's *Forrest Gump* and *Mission Impossible* "generated more box-office receipts internationally than in the U.S., and *Forrest Gump* broke pay TV sales records in numerous territories" (Viacom 1)—note here the substitution of "territories" for "countries." According to Viacom, Nickelodeon is now seen in more than one hundred countries around the world but few indigenous children's programs from Europe are seen regularly in the United States: The commercial traffic in films and filmic images of the child is largely one way.

CONCLUSION

There are in fact many ways of thinking about the "idea of cinema for children" including the way in which we might define a children's film. It's a complicated issue and involves a range of personal, pedagogical, critical, textual, institutional, and cultural/imperial points of view. There are films aimed at children, films about childhood, and films children see regardless of whether or not they are children's films. There are "children's films," but there is no such thing as a "children's film," regardless of what one might think watching *Return of the Jedi, A Bug's Life, Tarzan, Babe: Pig in the City, Back to the Future, Willy Wonka and the Chocolate Factory, The Princess Bride, The Wizard of Oz, Mighty Joe Young, E.T., The Rugrats Movie, The Lion King, The Goonies,* and *Baby Geniuses,* according to the Internet Movie Database website, the fifteen most popular kids movies searched today. Indeed, any attempt to universalize children's cinema, a children's film, or the nature of the child viewer, only reveals more closely the contradictions in which children's cinema finds itself situated. For example, American children rarely see children's films that contain a degree of "frankness about sex" (98), as in the case of *Mig og Mama Mia,* but have full access to R-rated movies and television shows such as the *Jerry Springer Show, Beavis and Butthead,* and *South Park,* shows critiqued as unsuitable for children because of their strong sexual content. Bazalgette and Staples remark, "Thus the hypocrisy of our society's much-vaunted concern for children and the sanctity of childhood is exposed" (108) through the "idea of cinema for children . . . under the age of about twelve" (92). Children's cinema and film indeed offers a metacommentary on film and society. Clearly, we need to talk more about the idea of children's cinema by situating children's films in their critical, historical, ideological, and pedagogical contexts. In the words of Jill May, "Film deserves a good deal of serious discussion" ("Audio-Visual Arts" 5).

NOTES

[1]Children's films in which psychiatrists play a role range from *Bright Eyes* to *Harriet the Spy.*

[2]The information that comprises the following map is taken from Viacom's website, www.viacom.com.

[3]Unsurprisingly in children's films, or films starring children, bicycles play important roles: think here of films like *The Bicycle Thief* (parodied in 1989 by Mauricio Nichetti's *The Icicle Thief*), *Pee-Wee's Big Adventure, E.T., Breaking Away, Milk Money, The Pagemaster, Last Action Hero,* and so forth. In *The Bicycle Thief,* for example, the search for the stolen bicycle (the disruption that initiates the narrative) is important, but so is the ensuing relationship between the father and son. In *Pee-Wee's Big Adventure,* the bicycle obviously means everything to Pee-Wee. The theft of the bike (disruption) sets Pee-Wee on a journey across America that ends only when the bike is found (resolution). The racing bike in the 1979 *Breaking Away,* starring Dennis Christopher as the working-class racing enthusiast Dave, is literally the means by which Dave wins a race against a group of middle-class university riders and symbolically the means by which he finds direction and purpose in a relatively mundane life with an over-protective but kindly mother and an authoritarian but well-meaning father. The multiple themes of growing-up, identity, class consciousness, parental authority, winning, and so forth are deftly woven together by English director Peter Yates, who came to Hollywood in the 1960s (having earlier directed television episodes of *Danger Man* and *The Saint*) and made award-winning films such as *The Deep* (1971), *Breaking Away* (1979), and *The Dresser* (1983). *Last Action Hero*'s most obvious homage to famous movies such as *E.T.* is the young rider/bike scene shot against a night sky and a silver moon.

[4]A defining feature of children's films as a genre is the motif of a lightning bolt that completely disrupts ordinary life (disruption) and leads to extraordinary events: Think here of *Home Alone, Back to the Future, The Pagemaster,* and so forth. On the one hand, the lightning bolt functions as a convenient plot device. It allows the director to split the story into three parts: those mundane, realistic

events leading up to the lightning strike, the dreamy, supernatural events that follow after the lightning strike, and the return to everyday life (resolution) at the end of the movie-the "happy ever after" ending. Variations on a theme would include *Jurassic Park, Jumanji, Angels in the Outfield,* and so forth. In *Jurassic Park,* a powerful storm that includes clashes of thunder, torrential rain, as well as blinding flashes of lightning, destroys the park's electrical systems which in turn set free the prehistoric animals. The end comes when the prehistoric animals are killed, the kids emerge alive from the destroyed park and are transported out of the Eden-turned-fallen world in a helicopter with their surrogate family, the doctors, the mathematician, and the grandfather.

Not only do children's films contain bolts of lightning thrown down from above, as in the case of *Fantasia,* that seem to strike animals and humans below at the most opportune moment, they also contain the opposite: beams of light. If the lightning strike signifies the beginning of cataclysmic change, a radical departure from the norm, the beam of light (*Land Before Time*) signifies the end of the disruption and the gradual return to normality. The appearance of the beam of light suggests that the journey of the protagonist is about to end, usually happily. Even in Adrian Lyne's 1990 *Jacob's Ladder,* the ghostly, heavenly appearance of Jacob's dead son (played by Macaulay Culkin) at the end signifies the release of ex-Vietnam Veteran Jacob's tortured, guilt-ridden soul to heaven—and thus the end of the movie (see also *Ghosts*).

The archetypal and biblical contexts for these oppositional but related motifs—the lightning strike and the beam of light—are clear. The bolt of lightning suggests an angry, Old Testament God displeased with the direction in which the human race seems to be traveling. This is made explicit in *The Pagemaster.* Sent by his father to buy some nails—in Campbell's archetypal terms this represents an example of the mythological hero answering the call to adventure and confronting his first test—Richie Tyler (again Macaulay Culkin) is prevented from going to the store by the local kids and has to go the long way round (stray from the path) to reach his destination. Instead he enters a dark tunnel—a return to the womb, the whale's belly, and so on—only to reemerge (rebirth, resurrection, and so on) in a fantasy land (unconscious) from which he must eventually escape in order to return home and, now a man rather than a boy, live happily ever after. The beam of light, in this instance the rise of the morning sun, suggests a more benevolent, New Testament God willing to accompany the transfigured child on his or her journey through life providing the child reciprocates with the appropriate gestures of servitude and gratitude. See Joseph Campbell, *The Hero with a Thousand Faces* 2nd ed. (Princeton, NJ: Princeton University Press, 1968).

[5]*The Exorcist* is important in any discussion of children's films because it raises so many child-related and cinematic issues. That the profanities uttered by Reagan, the throwing up of vomit, and the masturbation with the crucifix are actually spoken and done off-screen by Mercedes McCambridge and Eileen Dietz, doesn't diminish the power of the scenes or the importance of the issues.

Whilst it is not a children's films, and probably shouldn't be seen by children, it certainly stars a child—but then so do numerous other contemporary horror flicks kids get to watch such as John Carpenter's *Halloween.* Perhaps *The Exorcist* is less shocking today. Still, the British Board Film Classification (BBFC) continues to ban the release of the movie on video because "We also know that religious imagery is powerful for girls of around 12 to 15 . . . This film treats [religion and evil] seriously . . ." (Ferman quoted in Kermode 10). For a fuller discussion of *The Exorcist,* see Mark Kermode, "Lucifer rising," *Sight and Sound* July 1998: 6-11.

[6]Other body-switching children's films from the 1980s and 1990s would include those from the *Honey, I Shrunk the Kids* franchise.

[7]See Salman Rushdie's *Haroun and the Sea of Stories.*

[8]In an article called "The Daimler-Chrysler Deal: Here Comes the Road Test," Barrett Seaman and Ron Stodghill II argue that we live in an era of globo-cars because companies like DaimlerChrysler and GM/Opel/Saab operate in eighty-seven and 150 countries respectively. The fact that many children's films from corporate Hollywood are released around the world means we also can say that we live in an era of globo children's films.

PART TWO

Criticism

Taking Stock: The Politics of Children's Film Criticism[1]

This chapter does not attempt to survey all the works of children's film criticism published since 1895, which is clearly an impossibility. Some works get a fuller treatment than others and a further elaboration on individual theories of children's film criticism like Marxism or feminism can be found in Part Four: Ideology. I simply survey the landmark works of children's film criticism published in virtually every major film period since the silent era (1895–1927), and point out the broad critical, social, and cultural trends out of which those landmark works emerged. I want to take stock of the politics of twentieth-century children's film criticism.

MORAL 1910–20s

Set against the general intellectual, social, political, economic, and ideological turmoil that led to World War I (1914–18) and the Russian Revolution of 1917, one of the first full-length works of children's film criticism was *The Cinema: Its Present Position and Future Possibilities Being the Report of and Chief Evidence Taken by the Cinema Commission of Inquiry Instituted by the National Council of Public Morals* (NCPM). The NCPM was a composite of "religious, scientific and educational leaders" (vi). As its name implies, the function of the National Council, "one of those unofficial organisations which are the pride of the English endeavour" (v), was to examine whether the fabric of society was still tightly woven together or beginning to unravel. In this regard, the NCPM in June 1916 had published the National Birth-Rate Commission's report on the "causes and effects of the declining birth-rate . . ." (v).

Encouraged by newspaper articles in the United Kingdom and America that praised the report's "candid . . . outspoken . . . and impartial" (v–vi) nature, the NCPM, when approached by the Cinematograph Trade Council, turned its (supposedly) disinterested moral gaze on the state of the cinema and its effect on children and formed the Cinema Commission of Inquiry (CCI). Consisting of upstanding members of the community such as Lord Bishop of Birmingham, the Rev. Principal Garvie, Mr. C. W. Crook from the National Union of Teachers, and Mr. A. Newbould from the Cinematograph Exhibitor's Association, the CCI, under the auspices of the NCPM, was charged with conducting an inquiry into the "physical, social, educational, and moral influences of the cinema, with special reference to young people" (ix). As Europe struggled with war, revolution, and unrest, the CCI began its work on January 8, 1917 and ended on July 9, 1917, three months before the Bolshevik Revolution (sometimes known as the October Revolution) and the ascendancy to power of Lenin and the Communist Party.

The Commission's opening statements are interesting because they reveal how influential cinema in general had become by 1917 at both the national and the international level. The Commission reports that no one would see the cinema as "ephemeral" (xxi), yet no one is fully aware just how "strong and permanent [a] grip" (xxi) the "picture palace" has on the country as a whole (except presumably the CCI). For example, according to the Commission, there were approximately 4,500 theatres in the British Isles in 1916 (xxi). Over the course of any given year, approximately 1,075,875,000, people visited these theatres (xxi). Five thousand new films were issued each year and the "various branches of the [cinematic] trade" (xxi) in the United Kingdom alone employed between eighty and one hundred thousand workers. The Commission then compares the movie industry to an "international circulating library business of which each country forms a branch station" (xxi). Thus, after the United Kingdom, films literally travel around the world, "from China to Peru" (xxi): There were globofilms long before there were globocars! The Commission well understood that by 1917, merely twelve years after its birth in 1895, the movie industry had grown into a global business.

As the Commission's report unfolds, it becomes clear that what Bazalgette and Staples call the "idea of cinema for children" (92) is no simple matter—even in 1917. For example, from a moral standpoint, the Commission is forced to confront the issue of indecent conduct. They recognize that there is indecent conduct within the theater, a moral evil that is "incidental to the picture house," and the relative indecency of the films themselves, a moral evil "consequential on the kind of film shown" (xxv). Furthermore, the Commission recognizes, "A still more difficult problem persists itself in the moral influence of the films displayed" (xxix), and concludes that "it is impossible to set up a rigid standard of judgement" (xxix). What one person considers unacceptable for children to see another might consider acceptable. Indecency is illegal, vulgarity is not. The Commission's members agreed that, whilst children and young viewers should not see pictures that "lower the standard of reverence for women" (xxx) and/or that obtrude "sensuality" (xxx), banning immoral movies completely "must be confessed practically impossible" (xxx), despite the fact that the Cinematograph Exhibitor's Association provided brief summaries of most films scheduled for release. Finally, the Commission realizes that, because 90 percent of the movies shown in British theaters originate in America, banning them would have serious economic repercussions within the British film industry. The Commission acknowledges that, whilst in order to protect children there was probably a need for "stricter censorship than has been exercised in the past" (xxx), economic matters ironically dictated a less strict policy, or at least the maintenance of the status quo.

From a social viewpoint, the Commission tried to deal with the charge that "the picture house is responsible for the increase in juvenile crime" (xxxiv) and that an increase in juvenile crime leads necessarily to the unravelling of an otherwise tightly woven social fabric. But most witnesses brought before the Commission offered evidence to reject the rather simple-minded cause/effect explanation that youngsters watching crime films turned youngsters to crime. One witness, for example, argued that there are a range of "economic and social changes due to the war" (xxxvii) that must be recognized as "factors in the increase in juvenile crime" (xxxvii). Others suggested that the increase in juvenile crime reflected the tendency in recent years to broaden the definition of juvenile crime. Finally, the Commission realized that the picture house, with its darkened halls and sometimes immoral films, is better than the streets for most kids. The Commission reports, "We must recognize that the picture house fulfils a useful and needful function amid social conditions which press very hard not only the very poor, but even on the bulk of the working classes" (xlv). For "tens of thousands of poor kiddies" (xliv) and the "teeming masses" (xlv), the only alternative to the picture house is the slums, the mean streets, and the public house "with its constant temptation of strong drink and its no less polluted moral atmosphere" (xlv). For the young, better the polluted picture house than the polluted public house.

The Commission's report includes a discussion about the educational value of cinema for the young. Among educational topics discussed are whether there should be separate performances for children,[2] whether purely educational films are worth showing, and whether noneducational films, that is, entertainment films, also are educational. Based upon the evidence presented, the Commission reported that preventing all children from attending the cinema and forcing exhibitors to provide separate performances of educationally accepted pictures for children was neither desirable or possible (who decides what is educationally acceptable). Also, disastrous economic consequences might ensue if an exhibitor showed an educational film before what the Commission calls a "film story," what would today be called a feature-length, or blockbuster, movie. As the Commission's report states: "A film, however beautiful, of the life-history of a plant or insect sandwiched between a Charlie Chaplin film and a thrilling episode of the *Exploits of Elaine* has little chance of survival" (lix). In other words, whilst educational films—today these would be nonfictional videos by National Geographic, for example—dealing with "Scenes in foreign lands, Historical incidents, Travel and adventure, nature study, Pictured plays and novels, Industrial and agricultural life, and Noteworthy events of the day" (liii) have "educational value" (liii), they stood little chance with young audiences from a recreational point of view. Overall, the Commission concluded that: "The moving picture is intensely exciting, intensely realistic, and can cover an amazingly wide field of information. But these very characteristics, which may make it such a powerful instrument for evil, guarantee its future possibilities as a potent instrument of culture" (lxviii).

In recognition of cinema's global reach, the Commission includes in its report an appendix detailing the censorship regulations applicable in other countries. The Commission thus provides a fascinating glimpse into what adults and young viewers around the world were allowed and/or not allowed to watch. For example, Russian films representing the emperor were allowed only with special permission. Films showing strikes were absolutely forbidden. Under the heading of pornography, scenes in Russian films of "love-making may be shown provided there be no sign of licentiousness therein" (315)! In New Zealand, the Cinematograph Film Censorship Act of 1916 forbade scenes "against public order and decency" (320). In the United States, the by-laws of the National

Committee on Films For Young People, which were adopted in 1916, similarly insisted on "furthering the use of better films for the family group . . ." (325). In Norway, Sweden, New South Wales, and so forth, similar restrictions were placed on what films could be shown and to whom. Movie theaters were only to show uplifting films, those taken from the "best stories and plays of the world's literature" (lxii), those that presented "high qualities, such as courage, self-sacrifice and generosity" (liii).

Set against the changes that were taking place in the early decades of the twentieth century, the Commission's report makes the following main points, each of which is based upon a thinly disguised moral politics. First, there is the recognition that cinema in general and children's cinema in particular is firmly embedded in the national economies of nations as far-flung around the world as France, America, and New Zealand and that, precisely because of this globalization, moral matters will always sit uneasily alongside economic matters: Censorship leads to unemployment. Second, the Commission recognized that, whilst the international traffic in films was good for business, there was a concern that films around the world over which they had no regulatory control could educate young minds in the ways of democracy just as easily as they could educate young minds in the ways of revolution—an appropriate concern given the events in Russia in 1917. Third, unsurprisingly, in the minds of Commission's contributors, canonical films were deemed positively beneficial (good films lead to democracy), whilst "silly and sordid melodrama[s]" (lxii) were decidedly harmful (bad films lead to communism). Fourth, behind the Commission's mask of neutrality and impartiality in fact lay a great deal of class bias and racial discrimination. The Commission argued that the theater, or picture palace, is a better place "for the poor child than the street" (lviii), the class-based assumption being that all poor children were working class and therefore homeless and in need of rescue either by uplifting works, in this case canonical films, and/or by moralizing sermons (church attendance). In terms of race rather than social class, the Commission was similarly biased. Whilst discussing the educational value of the film story, the Commission reported, "The cowboy and Indian films, which are immensely popular with school children, have merits peculiarly their own. They are crude, but they represent a lower standard of civilisation, and appeal so directly to the primitive instincts and emotions that their position is secure" (lxi). At this point, perhaps, the Commission's true purpose is revealed. If the Commission sees the poor and other ethnic minorities as existing at the lower end of the social scale, it is reasonable to ask who the Commission sees as existing at the higher end of the social scale. Throughout the report the answer is clearly the "normally constituted youth and maiden" (xxx), the "normal schoolboy" (lxi). This answer is perhaps unsurprising given the following motto of the National Council of Public Morals: "The Foundations of National Glory are set in the homes of the people. They will only remain unshaken while the family life of our race and nation is strong, simple and pure" (vi).

SOCIAL SCIENCE 1930s

Two main strands of children's film criticism developed in the 1930s. Both were quite different from one another and from what came before in 1917. First, in the 1930s, the Motion Picture Research Council/Payne Fund Studies (PFS) were important, for they introduce a scientific approach to studying the effect of the movies on young viewers born out of the desire to more fully understand the power of mass communications. Second, back in 1913, the film magazine *Photoplay* had began circulation with an issue on child stars. Novelist, essayist, and reviewer Graham Greene continued this aspect of children's film criticism in the 1930s by looking at one particular child star—Shirley Temple—with particularly controversial results.

Children and the Movies (1996) is a recently published book about the Payne Fund Studies. More accurately, *Children and the Movies* "began as a quest for a missing book" (13).[3] That is, whilst the Payne Fund Studies are generally well known, the various personal and political histories and filmic debates out of which the PFS emerged are not. This is because, according to the contributors to *Children and the Movies,* Garth S. Jowett, Ian C. Jarvie, and Kathyrn H. Fuller, the Payne Fund Studies were discarded soon after their publication in 1933 owing to Henry Forman's journalistic, popularized, antimovie summary of the PFS findings called *Our Movie Made Children* (1935). *Children and the Movies* is an attempt to put back together the pieces of the puzzle that constitutes the history of the "twelve-volume series Motion Pictures and Youth, more commonly referred to as the Payne Fund Studies (PFS)" (17).

Like the NCPM in 1917, the Motion Picture Research Council (MPRC), the administrative organization behind the PFS, was very interested in how movies affected young viewers. In particular, the MPRC was concerned with whether or not immoral movies (define a moral/immoral film) were responsible for social problems (define a social problem). Also like the NCPM, the MPRC contained a mixture of interested parties: religious individuals such as William Harrison Short worked alongside lay academics such as Professor W. W. Charters, research director for the Payne Fund Studies. Both the NCPM and the MRPC consulted the opinions of children and young viewers whilst conducting their research, a trend that continues today in such works as Carole Cox's 1982 "Children's Preferences for Film Form and Technique." Methodologically and philosophically, both the NCPM and the MRPC were grounded in empiricist approaches to reality and language and mimetic theories of art.

Despite these similarities, there were a number of major differences between the NCPM and the MPRC. Whilst the NCPM included in its reports the firsthand observations of concerned citizens and various experts, the PFS, in the spirit of what they perceived to be the beginnings of "large-scale mass communications research" (*Children and the Movies* 2) systematically undertook a full and rigorous examination of whether the movies harmed children and thus, by extension, society as a whole. Moral rhetoric was to be replaced by scientific reporting that drew mostly from academic disciplines such as education, sociology, psychology, and so forth rather than anecdote. One contributor notes that rather than morality: "Facts were to be the effective rhetoric of reform" (118).

Children and the Movies reports that the PFS researchers met five times between 1928 and 1933. In each meeting, specific areas of research were assigned to specific researchers. In one of the first meetings, W. W. Charters was assigned to investigate the content of the films children see in an attempt to define what constitutes a good picture and, by implication, what constitutes a bad picture. In a 1929 meeting of the researchers, Charters employed Edgar Dale who "drew up a rather elementary list of major narrative themes" (75) any good film should include. Professor Christian Ruckmick and his assistants were assigned to study how children's emotions were affected by adventure films such as *Charlie Chan's Chance* or *The Feast of Ishtar.* To study the emotional impact of these and other movies on children, Ruckmick and his researchers in the psychology department at the University of Iowa "proposed attaching film watching children to heart monitors and psychogalvanometers to gauge suddenly accelerated heartbeats, blood pressure and galvanic resistance in children's skin associated with sweaty emotional reactions like excitement, arousal, fear and nervousness" (69). Children's beds were wired to study how films affected their sleep patterns (70). As a result of the 1930s meetings, youngsters in "isolated small towns" (75) were shown movies such as *The Birth of a Nation* to see whether or not their attitudes toward African-American and Chinese people changed because of the film. An equivalent study today might show kids "under the age of about twelve" films like *The Karate Kid, Rush Hour, The Indian in the Cupboard,* or *Air Force One.* Whether any more "isolated small towns" exist is debatable!

The members of the MPRC and the contributors to the PFS were not always wholly in agreement with one another. In fact, there were some sharp personal and political divisions within the MPRC that spilled over to the Payne Fund Studies. Short was primarily interested in moral issues and only sanctioned the social science approach of the PFS because he believed that science rather than rhetoric would conclusively prove to the population at large that movies generally corrupted the morals of young people and that consequently both the movies and young people needed censoring. By comparison, Charters was interested in scientific issues regardless of the outcome. Charters felt that the research function of the PFS was to measure scientifically how children were affected by the movies and publish the results regardless of what those results proved or disproved about the influence of the movies on children and society at large. Empirically tested and provable facts would shape public policy not religious dogma and moral rhetoric.

But in the history of children's film criticism, or criticism directed at films starring children, it is Forman's summary of the PFS, *Our Movie Made Children* (1935), that became popular, not the PFS work itself. Eschewing the social science methodologies preferred by Charters and his fellow academics for a more journalistic, popularized style of writing and presentation, Forman's successful book notes that though the movies have great potential—*Ben-Hur* "should be a source of pride to the industry" (Forman 2)—the "average is heavily weighted with sex and crime pictures" (275). In another example, Forman notes that, whilst "certain pictures have a socially desirable effect" (28), "crook and gangster and sex pictures" (280) are "most dangerous" (280). Given these generalizations, little wonder that Charters and his fellow researchers were reluctant to endorse Forman's study, which played to what people wanted to hear, not what the research indicated.

Forman's book was influential then and now. Summarizing the findings of the PFS in 1935, Forman argues that because "film is one of the most potent of all educational instruments" (3) children should see "commendable motion pictures . . . with exacting social standards" (2) such as *Ben-Hur,* and *The Hunchback of Notre Dame.* In a 1980s book such as *200 Selected Film Classics,* editors Francelia Butler, Phillip Sleeman, and Bernard Queenan argue along the same lines. They state, "A desperate need exists, then, for talented film writers to turn their attention to the wonderful material in the thousands of folktales of every ethnic group. . . . The second need in children's film programs is . . . to select from old books that have stood the test of time and that have been made into good films . . . that would be appealing and wholesome for each age group; grades K through 6, preteen and early teen, and young adults . . ." (7). Even the films Butler mentions are similar to those Forman cites: for Butler, "wholesome" films also include *Ben-Hur* (1959), *Abe Lincoln in Illinois* (1939), *The Hunchback of Notre Dame* (1939), and so forth.

Still, there are differences between, say, the work of Forman in the 1930s and Butler in the 1980s, differences that reflect changing social and historical conditions. Thus, continually looking for the slightest edge that will allow him to denounce the movies as immoral and antisocial, Forman writes that there are a "few indications" (221) that movies "play a part in female sex delinquency" (221). By comparison, each film Butler prescribes for students is assigned a thematic indicator: RKO Radio's 1939 production of *The Hunchback of Notre Dame,* for example, contains cultural, ethical and *feminist* (my emphasis) themes. Films such as MGM's 1939 *The Adventures of Huckleberry Finn* should be looked at for their cultural, ethical, and *racial* themes (my emphasis). The films remain more or less the same but, set against the background of the emerging identity politics of 1980s girl power and multiculturalism, the critical approach differs noticeably.

Taking a moral standpoint derived from the age-old unspoken authority of God and the King—in short, Protestant hegemony—the NCPM's 1917 report was published against the background of World War I (the United States declared war on Germany in 1917), the Russian Revolution, and other social and political changes: in 1918, for example, the Supreme Court rejected the Owen-Keating Child Labor Law of 1916 as unconstitutional, arguing that federal regulations restricting child labor violated the rights of individual states and parents. From a social science standpoint, the MPRC/PFS professional researchers and academics briefly rose to prominence in the late 1920s and early 1930s only to fade away given the rise to power in 1934 of the Roman Catholic Legion of Decency, the publication of Henry Forman's *Our Movie Made Children* in 1935 and Raymond A. Moley's reply, *Are We Movie Made?,* in 1938. Butler's work in the 1980s reflects the residual elements of what Zipes calls "the anti-Vietnam War movement and student protests of the late 1960s [which] along with the feminist movement and struggle for equal rights by various minority groups in the States and England during the 1970s, generated a fundamental change in attitudes toward childhood, children, and children's culture" (8). There have always been works of children's film criticism but each work is shaped by the particular historical conditions of the era.

Set against the background of both the Great Depression and the Hollywood star system, the 1930s is an important decade in the history of children's film criticism because of the publication of Graham Greene's reviews of Shirley Temple. Greene is perhaps best known for famous novels such as *Brighton Rock* (1938), *The Power and the Glory* (1940), *The Third Man* (1950), *Our Man in Havana* (1958), and *The Quiet American.* Less well known, but far more infamous, are Greene's reviews of Shirley Temple's films. In particular, Greene's review of *Wee Willie Winkie* in 1937 was controversial and resulted in a libel action brought by 20th Century Fox Film Corporation and Shirley Temple against Greene himself and the printer and publisher of *Night and Day,* the magazine in which the offending article first appeared. But what was the review all about? And to what extent does Greene's review suggest a new development in children's film criticism, the realization that not only do films and film stars affect children's behavior in both negative and positive ways, but that child stars themselves, particularly young female child stars, can affect adult behavior, particularly that of older men? These are, of course, related questions.

For the most part, Greene's two paragraph review of *Wee Willie Winkie* argues that Temple's "appeal is more secret and more adult" (233) than generally recognized. That is, among Temple's many admirers are "middle-aged men and clergymen" (234) who see in Temple something more than an innocent child dancing and singing her way through a film. In *Captain January,* men, particularly middle-aged men and members of the clergy, are attracted to Temple's Dietrichian "mature suggestiveness" (234). In *Wee Willie Winkie,* men in the audience are attracted to her "dubious coquetry, to the sight of her well-shaped and desirable little body, packed with enormous innocence" (234).

Greene had actually made the same point in an earlier review called *Under Two Flags/Captain January.* When *Captain January* was first released, Greene remarked that it was "sentimental" (128) but also a "little depraved, with an appeal interestingly decadent" (128). About Temple's popularity in general, Greene notes that it seems to "rest on a coquetry quite as mature as Miss Colbert's and on an oddly precocious body as voluptuous in grey flannel trousers as Miss Dietrich's" (128).

Why then did the studios seek libel action against Greene in 1937 when he published the review of *Wee Willie Winkie,* but not in 1936 with the review of *Captain January*? What is different about the two reviews? I think that the *Wee Willie Winkie* review incurred the wrath of 20th Century Fox not just because Greene pointed out that the "mask of childhood" (*Wee Willie* 234) was possibly only "skin-deep" (234), but because Greene makes explicit the link between the studios, the child stars the studios own, and the profit the studios derive from those child stars. Greene's review begins with the following comment: "The owners of a child star are like leaseholders—their property diminishes in value every year. . . . What is Jackie Coogan now but a matrimonial squabble?" (233). What irked the studios, in other words, was the fact that Greene compared them to leaseholders—and their child stars to property. Such a comparison situates the child star at the crossroads between economics and sexuality, what in a different context is called child prostitution with "middle-aged men and clergymen" (234) as paying customers.

In the history of children's cinema and film criticism, or at least criticism primarily directed at films starring children, Greene's reviews, particularly the one on *Wee Willie Winkie,* are obviously important. First, by looking at Shirley Temple herself, Greene temporarily shifted the emphasis away from what are basically circular arguments about whether or not immoral movies produced immoral kids to how kids in films affected adults in audiences. Second, albeit unintentionally, Greene opened up a relatively new area of study: that of the adult spectator, in this instance, "middle-aged men and clergymen" (*Wee Willie* 234), responding to apparently flirtatious child stars, in this instance Shirley Temple. Third, Greene's comments anticipate roughly the kind of arguments critics like Francis Clark Sayers in the 1960s and Laura Mulvey in the 1970s made about how the dominant, oedipal-driven, patriarchal gaze in Hollywood cinema (for Sayers it was Disney in particular, for Mulvey it was Hollywood in general) positions girls and women as objects of sexual desire. Fourth, Greene's comments foreshadow, in other words, the kind of discussions cultural critics like James Kincaid had in the 1990s about what Kincaid calls "allowable cultural pornography" (382).

CULTURAL 1950s

If moral, social science, and economic/sexual issues are the main characters in the history of children's film criticism up until the 1930s, from the 1950s onward a new protagonist enters the story: that of culture. Serious discussions about children and culture develop in a new direction in the 1950s with the publication of Margaret Mead's *Childhood in Contemporary Cultures* (1955). Not unlike Northrop Frye's *Anatomy of Criticism* (1957), Mead's book, and the essay within it by Martha Wolfenstein entitled "The Image of the Child in Contemporary Films," argues that, whilst there are many cultural differences among children around the world, there also are many similarities that can be studied synchronically rather than diachronically. These cultural similarities and differences, what another writer in *Childhood in Contemporary Cultures* calls "continuities and discontinuities" (Benedict 21), should be studied comparatively by researchers who should then look for patterns of behavior that fit "together to make a whole" (Mead 8)—much like Frye's attempt to fit all literary works into a single, unified theory of genre. For Mead, the theoretical models or disciplines that would accomplish this totalizing "interest in children in culture" (4) were a mixture of psychology, child-development research, and cultural anthropology—not morality. The moral issue did not disappear althogether. In the wake of the nuclear bombs dropped on Hiroshima and Nagasaki in the 1940s, it quickly became obvious that the problem was not violent movies but violent adults. The moral perspective lay low for a while as cultural issues emerged as dominant.

As an illustration of Mead's theories, Wolfenstein's essay considers a "series of contrasting images of children" (278) from 1940s and 1950s Italian, French, British, and American films. Noting that the cultural differences between Britain and America are "epitomized in the endings of [children's literature classics] *Oliver Twist* and *Huckleberry Finn*" (278), an argument that clearly anticipates Tony Watkins's 1992 use of *The Wizard of Oz* and *The Wind in the Willows* in "Cultural Studies, New Historicism and Children's Literature," Wolfenstein suggests that, whilst the images of the child in the Italian, French, British, and American films under discussion are different, each film nonetheless brings out that which is "common to the child protagonist of all four groups" (278), the child's Christlike sense of nobility and virtue. The predominant image of the child in Italian films is that of the savior. To support this argument, Wolfenstein examines films like *The White Line, Germany Year Zero, His Last Twelve Hours, The Bicycle Thief,* and *Without Pity.* Wolfenstein notes that in *His Last Twelve Hours,* a young girl saves her father by allowing him to achieve salvation. In De Sica's *The Bicycle Thief,* "it is the hurt look on the face of an innocent child which recalls an adult from the wrong path, or makes him aware of the depth of his fall from grace" (281). By contrast, French films tend to deal with the disappointments of childhood as in *The Seven Deadly Sins.* In British films, questions of trust between a child and an adult are paramount. For example, the theme of *The Fallen Idol* is whether or not the adult will "fall short of the child's expectations" (285). Wolfenstein reports that "In *The Browning Version,* a man's faith in himself depends on the genuiness of a boy's belief in him" (286). Finally, American films like *Shane* are characterized by the desire of the child "for an ideal man to appear from afar" (288). According to Wolfenstein "Children in the films of the four cultures considered . . . all have something in common" (291), a nobility often stronger than that of the adults with whom they interact.

There is a direct line of descent from Wolfenstein's 1955 "The Image of the Child in Contemporary Films" to Robin Wood's 1976 "Images of Childhood" and Kathy Merlock Jackson's 1986 *Images of Children in American Film: A Sociocultural Analysis.* Each situates the image of the child in contemporary films within a cultural context. Rather like Wolfenstein, Wood considers the image of the child in Italian, Swedish, American, and French films as an expression of the cultural concerns of those countries in the post-World War II era. As the title suggests, Jackson takes a sociocultural approach to the image of the child in American films from 1895 to the 1980s. More or less absent from these three works of children's film criticism are the kind of moral concerns that shaped the criticism of the National Council of Public Morals in 1917 and the social science concerns that shaped the criticism of the MPRC and the PFS in the 1930s.

FEMINIST 1960s

Set against the background of many of the major social and political and cultural developments of the twentieth century, including those that involve the arrival of contemporary feminist theory,[4] the 1960s sees the publication of one of the most famous post-World War II pieces of children's film criticism, one Lucy Rollin calls a "classic" (91). I refer of course to Frances Clarke Sayers's "Walt Disney Accused," an interview published in 1965 in the December issue of *The Horn Book Magazine.* More than thirty years old, "Walt Disney Accused" has matured well. It remains constantly discussed and endlessly cited, a touchstone of children's film criticism that brings together, albeit contentiously, a university academic, a public librarian, and an administrator.

"Walt Disney Accused," is an interview between Sayers, then Senior Lecturer in the Department of English (UCLA) and Charles M. Weisenberg, Public Relations Director of the Los Angeles Public Library.

Weisenberg was interviewing Sayers because earlier in the year she had written a letter to the *Los Angeles Times* complaining about Max Rafferty, California's then Superintendent of Public Instruction. Rafferty had earlier proclaimed Disney as one of the great American educators of the twentieth century. It is worth summarizing Sayers's attack on Disney—Rollin calls it a "personal blast" (91)—because as Weisenberg points out, educators and parents at the time were aghast that Sayers should so openly criticize Disney's mass-produced commercialization of the classic fairy tales.[5]

In her letter, Sayers first critiques Rafferty's "appraisal of Walt Disney as a pedagogue" as "absurd" (602). Sayers acknowledges Disney's "splendid films on science and nature" (602), but complains that his book adaptations of children's fairy tales, such as *Pinocchio,* for example, are debased, manipulative, and vulgar (602). Disney's books mutilate the tales, she argues. The illustrations are garish, the texts full of cliches. Finally, in the kind of language that recalls Graham Greene's remarks about Shirley Temple and foreshadows James Kincaid's observations in *Child-Loving* about children's bare "bottoms" (365), Sayers asks us to: "Look at that wretched sprite with the wand and the oversized buttocks which announces every Disney program on TV. She is a vulgar little thing, who has been too long at the sugar bowls" (602). In short, Sayers argues that Rafferty's encomium is thoroughly misplaced. What today we call "Disneyfication" is bad for kids.

Sayers develops these charges at length and more critically in the subsequent interview with Weisenberg. Sayers argues that Disney's picturebook adaptations of children's literature classics like *Mary Poppins, Treasure Island, Alice's Adventures in Wonderland,* and *The Wind in the Willows* are telescoped, reduced to "ridiculous lengths" and made very "obvious" (604). In relation to the illustrations in the books, Sayers argues that "a major crime has been committed" (605). Finally, Weisenberg quotes Rafferty's article which says that "Disney's . . . movies have become lone sanctuaries of decency and health in the jungle of sex, sadism and pornography created by the Hollywood producers. His pictures don't dwell on dirt. . . . The beatniks and degenerates think his films are square. I think they're wonderful" (quoted in Sayers 609). Weisenberg asks Sayers whether or not Disney's books, despite their shortcomings, aren't also "an oasis in a field of smut that fills the newsstands from one end of the city to another" (609). In a clever reply, Sayers replies that the only dirty book is one that falsifies life.

Overall, Sayers complains that Disney's film and book adaptations of the canonical children's fairy tales are overly simplistic and sentimental (A. Waller Hastings makes a similar argument in the 1990s), because they eliminate what is fundamental to an understanding not just of the original tales but of life itself: "a tragic tension between good and evil, between disaster and triumph" (610). Without these moral contrasts, the adaptations are just "sweetness and light," (610). Fed a steady diet of "sweetness and light" the mind of the child starves and, whilst a hungry mind might be good for marketing and merchandising, it is bad for morality and society. Subsequently, that which makes children's literature canonical and literary must be preserved even as educators like Rafferty welcome that which makes children's literature mass-produced and nonliterary.

Sayers's letter and interview are important in the history of children's cinema and film criticism for several, interconnected reasons. First, they challenge the generally favorable opinion the public had of the Disney Corporation in the 1950s and 1960s. Second, Sayers's criticisms can be situated in the context of what Toril Moi calls "Images of Women" feminist criticism. Third, Sayers's work looks back to Graham Greene and to some extent Martha Wolfenstein, but also forward to Jack Zipes and James Kincaid. Sayers's observation about Disney that it's all a "matter of merchandise" (605) surely foreshadows Zipes's discussion in *Breaking the Magic Spell* about the commodification and instrumentalization of fantasy by the culture industry. Fourth, a timeline in children's film criticism from the 1930s to the 1990s that is wide-ranging, eclectic, interdisciplinary, and increasingly political in that it refocuses the lens, as it were, away from the child to the adult, is important, because it goes some way toward establishing an authentic history of children's cinema and film, the subject of Part Three: History. We might adapt Eagleton's phrase here—"there is literature . . . there is criticism" (*Criticism and Ideology* 11)—and say that, because there is a history of children's film criticism, therefore there must be a history of children's films. Overall, Sayers's work occupies a central position in the history of children's cinema and film criticism.

IDEOLOGICAL 1970s

The progressive social and political changes of the 1960s—the civil rights, women's rights, and children's rights movments—evolved into the public policies of the 1970s and eventually began to shape children's literature criticism into what we recognize it as today. First, the Children's Literature Association (ChLA) was founded in 1971 by academics such as Francelia Butler, Anne Devereaux Jordan, Ben Brockman, Jill May, and others.[6] Formal panels on children's literature were introduced at the annual meeting of the Modern Language Association (MLA). Second, in conjunction with these developments, scholarly journals such as *Children's Literature,* the *Children's Literature Assocation Quarterly, Children's Literature in Education,* and *The Lion and the Unicorn* were founded. Journals such as *The Horn Book* had existed, of course, since the 1920s. The difference in the 1970s was an emergent belief that children's literature and related topics such as children's media should be studied and taught using feminist, Marxist, psychoanalytic, and other theoretical contexts. New Criticism did not completely fade away, as witnessed by the enduring presence of Rebecca J. Lukens's *A Critical Handbook of Children's Literature,* first published in 1976 and reprinted most recently in the 1990s. Still, criticism during the 1970s and onward was increasingly concerned with a text's ideological qualities.

Out of these important institutional and intellectual developments within the field of children's criticism, that look back to Sayers in the 1960s and forward to Kincaid in the 1990s, emerged Jack Zipes's 1979 *Breaking the Magic Spell: Radical Theories of Folk and Fairy Tales.* The book was indeed a turning point in the history of children's film criticism. It eschewed the moral, social science, and cultural anthropological approaches of previous critics like the NCPM, the MPRC, and Margaret Mead, though interestingly enough, in a 1987 *ChLA* article entitled "Fear of Faerie: Disney and the Elitist Critics," Lucy Rollin suggests that the criticisms of Disney by feminists and Marxists such as Jane Yolen, Kay Stone, and Zipes are "often more moral when they purport to be aesthetic" (90).[7] *Breaking the Magic Spell* courageously situated itself squarely in the Marxist tradition, particularly that of the Frankfurt School, to discuss questions of ideology.

ADAPTATION AND FILM HISTORY 1980s

Set against the right-wing, revolutionary political and ideological agendas of the Reagan and Thatcher administrations (back to basics in self, family, school, and society at large), the 1980s are particularly important in the history of children's film criticism. At the beginning of the decade, children's film criticism turned away from ideological, contextual approaches toward questions of adaptation. Thus, an important collection of essays by one of the major figures in children's film criticism during the early 1980s was *Children's Novels and the Movies* (1983), edited by Douglas Street. Each of the essays explores in some depth whether or not the film being discussed faithfully (or adulterously) adapts the essence of the literary original (back to the text, back to the family, etc). Adaptation issues were foregrounded in a 1982 special section of the *Children's Literature Association Quarterly* called "The Audio-Visual Arts and Children's Literature." For example, J. D. Stahl's "Children's Films: The Literature Connection," John Matoian's "Book to Film: The Process Explained" and Morton Schindel's "Working With Picture Book Artists in Adapting Their Work . . . - From Page to Screen" all discuss adaptational rather than ideological issues. Street's own article, "An Overview of Commercial Filmic Adaptation of Children's Fiction," came out in 1982.

A slightly different approach to children's film criticism emerged in the mid-1980s. It was Kathy Merlock Jackson's insightful 1986 book *Images of Children in American Film: A Sociocultural Analysis.* Jackson argued that film images of children should be studied from sociocultural perspectives.

With the exception of Jackson, whose book I want to return to momentarily, what Street and others in the children's literature community ignored at the time were the broader debates taking place in cinema studies and film historiography. What were those debates? Consider the following three quotes from David Shipman, Louis Giannetti, and William Palmer. Shipman writes: "I received a letter inviting me to write a history of the cinema" (9). Giannetti writes: "Film historians [today] scoff at the naive notion that there is *a* film history" (399). Palmer writes: "Social history, the major issues, and film history, the representation of those issues in motion pictures, constantly interact" (xii).

As these quotes suggest, the debate within cinema studies during the 1980s concerned how best to write a history of film. Shipman's comment suggests an attempt to write a single, complete, film history—a worthy goal. Giannetti's acerbic rejoinder suggests that totalizing histories of film are not impossible, just impossibly naive. How can a single historical overview incorporate within itself a discussion of all the films released and still treat them and the related filmic issues in depth? Ironically, such a wealth of general information about film history surely leads to an impoverished understanding of the history of film. Indeed, as the quote from Palmer, and the title of his book, *The Films of the Eighties,* suggests, the focus should be on detailed studies of specific periods-in his case, the 1980s.

What are essentially new historicist film studies emerged out of new historicist literary studies, itself a development within the politics of twentieth-century historiography. The study of history changed around the 1970s and early 1980s, changed irrevocably in part because important historical, social, economic, and political events like Thatcherism, Reaganism, Glasnost, Perestroika, and the end of the Cold War forced scholars to rethink traditional methods of historiography. History was being rewritten, likewise historiography, likewise film history and theoretical approaches to film. Tillyardian historiography was replaced by new historicism as exemplified and practiced by historians such as Michel Foucault and Hayden White, cultural anthropologists like Clifford Gertz, and literary critics like Stephen Greenblatt. Influenced by Marxist, feminist, psychoanalytic, structuralist and poststructuralist ideas, Greenblatt et al. tore down not so much the political barriers between Eastern and Western Europe but the academic and theoretical boundaries between, say, history, literature, criticism, and, eventually, film. As books like Veeser's *The New Historicism* (1989) and articles such as Tony Watkins's "Cultural Studies, New Historicism, and Children's Literature" (1992) point out: "New historicism [rendered] problematic the old critical distinction between literary text and history as foreground and background, renegotiating the relationship s between texts and other cultural practices within history" (Watkins 181).

Eventually, these debates spilled over to cinema studies and the writing of film history. Robert Ray, for example, argued that film finds itself "immersed" (6) in at least seven histories, those of technology, economics, competing commerical forms, filmmakers, other media, politics, and the audience. As a result, Ray points out, "[W]hat can a would-be film historian say?" (6).

A work of children's film criticism that more or less excludes the debates in film historiography is Street's overview of commercially successful adaptations of children's fiction. Acknowledging that his overview is neccesarily "superficial" (17), Street, in "An Overview of Commercial Filmic Adaptation of Children's Fiction," states that the historian of children's films, or rather what he calls "The attentive investigator . . ." (13), must in fact consider the growth of the two major mediums, or genres that constitute children's films per se: the live-action feature and the feature-length animated film, both of which developed simultaneously and "contributed immeasurably to the overall success of the commercial industry worldwide, and to the popularization . . . of literary gems glamorized by cinematic adaptation" (13). Street proceeds to do precisely that. Citing examples of films that relate to and exemplify the historical development of each medium. For example, Street notes that, during the 1930s, the only "artist to rival Disney" (13) was the Russian animatist Ptuschko, whose *Novil Gulliver* in 1935 and *The Little Golden Key* in 1939 suggested the "possibilities for successful filmic adaptation in animation of quality children's fiction" (13). Street points out of course that eventually Disney cornered the market because of his commitment to "artistic perfection" (14) and because of a number of significant technological developments made by the Disney Studios: Rotoscoping, for example. Street concludes his overview of the history of the animated film by briefly mentioning the controversy concerning the Disney Studios' adaptation of canonical fairy tales such as *Cinderella, Sleeping Beauty, Beauty and the Beast,* the domination of animation during the 1950s and 1960s by Eastern Europe, and the "rebirth of interest in the animated feature in America" (14) during the 1970s.

As well as briefly evaluating the history of animation, Street also hastily discusses feature length movies. Noting that, "The live-action feature based on children's fiction has a long heritage" (14), Street reviews the history of children's films in terms of when they were adapted from their original literary masterpiece. One of the earliest children's films according to Street was therefore Paul's 1901 *Scrooge,* an adaptation of Dickens' *A Christmas Carol.* Commenting upon the fact that after World War II, the major film companies and their child stars made numerous films for what at the time was considered a "family audience" (15), the remainder of Street's overview continues to list well-known, often classic movies, in relation to the period or year of their production and release: Cocteau's *Beauty and the Beast* is thus the "first true post-War cinema classic" (16), for example, whilst in order to outdo the ever increasing popularity of televison, "the sixties brought to the theatres a trio of high budget, musical adaptations led by Julie Andrews and the *Mary Poppins* crew" (16). The 1970s is noticeable for "nicely executed, unpretentious films" (16) like Lionel Jeffries 1971 adaptation of Nesbitt's *The Railway Children,* or the "pleasant though weak sequel to *Sounder,* directed by William Graham, *Sounder Part 2* . . . (16–17). Street concludes that "the medium is in for a commercially succesful and an artistically satisfying future" (17).

Though hardly concerned at all about the debates in cinema studies about film history, Street's essay nonetheless offers a useful starting point for the beginning student of children's film. Street raises, albeit briefly, questions concerning history, definition, technology, and ideology, for example, that do require answering. Street's essay suggests how the silent movies gave way to the talkies, how European animators succumbed to the technological and aesthetic demands of American innovators like Walt Disney, how literature gave way to film, which in turn gave way to television.

Like Street, Jackson more or less ignores the debates in cinema studies concerning film historiography. But unlike Street, Jackson acknowledges the need to situate the filmic images in an array of social and cultural (though not ideological) contexts. For Jackson, there is more to the image of the child than the image of the child. Noting that sociocultural works of film criticism have existed prior to the 1980s (she cites Siegfried Kracauer, Andrew Bergman, Martha Wolfenstein, and Robin Wood as examples), Jackson says that the value of sociocultural criticism is that it takes "film out of a vacuum and places it in the realm of history, politics, economics, literature, art, music, and other far-reaching cultural factors" (4). Jackson notes that "it is necessary to delve further into the relationship between children and the movies in order to determine how children—defined as pre-adolescents twelve years of age and under—have been portrayed in the movies, and how these portrayals reflect changing attitudes toward childhood and the historical trends in general" (8).

Still, although an extremely useful study, required reading for students of children's films, indeed, what Jackson ignores are the ideological contexts for the image of the child, precisely those that emerged as dominant in the 1970s. For example, whilst it may or may not be true that the image of the child as innocent dominates twentieth-century children's films, broader questions about that "innocence" remain: Whose reality does that image of innocence reflect? A middle-class reality? A working-class reality? Is the innocence of the child an ideological construct that attempts to mask, to gloss over, the truly dreadful experiences of children today? Recall that in his 1974 *The History of Childhood,* Lloyd deMause, quoting the following passage from Elizabeth Barrett Browning's *The Cry of the Children* (also a powerful silent-era movie that spoke out against child abuse), "Do ye hear the children weeping, Oh my brothers . . . ," writes that "The history of childhood is a nightmare from which we have only recently begun to awaken" (1).

Dudley Andrew intelligently argues in his influential 1984 *Concepts in Film Theory:* "One of the obvious duties of modern theory is to place more clearly the propositions of traditional theory" (11). Thus, just as Andrew neatly draws the distinction between traditional studies of film as exemplified by the formalism of Sergei Eisenstein and more modern approaches to the study of film as represented by the semioticism of

Christian Metz or the feminist psychoanalysis of Laura Mulvey, the historical break between these old and new approaches the social, economic, and political upheavals of the 1960s, I want to distinguish between an earlier, more traditional form of children's film criticism that was grounded in orthodox forms of historiography and mimesis and a later more contemporary form of criticism grounded in new historicist and poststructuralist forms of enquiry. The historical moment that marks the break between these different but not mutually exclusive ways of situating, interpreting, and perceiving the relationship between history and children's films is the early 1980s and the upheavals caused by the advent of Reaganism and the inexorable shift of the country away from the progressive liberalism of the immediate post-World War II period to the reactionary conservatism of the more recent past. That is, if Mitchell, Forman, and Greene mark the first wave, and Sayers in *The Horn Book* and Street, May, Nodelman, Cox, Stahl and others writing in the *Children's Literature Association Quarterly* mark the second wave of children's film critics reacting, albeit naively, to the coming of the Reagan years—liberal film critics talked about the adaptation of literature to film whilst conservative politicians talked about the adaptation of working-class lives to corporate culture—children's film critics like Kathy Jackson, Jack Zipes, Naomi Wood, Anne Morey and others, contributing to journals and books like *Children's Literature Association Quarterly, The Lion and the Unicorn, The Antic Art, Disney Discourse,* and *From Mouse to Mermaid* represent the third wave that situates children's films and the ever changing practice of children's film criticism within a formidable array of historical, cultural, and theoretical contexts most clearly articulated in the 1990s.

MEDIA STUDIES, CRITICIAL THEORY, AND BEYOND 2000

Several different trends have developed in children's film criticism between the previous decades discussed and the 1990s. First, overall there has been an acknowledgement of the importance of children's media studies, that theoretical model which allows critics to study television, advertisements, ratings, viewer responses, the production, distribution and reception of films, children's programming, and so forth. Second, critics recognize that whilst media forms aimed at children, including children's films, can and do bombard kids with traditional images and mainstream values, kids and teachers can fight back by being taught not just the politics of children's films (the place of children's films within the confines of the National Entertainment State) but the pedagogical, aesthetic, and historical role of independent films as forms of resistance to the dominant strain of Hollywood corporate entertainment for the young. These two trends, emerging out of a recognition of the importance of media studies (particularly the stabilizing/destabilizing power of the image), and the possibilities of a liberating pedagogy of film (including independent films), have coincided with a third: the use of other literary theories such as new historicism to discuss and ultimately politicize children's media and the related social and historical contexts of class, race, and gender.

Emerging out of poststructuralist and postmodern approaches to the text, the development of children's media studies in the past two decades has led, among other things, to journals such as *The Media Studies Journal* and a 1994 special issue entitled "Children and the Media." Noteworthy articles would be Ellen Wartella's "Electronic Childhood," and Renee Hobbs's "Teaching Media Literacy—Yo! Are You Hip to This?" Like *Potent Fictions: Children's Literacy and the Challenge of Popular Culture* (1996), Cary Bazalgette and David Buckingham's *In Front of the Children: Screen Entertainment and Young Audiences* (1995), or Michael Parenti's *Make-Believe Media: The Politics of Entertainment* (1992), Hobbs teaches kids how to deconstruct television images and thus politicizes that which the National Entertainment State television stations would no doubt rather keep apolitical. She also makes clear that deconstructing and demystifying for kids and teachers how television works as an ideological state apparatus to interpellate the subject is part of a broader political process in electronic education. To return to Miller—only by knowing our way around the information highway, can we map out new directions and therefore bypass the messages of consumerism upon which the information highway depends. Hobbs writes that "[A]ny meaningful critical discourse about media messages must include a careful and systematic examination of the economic and political contexts in which films, TV shows, newspapers and news programs are produced" (144).

The debates about the relationship between education, films, and children (rather than television and other media forms) were aired soon after the movies established themselves as a permanent feature of the American landscape. In the 1910s and the 1930s, the NCPM and the MPRC, for example, thought deeply about the educational aspects of cinema for the young from moral and/or social science perspectives. In the 1960s, with the advent around the world of what Jameson calls the "growth of the media" ("Periodizing" 207), the emphasis began to shift away from discussing the negative or positive values disseminated by films and whether or not those values were scientifically measureable, to how films might be taught to children so that they might learn to speak the language of film. It is fitting, given this global reach of cinema, that one of the first organizations to recognize fully the serious need and potential for teaching children's films in schools was the United Nations Educational, Scientific, and Cultural Organization, more popularly known as UNESCO. This organization published in 1961 *Teaching about The Film.* Written by J. M. L. Peters, the book is far-reaching because, using examples such as *The Fallen Idol,* it looks at the elements of film, how youngsters might make films, how film courses might be incorporated into schools, and how teachers themselves might learn to be film critics. Twenty years later, in the 1980s, Francelia Butler's *200 Selected Film Classics* made a similar attempt to incorporate the study of film into the school curriculum. Today, there are important conferences devoted to the teaching of children's cinema to youngsters. The Tisch School of the Arts at New York University, for example, will in 1999 host a conference, "Cinema Studies for the High School Teacher."

There are differences, of course, between the ideas and concerns of the MPRC/PFS, Peters, and Butler. At the beginning of the UNESCO report, for example, Peters takes issue with one of the main figures of the Payne Fund Studies research project, Professor Blumer. Blumer had argued that kids need to detach themselves somewhat from the movie they were watching. Peters, by contrast, argues that "nowadays we see more clearly that one may develop a critical attitude towards the cinema without at the same time becoming so detached that a film experience in which one participates as a deeply-engrossed spectator is forfeited" (14). And whilst the UNESCO report argues that kids from seven years old and upward might be taught the language of film, Butler argues that "many children as young as three would enjoy participating . . ." (13) in her film program.

If media studies and film classes are one aspect of children's criticism in the 1990s, another would be the use of critical theory to discuss Disney: The critical seeds sown by Sayers and Zipes in the 1960s and 1970s truly blossomed in the 1990s. For example, in a special issue of *The Lion and the Unicorn* (1993) called "Kiddie Lit(E): The Dumbing Down of Children's Literature," A. Waller Hastings's "Moral Simplification in Disney's *The Little Mermaid*" argues that Disney's "Manichean world of moral absolutes" (85) all but "eliminates the moral complexities of the original text" (90) and thus is part of the broader dumbing-down process characteristic of the modern culture industry. The echoes of Sayers and Zipes can clearly be heard in Hastings's argument, that Disney's simplification of classic works of children's literature, in this instance a moral simplification, is an example of the culture industry's instrumentalization of fantasy. Other critical studies have looked closely at Disney. Books like *From Mouse to Mermaid: The Politics of Film, Gender, and Culture* (1995), *Disney Discourse: Producing the Magic Kingdom,* and articles such as "Split Skins: Female Agency and Bodily Mutilation in *The Little Mermaid*" (1993) by Susan White, "Domesticating Dreams in Walt Disney's *Cinderella*" (1996) by Naomi Wood, and "Periods, Parody, and Polyphony: Fifty Years of Menstrual Education Through Fiction and Film" (1997) by Michele H. Martin, all demythologize the sexual politics of Disney and, by implication, the way Hollywood cinema as a whole constructs images of childhood designed to socialize children into the dominant mores of patriarchal, capitalist democracies.

One might argue that children's film criticism has finally shifted the focus away from children as the recipients of adult culture to adults as producers of children's culture. As Zipes says about the developments within children's literature criticism since the 1970s, "[I]nstead of accepting the literary canons and sanctioning the traditional socialisation processes, those who are trying to regulate children and images of childhood are the ones who are fortunately being questioned" (20). The real politics of children's film criticism is therefore not so much that it incorporates cultural studies, feminist, Marxist, and/or new historicist ideas into its forms of analysis, but that it does so in order to question the dominant media giants and the cinematic institutions like Hollywood as a whole and Disney in particular.

Interestingly, Disney is criticized also by nonacademics. In her newspaper story, "Snow White poisons kids' self-esteem," Susan D. Haas comments: "Would you fill a child's head with sugar-coated stereotypes? If the answer is no, don't take that cherished little psyche to see *Snow White.*" Other journalists such as Robert Welkos have criticized the similarities between Disney's *The Lion King* and a "Japanese-created American television cartoon series of the 1960s called "'Kimba, the White Lion.'" Still others like Evelyn Petersen have reported how parents themselves are upset over Disney. Newspapers like the *Wall Street Journal* regularly report on Disney/Cap Cities. Recently, Kimberley A. Strassel wrote that Mr. Joergensen, "Denmark's consumer ombudsman, is convinced that Walt Disney Co., an American icon of children's [programs threatens] the minds of Danish children." Marc Eliot's *Walt Dis-*

ney: Hollwood's Dark Prince alleges that Disney had pro-Nazi sympathies. Carl Hiaasen's *Team Rodent: How Disney Devours the World* critiques the homogeneity produced by Disney/Cap Cities' global business practices. Articles in journals such as *Rethinking Schools* offer not just scathing critiques of Disney's representation of minorities in films like *Pocahontas* and *Mulan* but discussions about how teachers can get students to take public action against Disney. Finally, on the World Wide Web, one can now read the full text of Walt Disney's October 24, 1947 testimony to the House Committee on Un-American Activities.[8] That the criticism of Disney should be political is appropriate: Disney was critical of politics himself, even though he would deny that his intentions were political—just patriotic, American, Godly.

What direction should children's film criticism take beyond 2000? As the research and writing of this book continued over the past few years, I have had to learn several new languages. The aesthetic language of film remains important, of course. But also there are other languages those critics interested in the politics of children's films must learn, or at least become familiar with. It is imperative, as Marx says in his *Theses on Feuerbach,* that the educator educates him or herself (12). Thus, children's critics need to become familiar with at least the following three areas of children's cinema and film: corporatism, technology, and foreign cinemas, films, and festivals.

The world of franchises, stock options, cash and short-term investments, mergers and acquisitions, operating budgets, territories, commodities, products, and so forth can no longer be inhabited only by corporate leaders, strategists, thinkers, and MBA students. Teachers must know these terms, what they mean, and their relation to the production, distribution, and reception of children's cinema and film. Imagine that the media giants such as Time Warner, Disney/Capital Cities, Viacom, DreamWorks SKG, and Pixar are exploitative factories rather than entertainment studios that produce "products" such as *Rambo, Star Trek, Lethal Weapon, 3 Ninjas, Free Willy, The Land Before Time, Home Alone, Rugrats, Toy Story,* and *Star Wars* designed to secure the dominant economic position of the media giant specifically within the moving picture industry and generally within the global economy.

It is important to understand and keep abreast of the terminology used to describe today's cinematic technological developments. *James and the Giant Peach* is produced through stop motion animation, whilst *Toy Story* is produced by computer generated images. This latter development, the introduction of computer technology into the making of a movie, extends to the way movies are shown. *Star Wars Episode 1: The Phantom Menace, USA Today* reports, will be shown on a movie screen without a "reel of film [because it] will play theaters in the cutting edge digital-cinema format" (Healey D1). The reel of film has been replaced by the beam of light, the on-site movie projectionist replaced by the off-site computer programmer.

Finally, critics, teachers, and students must become familiar with foreign cinemas, films, and film festivals. As I point out in Part Three: History, there is a thriving children's film festival industry around the world. Disney/Capital Cities has the financial resources (like Ford and General Motors have with cars or Microsoft and Apple and Dell have with computers) to make it appear that they alone produce and distribute all children's films—not so, as the small but imporant number of available foreign films and festivals attests.

CONCLUSION

Moral, social science, cultural, feminist, ideological, adaptation and history, media studies and critical theory: All these paradigms, denying their politics or proclaiming their politics, have at one time or another emerged, taken center stage, and played a dominant role in the history of children's film criticism. Given the initial appearance of the movie theaters within the cities, moral concerns were in ascendancy in the early years of children's film criticism, say 1895 to the late 1920s and early 1930s. Reformers like Jane Addams and institutions like the NCPM expressed concern that immoral movies caused immoral youngsters, which in turn caused a lack of the proper respect for institutions such as the family, the church, school, and society (similar arguments are made today). The moral arguments against the movies, preached in the early part of the 1930s by the Roman Catholic Legion of Decency and prominent Catholics such as Joseph Breen, culminated in the Production Code Administration, which "ruled the American film industry from its adoption in 1930 until it was replaced in 1966 by the current ratings system" (Black, *Hollywood* 1). The research and eventual publication of the Payne Fund Studies in the 1930s mapped out a new area of filmic investigation that included the social sciences. In the 1950s, cultural anthropology, itself a blend of psychology and child development research, further explored new territory, including that of the image of the child in children's films. From Francis Clark Sayers in the 1960s to Jack Zipes in the 1970s, Robin Wood in the 1980s, and critics like Henry Giroux, James

Kincaid, and Eric Smoodin in the 1990s, children's film criticism has gradually incorporated the broader theoretical developments in Marxism, new historicism, cultural studies, feminism, postmodernism, and postcolonialism, and turned toward a political understanding of the relationship between children and children's films.

This is not to argue that the work of Jane Addams (1916), the National Council of Public Morals (1917), the Legion of Decency and the Motion Picture Producers and Distributors of America, popularly known as the Hays Office (1930s), and the Motion Picture Research Council (1930s), for example, were apolitical. Quite the contrary. It is to argue that what post-World War II critics have done is reveal that since at least 1917 and no doubt before children's film criticism was tied to politics, even when it most vehemently denied it's political agenda. Macherey writes, "The speech of a book comes from a certain silence, a matter which it endows with form, a ground on which it traces a figure" (85). What Kincaid, Smoodin, Naomi Wood, Heather Neff, and others have done is make speak that which was otherwise silent, to borrow from Toril Moi, the sexual/textual politics of children's film criticism. In the process, what these critics have done is suggest something of the "real complexity" (Macherey 160) of children's film criticism and its relation to the history of children's cinema from around the world, the subject of Part Three of this book.

NOTES

[1]I refer here, of course, to Jack Zipes's article, "Taking Political Stock: New Theoretical and Cultural Approaches to Anglo-American Children's Literature in the 1980s." The article was published in *The Lion and the Unicorn* 14 (1990), 7-22.

[2]Staples argues that "It is often suggested that children's cinema began in 1900 in Mickleover, Derbyshire. In that town, at 5:30 p.m. on Tuesday, 7 February, there was a separate performance for children of the Great American Bioscope (and the accompanying magic lantern show)" (1–3).

[3]In a sense, I am trying in this essay to recreate a missing history of children's film criticism, or at least to weave together the unwoven strands of that history into a recognizable shape.

[4]A critical timeline shows that Sayers's work was only one of many feminist texts from the 1960s and 1970s that critiqued the representation of women by men as repressive and exploitative. For example, Betty Friedan had published *The Feminine Mystique* in 1963. Mary Ellman's *Thinking about Women* was published in 1969. Kate Millett's *Sexual Politics* appeared in 1970 along with Shulamith Firestone's *The Dialectic of Sex*.

[5]For a further discussion of the history of Disney criticism, see Eric Smoodin's *Disney Discourse: Producing the Magic Kingdom,* New York: Routledge, 1994.

[6]For a full discussion, see Jill May, "Literary Criticism and Children's Literature," *Children's Literature and Critical Theory.*

[7]Rollin's lively 1987 article is well worth reading, because she situates further the work of Frances Clarke Sayers, "a librarian, storyteller, and writer of children's books" (91), in the context of feminist approaches to Disney by critics such as Marcia Lieberman, Kay Stone, and Jane Yolen.

[8]Web address:<www.eserver.org/filmtv/disney_huac_testimony.txt>.

PART THREE

History

The category of children's films has, of course, always existed.

—Wood, *Hollywood* 163

Christian Metz wrote, "Historians of the cinema generally agree in dating the beginning of "cinema" as we know it in the period 1910–1915. Films like *Enoch Arden, Quo Vadis?, Fantomas, Cabiria, . . . The Battle of Gettysburg,* and above all *Birth of a Nation* were among the first films, in the acceptance we now give this word . . ." (95). Metz's quote, from *Film Language: A Semiotics of the Cinema,* suggests questions historians might ask about the "idea of children's cinema" (Bazalgette and Staples 92). Is there a date agreed upon by children's film critics when children's films, "in the acceptance we now give this word," began? Does children's cinema and film history begin in the years between 1910 and 1915 or before? At least one critic, Robin Wood, argues that "the category of children's films" has "always existed" (163). If so, what were the names of the first films? What children's films, canonical or otherwise, were made and released in subsequent film periods? Who are the child stars of children's films, the directors, the studios, and so forth? What social and political issues do children's films reflect in particular eras and throughout the twentieth century in general?

Some of these questions have already been answered. Solid, comprehensive overviews of films like Gerald Mast's *A Short History of the Movies* (1971), David Shipman's *The Story of Cinema: A Complete Narrative History from the Beginnings to the Present* (1982), Louis Giannetti's *Flashback: A Brief History of Film* (1986), and others usually consist of two or three important children's films (*The Wizard of Oz* in 1939, *The Yearling* in 1946, *Sounder* in 1972, etc.), a few canonized child stars (Shirley Temple and Jane Withers in the 1930s, Roddy McDowall and Elizabeth Taylor in the 1940s, Macaulay Culkin in the 1990s) but little else.

Brief histories of children's films have also been written by Goldstein and Zornow, Douglas Street, and Kathy Jackson. Goldstein and Zornow's history consists of a few introductory remarks at the beginning of their 1980 book *The Screen Image of Youth: Movies About Children and Adolescents.* Street's contribution to the history of children's cinema and film is an article called "An Overview of Commercial Filmic Adaptation of Children's Fiction" (1982). He primarily considers commercially successful adaptations of children's fiction from the silent era to the late 1970s. This is an important aspect of the history of children's cinema and film but, of course, begs the question what constitutes commerical success. Given that *Salaam Bombay* (1988) has only grossed $2.08 million so far in the United States and *Star Wars Episode I: The Phantom Menace* (1999) grossed $64.81 million on its opening weekend in the United States, what constitutes commercial success for overseas films might not be what constitutes commercial success for American films, the real phantom menace being capitalism, not Darth Vader! Jackson's contribution to children's film history is a book called *Images of Children in American Film: A Sociocultural Analysis* (1986).[1] She considers the image of the child in American children's films from 1895 to the early 1980s as a reflection of American attitudes toward children over the same period. That image is overwhelmingly one of innocence. Jackson's work is insightful work but again begs its own set of questions: Does the image of the child in American movies reflect how all Americans feel about children? Is the image of the innocent child an ideological construct designed to make money? Clearly many questions and answers concerning the history of children's cinema and film remain.

Part Three: History builds upon the work done by Goldstein, Zornow, Street, and Jackson, primarily by offering the reader a rather more comprehensive overview of the history of children's cinema and film from around the world. Each period discussed contains a summary of the extant histories by Goldstein, Zornow, Street, and Jackson. It's important, I think, to work from the concrete historical foundations they laid down in the 1980s. Second, I generally try to situate the following aspects of children's cinema and film—literary adaptations, other films, studios, directors, and child stars—in various social and political contexts. I try to show why certain adaptations, films, images of the child, and so forth are historically and politically important and relevant to a comprehensive world overview of the history of children's cinema and film.

1895–1927: THE SILENT ERA AND THE BEGINNING OF CHILDREN'S CINEMA AND FILM IN AMERICA AND BRITAIN

The first period in film history is generally known as the silent era. The silent era more or less extends from December 28, 1895, when the Lumière Brothers showed the first movies to a paying public in the Salon Indien, a basement room of the Grand Café in Paris, to 1927, when the Warner Brothers released *The Jazz Singer,* the movie said to have ushered in the era of the talkies (Shipman 201). Shipman's *The Story of Cinema* has chapters covering "The Rise of the American Industry," "Germany in the Twenties," "The U.S.S.R: Montage and Message," "The Twenties: Britain and France," and so forth. Giannetti's *Flashback: A Brief History of Film* discusses issues such as "American Cinema in the 1920s" and "European Cinema in the 1920s." David Parkinson's *History of Film* has two chapters dealing with the Silent Era: "The Foundations of Classical Hollywood" and "Film Art: 1908–1930." French critic Andre Bazin argues, "By 1928 the silent film had reached its artistic peak" (155).

Mast, Shipman, Giannetti, and Parkinson argue that the founding "mothers" and "fathers" of the cinema were scientists and entrepreneurs like Etienne Jules Marey, Eadweard Muybridge, George Eastman, Thomas Edison, W. K. L. Dickson, August and Louis Lumière, and film directors and actors like Georges Méliès, Ferdinand Zecca, Edwin Porter, Cecil Hepworth, Margaret Sanger, Lois Weber, Charlie Chaplin, Cecil B. De Mille, D. W. Griffith, Sergei Eisenstein, and others. Marey invented the photographic gun—hence the term "shooting a scene." Muybridge invented the Zoopraxiscope. Eastman developed the celluloid roll film which Edison and Dickson used first in their Kinetograph and Kinetoscope parlors (Mast 15). Edison, whom Mast calls the "American father of the movies . . ." (14), and Dickson, whom Robinson calls the "genius . . . too often overlooked" (15), built the first studio, the Black Maria. In the Black Maria, Edison and Dickson made films such as *The Rice/Irwin Kiss* (1896) and *Fred Ott's Sneeze.* Famous films from the silent era include the Lumières' *Sortie des Ouvriers de l'Usine Lumière* (1895) and Méliès' *A Trip to the Moon* (1902) from France; Porter's *The Great Train Robbery* (1903), Griffith's *Birth of a Nation* (1915), and Chaplin's *The Tramp* (1915) from the United States; Sergei Eisenstein's *Bronenosets Potyomkin* (*The Battleship Potemkin*) (1925) from the former Soviet Union. Without doubt, these and other silent-era movies from around the world establish the major film genres (fantasy, adventure, comedy, historical epic, and so forth) and techniques (long-shot, dissolves, close-up, fade-out, montage, etc.) directors worldwide still employ. Some filmmakers, such as Eisenstein (1898–1948), for example, were also film theorists whose combined ouevre and critical writings granted to cinema and film aesthetic legitimacy and political significance. A selection of the writings of Eisenstein and other film theorists are printed in anthologies such as *Film Theory and Criticism* (1992).

About the relationship between the silent era and children's cinema and film in particular, Street mentions commercially successful silent-era literary adaptations such as Cesare Antamaro's 1911 version of *Pinocchio* and Hepworth's 1903 *Alice in Wonderland.* Goldstein and Zornow set the time of the birth of children's cinema at 1898. They argue that "Long before *The Kid,* filmmakers had been attracted to the charms of infancy" (xiii) and cite Louis Lumière's 1898 *Le Dejeuner de Bébé* as an example of that attraction. The remainder of their discussion concerning the silent era consists of four short paragraphs in which they cite films such as Griffith's *The Adventures of Dolly* (1908), John Ford's *Just Pals* (1920) and C. B. De Mille's *The Godless Girl* (1929), and movie magazines such as *The Moving Picture World* as constituting children's cinema and film in the silent era.

Though short, Goldstein and Zornow's discussion is important nonetheless for at least two reasons. First, it answers Metz's question by suggesting a date for the beginning of children's cinema. Second, it suggests that the history of children's cinema and film includes not just the adaptation of classic works of children's literature but also other films, magazines, and related cinematic issues—including those of culture and politics.

Jackson resets the origins of children's cinema further back than Goldstein and Zornow, to 1895 and the Lumière Brothers' *Watering the Gardener.* In this film, Jackson reports, "A young boy places his foot on a garden hose, thus blocking the flow of water. When the gardener examines the clogged hose to determine the problem, he gets soaked by a quick torrent of water" (31). By implication, Jackson introduces here the issue of genre. Consisting of a practical joke, *Watering the Gardener* is one of the first comedies of the cinema and, because it stars a young boy, children's cinema. Jackson also argues, quite rightly, that the film introduces the child in "trickster roles" (31). Along with the image of the child as a trickster, according to Jackson, is the image of the "child fix-it character" (33), the idea of the "innocent child in jeopardy" (35), and, outside of film, an interest in childhood that reflected the Progressive-era politics of pre-World War I America and Europe.

Literary Adaptations

Children today see G- and PG-rated films such as *The Nightmare Before Christmas, James and the Giant Peach, The Hunchback of Notre Dame,* and *Harriet the Spy,* and R-rated films such as *The Matrix* (loosely based upon *Alice's Adventures in Wonderland*), but filmed adaptations of canonical works of children's literature appeared as early as 1899, when George Méliès completed a version of *Cinderella* (*Cendrillon*), one of his experimental "*feeries* or trick films" (Zipes 4). In 1901, Méliès made *Barbe Bleue* (*Bluebeard*) and *Le Petit Chaperon Rouge* (*Little Red Riding Hood*). In 1903 Méliès produced *Kingdom of the Fairies* and in 1912 remade *Cinderella* (see Figure 3).

Méliès's *A Trip to the Moon* (1902) was inspired by Jules Verne, a writer whose books are read by children and often adapted to the screen: Jeremy Lyons recommends the 1956 film version of Verne's *Around the World in 80 Days* for kids six and older (19) and the 1954 adaptation of Verne's *20,000 Leagues Under the Sea* for kids eight and older (256). Verne's work also was popular in the 1960s as the adaptations of *Five Weeks in a Balloon* (1962) and *The Mysterious Island* (1961) attest. A contemporary of Méliès, influential French director Ferdinand Zecca made *Ali Baba et les 40 Voleurs* (1902), *Puss 'n Boots* (1903), and *Aladin* (1906). In terms of literary adaptation, there were many children's films long before 1910 or 1911, the dates set down by Street or Metz.

Hollywood adapted so many canonical works of children's literature during the silent era for a variety of aesthetic and political reasons. In his 1944 essay "Dickens, Griffith, and the Film Today," Eisenstein remarks that both fiction and film contain an "optical quality" (396) manifest most completely in the "individual cinematic craftsmanship" (396) of pioneering American filmmaker Griffith's use of montage. For Eisenstein, "Griffith arrived at montage through the method of parallel action, and he was led to the idea of parallel action by Dickens" (395). The work of Dickens, in particular *Oliver Twist,* has a visual quality that Griffith, according to Eisenstein, was able to translate into film.

The aesthetic reasons why Hollywood so frequently adapted canonical works of children's literature parallel a broader set of political issues surely relevant to any comprehensive world history of children's cinema.

Figure 3. Georges Méliès' 1912 remake of *Cinderella* (*Cendrillon*). Photo courtesy of the Museum of Modern Art/Film Stills Archive, New York.

Eisenstein asks: "What were the novels of Dickens for his contemporaries, for his readers"? (395) and answers, "There is one answer: they bore the same relation to them that the film bears to the same strata in our own time" (396). This is not the place to rehearse the arguments about the "rise of the novel" and the "rise of the middle class." Sufficient here to note that the aesthetic and political function novels fulfilled for nineteenth-century readers was fulfilled for early twentieth-century viewers by children's films, at least those that were adapted from canonical works of children's literature.

Other examples show adaptations from the silent era starring children emerging out of the cultural politics of the period. First, American director Porter used "Goldilocks and the Three Bears" in *The 'Teddy' Bears,* his 1907 satire of then Vice President-elect Theodore Roosevelt. Second, in *The Emergence of Cinema: The American Screen to 1907,* Charles Musser writes, "The most popular and influential Méliès film was *Cinderella,* which first appeared in the United States during the 1899 Christmas Holidays" (277). Musser further notes that this and other experimental films from Méliès began "filling the movie theaters and delighting American audiences just as the vaudeville workers went on strike in what became known as the White Rats Strike" (276). In an ironic foreshadowing of how art and politics, technology and audience relations, would shape the development of children's cinema and film in the twentieth century, here in 1899 striking films replaced striking workers. Third, in "The Politics of Children's Films," I stated that "Knowing . . . millions of families were being torn asunder during the First World War, what better images . . . were there for those ravaged families than images of lost boys finding homes? The filmed version of *Oliver Twist,* for example, perfectly reproduces late nineteenth-century ideology on the early twentieth-century screen" (223). In short, the actual number of canonical children's literature texts used by Hollywood, fairy tale or otherwise, is less important than the various histories in which those films find themselves embedded: those of aesthetics (montage) and politics (strikes).

A Trip to the Moon (1902) and *Aladin* (1906) are important landmarks in the history of children's cinema and film, not just because they are two of the earliest adaptations of children's literature, but because in them Méliès and Zecca respectively invented and developed what we now call special effects. According to Parkinson, "Producer, director, writer, designer, cameraman and actor, Méliès is attributed with the first use of dissolves, superimposition, time-lapse photography, art direction and artifical lighting effects" (18). Méliès (and later Zecca) used these techniques to create special effects in films such as *Cinderella, Bluebeard, Little Red Riding Hood,* and *Kingdom of the Fairies.* The history of special effects in the movies begins in the silent era with the adaptation of children's literature classics.

Child Stars

No comprehensive survey of children's cinema and film would be complete without a discussion of the silent-era's child stars. Film historians traditionally mention famous child stars such as Mary Pickford, Lillian Gish, and Jackie Coogan as child stars from the silent era. Mary Pickford made numerous films, including many adapted from works of children's literature. She starred in *Cinderella* (1914) and *Little Lord Fauntleroy* (1921), for example. In an early example of what will become a recurring feature of children's cinema and film, whereby adults play children and children play adults, Pickford, when she was a twenty-seven-year-old woman, played a twelve-year-old girl in *Pollyanna* (1920).[2] In 1926 she starred in *Sparrows,* a film that, according to Richard Corliss, "luxuriates

Figure 4. Charlie Chaplin's *The Kid,* starring Jackie Coogan. Photo: The Museum of Modern Art/Film Stills Archive, New York. Courtesy of First National.

in dramatizing the evil done to children—and the life of fantasy that allows children to cope with evil" (60).[3] Pickford was eventually known as "America's Sweetheart." Known as "The First Lady of the Silent Screen," Lillian Gish began as a child star at the age of five. She acted in a melodrama called *In Convict Stripes.* Perhaps her most famous role was as

Elsie Stoneman in Griffith's *Birth of a Nation* (1915). Born John Leslie Coogan in 1914, Jackie Coogan became an international child star after acting in Charlie Chaplin's *The Kid* (1921) (see Figure 4).

Coogan also starred in versions of *Oliver Twist* (1922) and *Little Robinson Crusoe* (1924). By 1927, his career as a child star was over, though he acted in an adaptation of *Tom Sawyer,* for example, in 1930. Like Mary Pickford before him, he was suddenly redundant, out of work not ten years after his career had begun. He became a television actor, playing Uncle Fester in *The Addams Family* (1964–66).

Jackie Coogan's relevance to the history of children's cinema and film rests both on *The Kid* (1921), a "landmark film for child performers" (Jackson 47), but also the off-screen role he played in the 1930s determining the passage of the California Child Actors Bill. Like most child stars of the era, Coogan earned an enormous salary. When switching contracts from a studio such as First National to Metro, Coogan received a half-million-dollar signing bonus plus a $1 million contract and a percentage of the profits. Other profits, though partially embezzled by his mother and stepfather, were invested in Jackie Coogan Productions. Eventually Coogan received only half of the $252,000.00 remaining monies. Nonetheless, the end result was the Child Actors Bill, popularly known as the Coogan Act.

Beyond Mary Pickford, Lillian Gish, and Jackie Coogan, there existed less famous child stars who appeared in movies that incorporated new film techniques. Porter's *The Life of an American Fireman* (1903), for example, hightens the drama by cutting back and forth between the fire-engine and the child and the woman that needed rescuing: "[T]film remains significant for a number of genuine innovations" (19), David Parkinson argues. David Shipman attributes the success of Hepworth's *Rescued by Rover* (1905) to the "cross-cutting which increased audience tension as it slipped back and forth between the baby's fate and the parent's agitation" (26). Wallace McCutcheon's *The Lost Child* (1905), a movie about a child kidnapper pursued by passers-by, employs a different film technique to develop tension within its narrative: the close-up. Between 1903 and 1905, children starred in movies considered aesthetically and technologically cutting-edge.

The history of the *Our Gang* series, which starred numerous child actors over the years, began in the silent era in the United States. The historical roots of *Our Gang* are in the *Sunshine Comedies* of 1921 and 1922. With the acting of African-American child star Ernie Morrison, the show blossomed into the *Our Gang* series, which ran from 1922 to 1944 under the direction of Hal Roach. The child stars of the original *Our Gang* series were Joe Cobb, Mary Kornman, Mickey Daniels, Allen Clayton Hoskins, Jackie David, Jackie Condon, and Pete the dog. As these children grew older they were replaced by child actors like Jackie Cooper, Norman Chaney, Bobby Hutchins, and Matthew Beard. During the 1930s, Spanky McFarland, Carl "Alfalfa" Switzer, and Darla Hood appeared. Many of these children, like Jackie Cooper, became stars. Others faded away. After 1944, the series appeared on syndicated television and cable under the name *The Little Rascals.* Recently, many of the original *Our Gang* and *The Little Rascals* series have been rereleased on video. The Universal Pictures production of *The Little Rascals,* directed by Penelope Spheeris, was released in 1994 and starred Travis Tedford, Bug Hall, Brittany Ashton Holmes, Kevin Jamal Woods, and Zachary Mabry as Spanky, Alfalfa, Darla, Stymie, and Porky respectively.

Who were the child stars from overseas? Whilst the most famous child stars of the silent era were undoubtedly American, foreshadowing the powerful influence the image of the child in U.S. cinema would have around the world, particularly in the 1970s and 1980s, some were English. Born in London in 1895, the year cinema is said to have begun, Alma Taylor acted in films such as *The Little Flower Girl* (1908), *Oliver Twist* (1912), *David Copperfield, The Old Curiosity Shop* (1913), and others. In 1922, she starred in two Cecil Hepworth films: *Mist in the Valley* and *Comin' Thro' the Rye.* According to Roy Armes, Taylor plays a "young convent-educated girl" (62) in the former and in the latter "the ugly duckling of the family who grows into a beautiful young woman [who] captures the love of the handsome Paul" (62). Both films are "sober and tasteful but rather prosaic" (63).

Studios

As mentioned earlier, the first studio was probably Dickson's Black Maria. By the end of the silent era, most if not all films in the United States were produced and distributed by seven major studios: MGM, Paramount, RKO, Universal, 20th Century Fox, Columbia, and Warner Brothers. These seven studios were "large-scale, tightly controlled vertical monopolies that produced, distributed, and exhibited films" (Black, *Hollywood* 26). The monopoly of the moving picture industry by these major studios, which had begun in 1908–09 when the Motion Picture Patents Company consisting of Edison, Biography, Vitagraph, Selig, Kalem, Essanay, and Lubin controlled the manufacturing, production, and distribution of movies, ended with the federally mandated antitrust laws of 1948. The Walt Disney Company was founded in the early 1920s.

Directors

Who were the directors of children's films in the silent era, the equivalent of contemporary directors such as Carroll Ballard (*The Black Stallion*), Don Bluth (*The Land Before Time*), Tim Burton (*Edward Scissorhands*), John Hughes (*Curly Sue*), and Penelope Spheeris (*The Little Rascals*)? The famous directors of the silent era were Hepworth, Griffith, Chaplin, Lois Weber, Margaret Sanger, and others. They made films that either starred children, dealt with children's issues, or were otherwise child-centered. As well as *Birth of a Nation* and *Intolerance,* the two films for which he is most famous, Griffith made *The Adventures of Dolly* (1908), *The Lonely Villa* (1909), and *The Battle at Elderbush Gulch* (1913). *The Adventures of Dolly,* Griffith's first one-reeler for Biograph, involves the unsuccessful kidnapping of Dolly by a gypsy. As mentioned, Chaplin's *The Kid* (1921), according to Goldstein and Zornow the first "important film about a child" (vii), showcased the considerable talents of Jackie Coogan (see Figure 4).

Chaplin was not the only director to deal with important social issues in film. Despite tremendous opposition, Margaret Sanger introduced birth control to the United States. Sanger's magazine, *The Woman Rebel,* was banned by Postmaster General Anthony Comstock because the mentioning of contraception through the mail was deemed pornographic. When Sanger opened her first clinic in Brooklyn in October 1916, the vice squad promptly arrested her. Even so, Sanger persevered. Quite rightly, she is known as the mother of birth control.

Determined to introduce birth control, Sanger drew on her own nursing experiences in the Lower East Side of New York to make an antiabortion, pro–birth control film called (not unsurprisingly) *Birth Control.*

The reception of *Birth Control* was mixed. The National Board of Review approved it because they felt the message worthwhile and Sanger's acting sincere, not sensational or exploitative. The New York City License Commissioner George Bell, however, considered the film "immoral and indecent" (Brownlow 50). The film was withdrawn from public circulation. Sanger showed the film privately to the press who overwhelmingly supported its release. Still, the Appellate Division of the New York State Supreme Court upheld the earlier decision by Bell to ban *Birth Control.* Though seen by people attending her lectures, the film remained illegal until 1965, the year the Supreme Court overturned state laws that had made the spreading of birth control information a crime.

Social and Political Issues

Kevin Brownlow remarks: "The movies were born into an era of reform, which (roughly) opened with the inauguration of President Theodore Roosevelt in 1901 and closed with the entry of the United States into the First World War in 1917" (xvi). In the spirit of reformism, social problem films such as *Children Who Labor* (1912) and *The Blood of the Children* (1915) revealed something of the economic exploitation and abuse endured by children in factories and mines around the country: The number of child laborers in the United States in 1900, for example, was approximately 1,790,000 (Brownlow 426). These and other films from the silent era, such as *Birth Control, Where Are My Children,* and *The Hand That Rocks the Cradle,* generally took reformist positions though, as Brownlow also reports, "The fact that child labor should still be an issue at the end of the Reform Era is an indication of the strength of the opposition" (427). Die-hard conservatives, for example, resisted federally mandated child labor laws, staunchly arguing that children often worked down mines with the full knowledge of their parents and that what constitutes child labor is ethnically and culturally determined.

EUROPEAN CHILDREN'S SILENT CINEMA

Terry Staples's 1997 *All Pals Together: The Story of Children's Cinema* considers the history of children's cinema in Britain rather than in the United States. First, like Goldstein, Zornow, and Jackson did in relation to American children's cinema, Staples locates the emergence of children's cinema in England at the turn of the twentieth century. He writes: "It is often suggested that children's cinema began [in England] in 1900 in Mickleover, Derbyshire. In that town, at 5:30 p.m. on Tuesday, 7 February, there was a separate performance for children of the Great American Bioscope" (1–3). Second, according to Staples, kids were charged half price, though for economic rather than altruistic reasons: more kids, more money. Staples also makes a third point relevant to a global history of children's cinema and film, the tragic deaths of kids in the theaters. Staples relates three such incidents, in 1908, 1917, and 1929, when children died. In 1908 in Barnsley, over one thousand children crowded into a theater. Many kids waited impatiently outside. Staples says that in the ensuing confusion, "Of the sixteen children who suffocated that day, four were aged eight, three were seven, two were six, five were five, and two were four" (6). In 1917, four kids were crushed and suffocated when children panicked upon hearing somebody shout fire (19). In 1929 "seventy children" (27) died when smoke filled the theater, in part because the exit doors were all locked to prevent other kids from sneaking in "without paying" (28). The birth of children's cinema in England was accompanied by the death of numerous children.

Despite these deaths, kids continued attending the movies in England. What did they see? From 1910–14, kids watched a series of two-reelers involving a character called Lieutenant Rose (8). At about the same time, Cecil Hepworth produced a series of films for girls featuring two tomboys named Tilly and Sally: *Tilly and the Fire Engines* and *Tilly the Tomboy Goes Boating*. Generally, in these early years of the cinema, kids saw "music hall items such as *Tiller's Six Diamonds* . . . comedies such as *Four to One* . . . dramas such as *An Affair of Honour* . . . and character sketches such as *A Jolly Old Couple*" (3). Staples notes that by the 1920s, animals were again stars. Hepworth's *Rescued by Rover,* a favorite movie for kids and adults in the early 1900s, was replaced by the movies of a German shepherd named Rin Tin Tin in the 1920s: *Where the North Begins* (1923), *Find Your Man* (1924), and *Clash of the Wolves* (1925) were all popular at the time. As well as animal movies, kids watched European comic actors such as Frenchmen Max Linder and André Deed. Overall, kids saw films that, according to one advertisement, were "free from vulgarity throughout" (quoted in Staples 3).

Toward the end of the silent era, Staples says, "In the main . . . the films that children saw [in England] at matinees were the same that [*sic*] everyone else saw . . . : Charlie Chaplin, Buster Keaton, Harold Lloyd, Jackie Coogan, Mary Pickford, Douglas Fairbanks, the Keystone Cops" (22). Though Staples does not say so, the point is worth making anyway: The dominating influence of American cinema on movie-minded children in Great Britain was well established by the end of the silent era.

Summary

American and British children's cinema is as old as cinema itself. For some, children's cinema begins in 1895. For others, it begins in 1898, or 1900. Immediately, Hollywood begins to make numerous literary adaptations of classic children's literature texts and begins a relationship (albeit a problematic relationship) that to varying degrees continues to this day with films such as *The Indian in the Cupboard, Madeline, Harriet the Spy,* and, for young adults, *The Bloody Chamber, Freeway,* and *The Matrix.* Films generate stars. Pickford, Gish, and Coogan emerge as highly paid, internationally recognized child stars who function as ambassadors for American capitalism as much as American films. Child star Alma Taylor was popular in Britain. *Gertie the Dinosaur,* in 1909, ushers in the art of animation in the United States. In the early 1920s, Walt Disney introduces the "Alice" shorts, the Silly Symphony cartoons and characters like Mickey Mouse, Donald Duck, Pluto, and Goofy. The history of the Disney Corporation from fledgling family business to corporate empire is well documented. Magazines like *The Moving Picture World* and *Photoplay* are established. *Photoplay* in 1913 begins circulation with a cover story on child stars. Films starring children are at the center of the censorship debate in the first decade of the twentieth century (*Birth Control,* 1917) just as they are in the last decade of the twentieth century (*Kids,* 1995). No doubt reacting against the social and political changes taking place in the early years of the twentieth century, institutions in England such as the National Council on Public Morals investigated the ways in which the movies affected children by causing lack of sleep, juvenile delinquency, and even death. In the United States, reform-era politics were reflected in reform-era movies such as *Broken Blossoms* (parent-child abuse) and *Children Who Labor* (child labor). In short, out of the "confluence of film history and social history" (Palmer 10) is born not just the history of cinema (Metz 95) but the history of children's cinema and film.

1930s CHILDREN'S CINEMA AND FILM: LITERARY ADAPTATIONS, CHILD STARS, AND CENSORSHIP

David Parkinson argues that the period generally known as the "Golden Age of Hollywood" extends from 1927–41. This period is arguably the most influential period in the history of cinema and children's cinema and film. During this time, major studios from the silent era such as Edison, Vitagraph, Biograph, and Essanay, who had once formed the powerful Motion Picture Patents Company, dissolved and disappeared. Essanay, for example, famous for its westerns and comedies, disbanded soon after Charlie Chaplin left to form the Mutual Film Corporation in 1916. Mutual evolved into Radio Keith Orpheum, more popularly known as RKO. When these studios disappeared, in their place appeared Metro-

Goldwyn-Meyer, 20th Century Fox, Warner Brothers, Paramount, Columbia, Disney, Universal, and United Artists.

According to the editors of the influential French film journal *Cahiers du Cinéma,* these major studios were beholden to the "major banking groups [such as] Morgan, Rockefeller [and] DuPont" (497). Acording to the *Cahiers* editors, 20th Century Fox, for example, was directly "under the aegis of the Chase National Bank . . ." (497). Today, the major studios are owned by global media corporations such as Time Warner (Warner Brothers), Disney/Capital Cities (Touchstone Pictures, Miramax, etc.), and Viacom (Paramount, Nickelodeon, etc.), and banks such as the Credit Lyonnaise in France (MGM/Pathé).

In the 1930s, no doubt under the influence of the banks, who were themselves no doubt under the influence of the Great Depression, the studios regrouped (today it would be called "downsizing") and gradually attained economic stability by overhauling their production processes and turning their studios into efficient dream factories. The Golden Age of Hollywood is synonymous with the Studio Era. Businesslike, the studios employed stars like Bogart, Cagney, Dietrich, and Astaire to work in genres like the musical, the screwball comedy, and the gangster movie. Ray writes: "Understandably, therefore, film historians have designated the years 1930–1945 as the Classic Period of American movies. For despite the American Cinema's enormous silent-era success, the arrival of sound saw Hollywood reach the peak of its narrative and commercial efficiency" (25). After discussing the fact that between 1930 and 1945, "the movies averaged 80 million in weekly attendance, a sum representing more than half of the U.S population of the time" (25), Ray concludes: "We should realize, therefore, that in examining the movies of Hollywood's Classic Period, we are studying the single most important body of films in the history of the cinema, the one that set the terms by which all the movies before or after, would be seen" (26). Given that this period sees the release of influential films like *The Jazz Singer* (1927), *Scarface* (1932), and *Top Hat* (1935), and directors like Howard Hawks and John Ford (the latter made *Mr. Smith Goes to Washington, Stagecoach,* and *Young Mr. Lincoln* in 1939, and *How Green Was My Valley* in 1941), Ray's emphasis on Hollywood's ability to show and tell with businesslike efficiency is well placed.

The 1930s in the United States are no less important in the history of children's cinema. As the Great Depression swept across America, the Golden Age of children's cinema and film might be said to have swept across Hollywood. MGM, Universal, RKO, and so forth, produced what Street calls "three historically significant features, all adaptations" ("Overview" 13): *Snow White and the Seven Dwarfs, Gulliver's Travels,* and *Pinocchio.* According to Street, these three animated films were "technical masterworks" but "travesties of their literary sources" (14). Regardless, they made a great deal of money: *Snow White and the Seven Dwarfs,* for example, made $37 million when released (Case 1054), became one of the top movies of the 1930s (Ash 22), and in 1998 was rated forty-ninth on the American Film Institute's (AFI) roll call of *100 Greatest American Films* (Watson 17). In terms of feature-length movies adapted from children's literature texts, there were "three major family triumphs" ("Overview" 15) according to Street: *David Copperfield* (1935), *Captains Courageous* (1937), and *Christmas Carol* (1938). Jackson, focusing on images of the child, notes that the 1930s was the beginning of the "child-star era" (56) epitomized by child stars such as Shirley Temple, Jane Withers, Baby Peggy Montgomery, and others. Jackson notes "Shirley Temple's phenomenal popularity during the Depression years" (62) and accounts for it by arguing that "She embodied Americans' hope in the power of youth to right wrongs and ensure a better world" (64).

Literary Adaptations

As well as *Snow White and the Seven Dwarfs, Gulliver's Travels, Pinocchio, David Copperfield,* and so forth, many other adaptations were released during the 1930s. A useful book in this regard is Francelia Butler's *200 Selected Film Classics for Children of All Ages* (1984). She cites numerous literary adaptations, including many from the 1930s. Jack Conway's adaptation of Dickens *A Tale of Two Cities* (US, 1935), James Whale's adaptation of H. G. Wells *The Invisible Man* (US, 1933), Merian Cooper's adaptation of Edgar Wallace's *King Kong* (USA, 1933), George Cukor's remake of Shakespeare's *Romeo and Juliet* (US, 1936), and Norman Taurog's 1934 adaptation of Alice Hegan Rice's 1901 *Mrs. Wiggs of the Cabbage Patch* are mentioned as significant. MGM also financed and produced versions of *Tarzan the Ape Man* (1932) and *Wuthering Heights* (1939). United Artists made a version of *The Prisoner of Zenda* (1937). Numerous other literary adaptations such as Victor Fleming's 1934 *Treasure Island* and William Dieterle's *The Hunchback of Notre Dame* (US, 1939) appeared. Charles Laughton played Quasimodo in *The Hunchback.* Michael Curtiz and William Keighley directed

Figure 5. King Vidor's *The Champ*. Photo: Museum of Modern Art/Film Stills Archive, New York. Courtesy of MGM.

The Adventures of Robin Hood, a film Jeffrey Lyons calls "an action-packed story children will love" (16). Arguably, the decade belongs to the writer Rudyard Kipling. Versions of *Elephant Boy, Captains Courageous,* and *Gunga Din* were all made during the 1930s.

Some famous 1930s literary adaptations dealt specifically with the Great Depression. Films like William Wellman's 1933 *Wild Boys of the Road* (adapted from Daniel Ahearn's *Desperate Youth*), King Vidor's 1931 *The Champ* (based on a story by Frances Marion), Hamilton McFadden's 1934 *Stand Up and Cheer,* and Norman Taurog's 1938 *Boys Town* (adapted from a story by Dore Schary and Eleanore Griffin) are set against the backdrop of the Great Depression (see Figure 5).

At the height of the Great Depression, the most famous and enduring commercially successful literary adaptation of all was released: Victor Fleming's adaptation of L. Frank Baum's *The Wizard of Oz.* Thomas J. Harris calls *The Wizard of Oz* the "perfect embodiment" of the "ideal children's musical-fantasy film" (5). Joel D. Chaston sees *The Wizard of Oz* as responsible for the "Ozification" of American children's fantasy films (13).

Jackson calls it a "capstone film of the entire Depression period" (71). Indeed, in 1939, the film grossed $5.5 million for MGM (Case 1053).

Other than literary adaptations, film genres born in the silent era were full-grown by the 1930s. Hepworth's *Rescued By Rover* (1905), which had evolved into the "Rin Tin Tin" features of the 1920s, again evolved, this time into William Wellman's 1935 *Call of the Wild,* an adaptation of the writings of Jack London starring Clark Gable as Jack Thornton and a dog called Buck. The film was produced by 20th Century, which became 20th Century Fox in 1935. Street considers *Call of the Wild* "more than an animal movie; the film and its star Clark Gable were acclaimed major successes of 1935" ("Overview" 15).

Literary Adaptations and Film Historiography

In the context of poststructuralism and postmodernism and the emerging theoretical debates about film historiography (referred to in Part Two: Criticism), literary adaptations like *Boys Town* and *Snow White and the Seven Dwarfs* are particularly interesting examples of how quite different historical conditions produce different filmic meanings. In *A Second Look,* Leonard Quart argues that, whilst *Boys Town* is the kind of "mawkish, contrived Thirties social melodrama that normally does not deserve a second look" (55), the film is also a favorite of "America's self-appointed political savior and conservative revolutionary, Newt Gingrich" (55). Quart notes that, in *Boys Town,* "Father Flanagan simply wants to save children, whom he sees as inherently good, from the poverty and hopelessness of their daily lives. And he's willing to do it without paying the slightest bit of attention to Gingrich-like commitments to balanced budgets or financial discipline. For Father Flanagan, social need takes place over cost-effectiveness" (55). Quart quite rightly points out that the film reflects a commitment to collective action, but that Gingrich uses the film in the 1990s to reflect a commitment to individual choice. Mildly critical of capitalism in the 1930s, the film is made to support capitalism in the 1990s. Filmic meaning changes according to changing historical conditions. Different time period, different film meaning.

The meaning of *Snow White and the Seven Dwarfs* also changes dramatically when we situate it within history in general but in particular the economic decisions and sound technologies that produced *The Jazz Singer.* Considering *Snow White* this way allows us to see something of Disney's complex and "secret . . . relationship with history" (Macherey 160). "Talkies!" (200) declares Shipman. Parkinson writes that "However, undeniable proof that the sound era had dawned came in [1927 in] the form of *The Jazz Singer*" (85). Traditional film histories indeed see *The Jazz Singer* as the film that ends the silent era and begins the era of the talkies. Film historians point to *The Jazz Singer* as proof positive that silent movies were a thing of the past and talking movies a thing of the future. As Shipman himself notes, after discussing how Jolson was paid $75,000 for appearing in *The Jazz Singer*: "The rest is history . . ." (201). Film historians like Peter Wollen in "Cinema and Technology: An Historical Overview" and Douglas Gomery in "Towards an Economic History of the Cinema: The Coming of Sound to Hollywood" argue that privileging *The Jazz Singer* as the movie that marks the difference between an era of silence and an era of sound is symptomatic of how traditional film histories often simplify otherwise traditional histories of film. Gomery writes: "Gone, I hope, is the undue emphasis on *The Jazz Singer* and other firsts. The coming of sound was a much more complex process than simply filming Broadway plays, as previous histories led us to believe" (45).

The differences between Shipman and Parkinson and Wollen and Gomery are really the differences between old and new approaches to film historiography. Typical of older approaches, Shipman's chapter "Talkies" sets the historical scene (as it were) by directing our attention to the aesthetic developments inaugurated by *The Jazz Singer.* Shipman briefly notes how "Edison in the U.S. and Gaumont in France" (200) tried to solve the two chief problems associated with sound, those of synchronization and amplification. But Shipman's discussion then becomes a mere listing of what he considers to be the countries and films most deeply indebted to *The Jazz Singer.* This tells us what *The Jazz Singer* influenced but not the historical conditions that influenced *The Jazz Singer.* Similarly, Parkinson notes the commercial success of *The Jazz Singer,* but then tells us that the film led to several new genres such as the musical, the gangster movie, and the screwball comedy, and Disney's experimentation with sound throughout the 1920s. Macherey writes that "The various 'theories' of creation all ignore the process of making; they omit any account of production" (68). Shipman and Parkinson tells us about what aesthetic creations *The Jazz Singer* authored, not what historical and economic conditions produced *The Jazz Singer*.

Wollen and Gomery see sound and *The Jazz Singer* less in terms of an aesthetic history of film more in terms of a materialist history. Wollen, for example, notes that "Technically, sound . . . introduced new possibilities [and] new obstacles" (17). Wollen points out that whilst it is true that the two chief problems associated with sound—synchronization and amplification—were solved, subsequent developments affected the film industry both positively and negatively. The beginning of recorded sound in the form of *The Jazz Singer* signified the end of live entertainment in the form of orchestras. This in turn meant labor-saving costs (Wollen 16) for the production companies but unemployment for the workers. As sound technologies developed studio laboratories became increasingly standardized and "divorced from the work of the director and the cinematographer" (17). In other words, the advent of sound and its culmination in *The Jazz Singer,* which reaped huge profits for the production companies and literally "saved the American cinema in the wake of the 1929 Wall Street Crash" (Parkinson 85), also signified the industrialization and standardization of movie production. Mythologizing *The Jazz Singer* ahistoricizes and thus conceals the material conditions of production (technology, labor, etc.) that produced *The Jazz Singer.* We remember *The Jazz Singer* because it influenced a number of subsequent films and film trends, but we forget the work that went into the making of *The Jazz Singer.* In this way, we learn about film history as a series of aesthetic sucesses (sound liberated film) rather than a series of political failures (sound oppresses film workers). Mary Ann Doane makes the point nicely when she remarks in "Ideology and the Practice of Sound Editing" that "The effacement of work which characterizes bourgeois ideology is highly successful with respect to . . . sound . . ." (47). Idealist histories of film efface realist film histories.

These issues impact directly upon children's cinema and film. Parkinson notes that "Debuting in the silent *Plane Crazy,* Mickey found his voice in *Steamboat Willie* later that year, by which time Disney had begun a series of experiments to perfect sound and image synchronization. The last of the resultant "Silly Symphonies" was an immensely popular all-colour version of *The Three Little Pigs* (1933) and . . . *Snow White and the Seven Dwarfs* . . . (94). Two recently published essays will help us understand the economic issues Parkinson's comment effaces.

First, Douglas Gomery points out in "Disney's Business History: A Reinterpretation" that Disney's sound experiments were accompanied by Disney's corporate experiments. The Disney Corporation allied itself with "Columbia Pictures (1929–1931), then United Artists (1931 to 1936), and then RKO (1936 to 1954)" (72). Sound innovations were accompanied by sound investments. Aesthetic developments went hand in hand with economic developments.

Second, Richard Neupert's "Painting a Plausible World: Disney's

Color Prototypes" notes a number of connections between the world of aesthetics and the world of capital. According to Neupert, Technicolor Inc. developed and produced throughout the late 1920s and early 1930s a "three-strip color motion picture process . . . which improved upon their earlier two-strip process by adding a blue component to what had previously been only a red and green system" (106). To prove to the major Hollywood studios that color processing was worth the extra investment, Technicolor Inc. "looked to animation [i.e., Disney] and industrial clients" (106) to pay their production and development costs.

At the same time, Neupert writes, "Disney . . . embarked on a program to train its animators and story writers alike in color theory" (107): Pixar Animation today insists upon a similar training program for animators at Pixar University. As a result of these collaborations between Technicolor Incorporated and the Disney studios, Neupert argues, the coloring in *Snow White and the Seven Dwarfs* satisfied "conventional aesthetic norms of harmony, balance, and variety, while keeping the central figures as focal points for our attention as unifying points for the color pattern" (117). *Snow White* succeeded not just because it used color but because the colors used satisfied aesthetic norms, norms that correctly position audiences to see and appreciate a film. In sum, that which we take for granted today, sound and color, are grounded in what Fredric Jameson calls a "combinatoire" ("Marxism and Historicism" 152) of economic and aesthetic histories, those of corporate business agreements and mimetic theories of representation. Any history of children's cinema and film that effaces such determinants simplifies film historiography. *Snow White and the Seven Dwarfs* is important, not because it was a first, but because it represents a synthesis of economic and aesthetic conditions grounded in the dialectics of history and art.

Child Stars

The history of children's cinema and film in the 1930s must consist of more than a discussion about literary adaptations, and so forth. The 1930s are also known for a number of famous child stars such as Baby June Hovick, the Parrish Children, Mickey Rooney, Shirley Temple, Deanna Durbin, Jane Withers, Freddie Bartholomew, Jackie Cooper, Judy Garland, and Sabu Dagistur.

Though much has been written about these child stars, the degree to which the studios used them financially has nevertheless been neglected. Deanna Durbin starred with Judy Garland in *Every Sunday* in 1936 but, just as Temple's films during the 1930s saved 20th Century Fox from financial ruin, it was *Three Smart Girls* starring Durbin that saved Universal Pictures from bankruptcy. The work of Temple and Durbin literally prevented the economic collapse of their respective studios.

European Children's Cinema

In the 1930s and early 1940s, several important developments took place in Europe in relation to children's cinema and film. Staples reports that "Early in the thirties, the USSR had believed it was necessary to produce films specially [*sic*] for children, and set up a Children's Film Studio in Moscow" (88). As Great Britain, Russia, and America joined forces against Hitler, a distribution company called Anglo-American was formed. They imported from the Children's Film Studio for United Kingdom youth audiences what they felt were pro-Western films, such as *The Magic Fish, The Land of Toys,* and *The Little Humpback Horse* (88)

In relation to the studios and theaters in England, J. Arthur Rank acquired control of Gaumont-British in 1942. In the same year, Oscar Deutsch, the owner of the Odeon chain of theaters, died. His 230 theaters were acquired by Rank. According to Staples, the only other competitor to Rank at the time was the ABC chain.

Rank was the British equivalent of, say, MGM, Universal, or Walt Disney. Indeed, just as Disney had the Mickey Mouse Club in America, so Rank created the Odeon National Cinema Club in England for kids.

Summary

Though Disney initially appears in the 1920s with the "Alice" shorts, the Silly Symphony cartoons, and characters like Mickey Mouse and Donald Duck, during the 1930s these relatively minor cartoon characters evolve into major economic stars. The Disney Corporation becomes a major force in the film industry and, as we shall see, a major force in children's social and cultural lives. In their search for profits, studios made redundant silent-era child stars such as Mary Pickford, Lillian Gish, and Jackie Coogan, and replaced them with "talking" child stars like Deanna Durbin, Shirley Temple, Jane Withers, Sabu Dagistur, and Freddie Bartholomew. Temple spent most of the 1930s under contract to 20th Century Fox, at one point earning as much as $1,000 per week. By comparison, *Time* reports that Macaulay Culkin was paid a "low six figures for *Home*

Alone" (79). Little wonder Temple Black, as she would later become, refers to herself in her autobiography *Child Star* as a "tiny commodity" (Black, *Child Star* 28). Ironically, her innocence reaches its height during the experience of the Great Depression. Street comments that Freddie Bartholomew was "the hottest child property in Hollywood" ("Overview" 15) at the time. A number of important works of children's film criticism were published during the 1930s, among them Graham Greene's libelous discussion of Shirley Temple's *Wee Willie Winkie*. More generally, the debates about the power of film to affect children either positively (good films turns out good kids) or negatively (bad films turn out bad kids), raised originally in the silent era with the 1917 publication in England of the research of the National Council of Public Morals, became full-blown in the 1930s with the publication of the Payne Fund Studies (PFS).

Significantly, Shirley Temple's career finished in the early 1940s, just as the United States become embroiled in World War II, a truly epoch-making event that pulled America, Europe, and Asia out of their respective economic depressions and set a chain reaction of social (1950s urbanization, 1960s social revolt, etc.), political (Cold War), and cultural (Maoism, etc.) explosions. Previously, the complex affairs of the world as shown in Temple's films were ultimately resolvable by her prayers, luck, good fortune, will-power, enthusiasm, hard work, determination, and a pretty smile that forced the doting adults around her to use their power for the good of all rather than one individual: think here of *Stand Up and Cheer.*

But in the post-World War II era, a winning and engaging personality were no longer enough. As Temple Black herself forsook the world of entertainment for the world of politics, so audiences also were forced to grow up and confront a world that was forever changed by the political, military, and ideological conflicts of the 1940s out of which emerged the United States as a dominant world power.

Unsurprisingly, in the post-World War II era, we will see children's cinema and film emerge as a site of phenomenal commercial success and deep ideological commitment to conservative family values. Corporate Hollywood's use of film to highlight social injustice, so prevalent in the silent era and the early 1930s, fades entirely in the post-World War II era. Film as a tool for promoting social equality is assigned to Italian Neorealism (1940s), Third Worldism and Black Cinema (1970s), Independents and women directors (1980s and 1990s). In the post-World War II era, Hollywood got in it for the money alone.

WORLD WAR II: DISNEY, AMERICAN FILM NOIR, ITALIAN NEOREALISM, AND FRENCH CLASSICISM

World War II and its aftermath had a major impact on America and Europe and their respective film industries, including those geared toward children's cinema and film. The war begun in Europe on September 3, 1939, when Britain and France declared war on Germany, which three days earlier had invaded Poland. Franklin Delano Roosevelt was elected to an unprecedented third term of office in 1940. America had also changed its policy of neutrality to one of nonbeligerence. This policy again changed when, on December 7, 1941, Japan launched a surprise attack on Pearl Harbor, Hawaii. America retaliated by declaring war on Japan. Effectively, America entered World War II. In June 1944, the Allied forces—Americans, British, Canadians, South Africans, and New Zealanders, for example, all of whom had film industries—entered Rome to begin the process of liberating Italy. The historic D-Day, when the Allies landed on the Normandy beaches to begin the liberation of France, took place on June 6, 1944. By August of that year, Paris had been liberated from German occupation. As the Soviet Union, the United States, and Great Britain subsequently carved up Germany, Poland, and the Far East between them at Yalta, American bombers in August 1945 began the virtual total destruction of Japan. On August 6, 1945, the Enola Gay dropped a nuclear bomb on Hiroshima and, a few days later, on Nagasaki. Japan surrended in September. World War II ended in Europe on May 7, 1945, VE Day (Victory in Europe Day). World War II ended for the United States on September 2, 1945.

During World War II, a tremendous loss of life was suffered by United States and the countries of Europe. During the Bataan death-march, an estimated five to ten thousand U.S. soldiers lost their lives. By February 1943, some sixty thousand American soldiers were feared dead. By 1945, four hundred thousand American soldiers had died in the conflict. Needless to say, Europe, China, and Japan were devasted. The Soviet Union, for example, lost twenty million people during World War II.

Almost immediately after the end of World War II, the Cold War, a term coined by Winston Churchill in 1946, began. The Cold War froze American and Russian relations during the 1950s, in part because the United States feared Russian expansion in South America, Europe, the Middle East, and Asia, whilst Russia feared U.S. expansion in precisely those areas plus Africa. Certainly by 1959, Castro had taken over Cuba (the Bay of Pigs in 1961 and the Cuban Missile crisis in 1962 are but a few years away). On the other hand, in 1950, the United States became embroiled in the Korean War, backing South Korea against the Communist North (the Vietnam War followed thereafter). The Korean War ended in 1953.

As a result of the Cold War, the arms race started. In 1946, for example, American scientists, politicians, and corporate interests saw nuclear testing continued at Bikini Atoll. In 1949, the Soviet Union detonated its own bomb and thus shifted the balance of power among the Cold War superpowers, principally Russia and America, but also Great Britain. In 1951, American detonated an H-bomb in the Marshall Islands. In 1952, Britain tested its first atomic bomb in Western Australia and in 1954, the United States tested the H-Bomb at Bikini Islands.

Other social and cultural events dominated the domestic landscape at this time: From the vantage point of the 1990s, the 1950s seem like a pressure cooker waiting to explode. America's dropping of the bomb on Hiroshima and Nagasaki in 1945, and its continued nuclear testing in the Pacific in the 1950s, also produced the Peace Movements of the 1960s: Atomic power was met by flower power. Television had become immensely popular. By 1954, twenty-nine million homes were watching shows like *Leave It to Beaver,* although, as Stephanie Coontz points out, not everyone shared in the "consumer expansion that provided Hotpoint appliances for June Cleaver's kitchen and a vacuum cleaner for Donna Stone" (29). One of the most important events of the 1950s, though, was the ruling by the U.S. Supreme Court in 1954 that segregation by color in public schools was a violation of the 14th Amendment. As Bob Dylan would sing in 1964: "The Times They Are A-Changin'."

How did these terrible events of World War II and after affect American and European moving picture industries? David Shipman's lengthy *The Story of Cinema* discusses American and European 1940s war films in chapters such as "The British at War," "Hollywood's War Effort," "French Cinema during Occupation and Readjustment," "The M.G.M. Musical," "Postwar Hollywood: The Directors [and] Studios," and "Production in Austerity Britain." John Russell Taylor's chapter on the 1940s in *1930–1990 Hollywood: Sixty Great Years* discusses "The Business of War," "Movie Mobilization," and "Brave New World 1948–9," in relation to films such as *The Bridge Over the River Kwai, Mrs. Miniver,* and *The Great Dictator* (1940). Gerald Mast's *A Short History of the Movies* comments briefly on World War II in "Hollywood in Transition: 1946–1965." Koppes and Black's *Hollywood Goes To War: How Politics, Profit, and Propaganda Shaped World War II Movies* fully details Hollywood's investment in war.

The Cold War politics of the 1950s are reflected in the films of the 1950s. War films such as *Paths of Glory* (1957) and *The Bridge Over the River Kwai* (1957) were immensely popular. Starring Kirk Douglas (whose hiring of blacklisted writer Dalton Trumbo for *Spartacus* signified the end of the McCarthy witchhunts), directed by Stanley Kubrick, and set on the French and German front during World War I, *Paths of Glory* shows the futility of war as does *Bridge Over the River Kwai,* a film set in a Japanese POW camp. Westerns such as *High Noon* (1952) and social realist movies such as *On the Waterfront* are often seen as critical of McCarthyism. Not all films from this period questioned the war: witness *The Steel Helmet* (1950), *Retreat Hell* (1952), and *Big Jim McLain* (1952). In this latter film, John Wayne made his right-wing sympathies clear as his character conducts a McCarthy-like campaign in Hawaii.

Beyond the politics of the Cold War, films such as *From Here to Eternity* reflected a much more mature approach to sexual relations and Stanley Kramer's *The Defiant Ones* (1958), starring Tony Curtis and Sidney Poitier, comments on American race relations during the 1950s. In retrospect, *The Defiant Ones* exemplifies what has recently become a trend in Hollywood movies such as *Lethal Weapon, Money Train,* and *Enemy of the State.* These and other buddy movies pair a black man with a white man, presumably in an attempt to ellide the politics of racial strife that smoldered briefly in the 1950s, erupted finally in the 1960s, and continues today. Fall-out from the Cold War included the McCarthy witchhunts. Senator McCarthy targeted Hollywood, accusing many of its writers, directors, and actors as either Communist sympathizers or bleeding-heart liberals. McCarthy was finally censored in 1954, but not before the "Red Scare" had been seen on television. Talking about the 1950s, Adrian Turner comments: "The political, social, and creative tensions [of the 1950s] produced one of the most fascinating periods in Hollywood's 75-year history" (235).

What impact did World War II have on the evolution of American and European children's cinema and film history? According to Goldstein, Zornow, and Street, none. Goldstein and Zornow do not mention World War II at all in their introduction and Street moves quickly from movies made "in the years before World War II" ("Overview" 16) to "screen adaptations of children's fiction in post-war years through the fifties" (16). There is nothing much said about World War II and children's cinema and film.

Literary Adaptations

Perhaps the most famous literary adaptation of the immediate post-World War II period was George Stevens's *The Diary of Anne Frank* (1959). Less famous but still important were Byron Haskins's *Treasure Island,* Disney's *Cinderella* and *Alice in Wonderland,* and Luigi Comincini's 1952 adaptation of Johanna Spyri's *Heidi.*

Many other children's films that have either become classics of their genre or remain important for other reasons were released during the late 1940s and early 1950s. Audiences could see Westerns such as *Shane* as well as *High Noon.* Charles Laughton's psychological thriller *The Night of the Hunter,* starring Robert Mitchum, Shelley Winters, and Lillian Gish, was released. Laughton's only directorial effort, *The Night of the Hunter,* is considered a masterpiece of German expressionism and American realism. The 1950s saw the release of sports movies involving children: *Angels in the Outfield* (1951), *It Happens Every Spring* (1949), *The Jackie Robinson Story* (1950), *Jim Thorpe: All American* (1951), and *The Kid from Left Field* (1953). Two musicals from this period are significant: *Brigadoon* (1954) and *A Connecticut Yankee in King Arthur's Court* (1949). In 1956, French director Albert Lamorisse made *The Red Balloon,* a film Jeffrey Lyons calls "one of the strangest, most beautiful children's movies ever made" (206). Neither were children's films unaffected by the developments in film technology. *Bad Day at Black Rock* (1955), according to Lyons, "a tough, gritty little movie [that] will win the hearts of young adults" (22), was one of the first films made in "the new process called CinemaScope" (22).

Social and Political Issues

World War II and the aftermath affected children's cinema and film in other ways. The McCarthy witchhunts resulted in the blacklisting of the famous "Hollywood Ten," writers, actors, and directors who refused to cooperate with the House Un-American Activities Committee (HUAC). The HUAC tried to expose Communist influences in Hollywood. Specifically, the HUAC had three functions. First, it wanted to prove that the Screen Writer's Guild (or union) had Communist members. Second, it wanted to prove that these Communist members of the Screen Writer's Guild were trying to insert subversive (Communist) propaganda into Hollywood made films. Third, it wanted to prove that President Roosevelt had encouraged pro-Soviet Union films during World War II. During the committee's hearings, friendly and unfriendly witnesses were called. Friendly witnesses, those who testified about any Communist activity they had heard of, were people like Jack Warner, Gary Cooper, and Ronald Reagan.[4] There were nineteen unfriendly witnesses, unfriendly because they were considered Communists. The famous ten were Alvah Bessie, Herbert Biberman, Lester Cole, Edward Dmytryk, Ring Lardner, Jr., John Howard Lawson, Albert Maltz, Samuel Ornitz, Adrian Scott, and Dalto Trumbo. These and others fled abroad, never worked again, or were forced to write under pseudonyms.

Of the ten, Lester Cole and Edward Dmytryk are of particular interest to the children's film historian. A screenplay writer and union activist who helped found the Screen Writer's Guild in 1933, Cole adopted the pseudonym Gerald L. C. Copely in 1966 when he wrote the screenplay for *Born Free.* Born in Canada to Ukranian immigrants and abused as a child, Dmytryk, who directed the anti-fascist *Hitler's Children* in 1943, went into self-imposed exile in Britain after being found guilty of Communist affiliations by the HUAC in 1947. Jackson notes that *Hitler's Children* was the "eleventh-biggest money-maker of 1942–1943 . . . and fortells the horror of children exposed to a very different sort of environment" (76–77)—that of Nazism.

The McCarthy witchhunts affected not just writers of children's films but the children of the writers. In "I'll Always Be An American," Patrick McGilligan, writing a book to coincide with the fiftieth anniversary of the House Un-American Activities Committee, interviewed Jules Dassin, one of many writers other than the famous ten blacklisted by the HUAC. Whilst recalling the betrayal of actors like Lee J. Cobb and directors like Robert Rossen, Dassin remarks: "When I think of Bob, I think of his kids. That's one of the things people don't talk about much—the problems we had with our children. You'd find writings on the walls of your house. Other kids would say terrible things. How do you explain what was happening [the witchhunts] to your own kids" (quoted in McGilligan 42–43). Dassin's comment reminds us that a discussion of the Cold War must include a discussion of the politics of children's lives.

Disney

From the point of view of a history of children's cinema and film, the role played by the Disney Corporation during World War II and the years immediately following is significant. Critics such as John Taylor note how Walt Disney's films were at the "forefront of escapist cinema in the dark days of 1942–3" (154). This commonsensical approach to film history—fantasy films function merely as escapist entertainment—rings true if we consider only the famous movies the Disney Corporation produced at this time. The most well-known were *Fantasia* and *Pinocchio* in 1940 and *Bambi* in 1942. On the surface what connection could there be between the dystopian landscapes of Pearl Harbor, Bataan, Hiroshima, Nagasaki, and the utopian landscapes of *Fantasia, Pinocchio,* and *Bambi*? Disney offered pure, escapist entertainment during the 1940s just as it appears to do in the 1990s with films such as *Pocahontas* and *Mulan.*

In fact, during World War II and directly after, the Disney Company continued where it left off in the 1920s and 1930s by advancing both its political and corporate interests simultaneously. Recognizing that, as a corporation, robust profits were intimately linked to a vigorous, healthy U.S. economy, the Disney Company threw its considerable production forces into the war effort. Thus, as American war production of planes, boats, and bombs reached its zenith during the early 1940s, Disney cartoon production reached its own peak. The B-24 factory at Willow Run, Michigan produced some five hundred planes per month to aid the war effort, whilst Disney was mass-producing cartoons such as *Donald Gets Drafted, The Army Mascot, Private Pluto* (1942), and *Commando Duck* (1944). Cartoons such as *The Lone Raider* caricatured the Japanese, whilst *Reason and Emotion* (1943) and *Education for Death* (1943) showed the evils of Nazism. Anthony Rhodes' *Propaganda: The Art of Persuasion, World War II* reproduces a poster advertising *Der Fuehrer's Face* and another showing Mickey Mouse dressed as Goebbels. Disney responded to the war by making instructional films such as *Victory through Air Power* (1943). Feature-length animated films such as *Saludos Amigos* (1943) and *The Three Caballeros* (1945) were designed, among other things, to sell North American "Good Neighborliness" to South America on behalf of Nelson Rockefeller's Office of the Coordinator of Inter-American Affairs. Initial sketches and finished drawings from these cartoons and films, as well as others the Disney Company halted production on, can be found in Charles Solomon's *The Disney That Never Was.* Allied with various government agencies—Agriculture, Treasury, Army, and Navy, for example—the years between 1922 and 1946 became Disney's Golden Age, its corporate interests more or less perfectly wedded to its political interests.

Capitalism and communism, finance capital and manual/mental labor, management who strike at workers and striking workers who insist upon unionization, class struggle, and self-determination: In 1941, the

Disney Company clashed with workers and found itself embroiled in a prolonged, bitter strike. The strike began in the early 1940s, although the events that led up to the strike can be traced back to the 1930s when President Roosevelt's New Deal policies created the National Labor Relations Board and made union organization within and without Hollywood easier. Studio bosses such as Louis Mayer of MGM and Jack Warner of Warner Brothers, however, equated unions with communism, union members with communists. In the late 1930s and early 1940s, these filmic and political perspectives clashed. In 1941, Herbert Sorrell, the head of the Screen Cartoonists Guild, itself part of the Painters and Paperhangers Union that was affiliated with the NLRB, told Disney that he had signed enough Disney employees to turn the studio into a closed shop (Mosley 193). Disney tried to resist the workers but failed. The boycott of the Disney studios began on August 18, when the studios closed down for four weeks (Watts 225).

There were several outcomes from the strike. First, appropriate screen credits were finally given to the Disney animators.[5] Second, disgusted with what he saw as communist infiltration, Disney flew to South America to make cartoons that would counter "pro-Nazi and anti-American propaganda in Brazil and South American states" (Mosley 196). *Saludos Amigos* and *The Three Caballeros* are the result of Disney's trip.

Third, when the HUAC called Walt Disney to testify on October 24, 1947, clearly he was ready to seek revenge upon anyone he thought was a Communist, particularly Sorrell and others who had crossed him during the stike. At the beginning of the testimony, Disney admits that his cartoons for the "Treasury on taxes" (3) were effective propaganda. Soon thereafter, Disney begins to talk about the strike at his studio, citing in particular Mr. Sorrell as a communist troublemaker. But Disney then names, apparently without foundation, people such as David Hilberman, Mr. Pomerance, and Mr. Howard as Communists. The ludicrousness of the accusations can be seen in the following comment by Disney, who says he looked up Hilberman's record and "found that, number 1 . . . he had no religion and, number 2, that he had spent considerable time at the Moscow Art Theatre studying art direction" (6)! As the testimony continues, Disney consistently places communists against "one-hundred-percent-Americans" (6), "solid Americans" (6), those who believe in "good, American rights" (7). At the end of the testimony, Chairman J. Parnell Thomas remarks to Disney: "I want to congratulate you on the form of entertainment which you have given the American people and given the world and congratulate you for taking time out to come here and testify before this committee" (7). In this repressive cinematic and political climate, Sayers' enlightened criticisms of Disney in 1965, discussed at length in Part Two: Criticism, were brave indeed and entirely in keeping with the rebellious spirit of the times.

Walt Disney's pronationalist and anticommunist wartime activities raise issues concerning not just a general history of children's cinema and film, but also the interpretation of specific Disney films. Should Disney's wartime activities be included in a history of children's cinema? Are those wartime activities relevant to interpretations of Disney's films, those released prior to and after World War II? Are films such as *Saludos Amigos* and *Der Fuehrer's Face* entertainment or instruction, art or propaganda? Using Mickey Mouse to parody Goebbels might be good propaganda, but is it good children's cinema? Is it appropriate for children? The sexual imagery and political function of *The Three Caballeros* suggests a film more appropriate for adults than children. What legal, ethical, and curricular issues are involved when teachers show students that "The celebrated innocence of the Disney Empire is merely the cultural ideology of an achieved neo-colonialism [and that] The infantile, narcissistic, and violent underside of Disney culture arises directly from the real world brutalities of capital accumulation" (Phillips & Wojcik-Andrews 85).

American Film Noir

First identified in 1946 by French critics who noticed in American cinema a "new mood of cynicism, pessimism and darkness" (Schrader 53), American film noir in general, along with contemporaneous film movements such as Italian Neorealism and French Classicism, is a response to the dark days of World War II. Schrader suggests that immediately after World War II, disillusionment set in and American films became increasingly "sardonic" (54) and realistic as they began to take a "harsh view of America" (55). What Alain Silver calls an "indigenous American form" (5), film noir in the 1940s self-critically "turns with a new viciousness toward . . . American society itself" (Schrader 55), no doubt thoroughly disturbed and distraught by "The unprecedented social upheaval of two world wars compounded by economic turmoil and genocides on every continent . . ." (5).

Partly because American film noir is usually associated with classic, canonical films such as John Huston's *The Maltese Falcon* (1941), Billy

Wilder's *Double Indemnity* (1944), and Fritz Lang's *The Woman in the Window* (1945), it remains a neglected area of children's cinema and film history. Street's omission of a discussion of film noir is surprising. At least one film noir from the 1940s had a child protagonist and was a commercially successful, literary adaptation. I refer of course to *The Window,* Ted Tetzlaff's adaptation of Cornell Woolrich's novelette *The Boy Cried Murder.* Jackson's omission is equally surprising. *The Window,* and a more recent film noir such as *Rumble Fish,* are surely relevant to sociocultural film historians interested in the image of a child star and what that image reflects about the attitudes of Americans toward children in any given historical period. Of particular interest would be the issue of juvenile deliquency in film noir.

Italian Neorealism

Gerald Mast writes: "After the Second World War, European directors did exactly what they did after the First World War. They climbed out from under five years of wartime rubble and disrupted production, somehow scraped enough money and film stock to [make] films that showed extraordinary sincerity, perceptivity, and artistic control" (315). Making films that markedly "contrasted with the typical American film" (315), Italy and France, along with Sweden, Britain, and Czechoslovakia, made particularly important contributions to children's cinema after World War II. Postwar Italy saw the rise of Italian Neorealism, whilst postwar France saw the rise of French Classicism. The 1950s in Sweden saw the rise to prominence of Ingmar Bergman, whilst the British film industry produced a number of significant adaptations, comedies, and social realist films. Czechoslovakian animation dominated the industry "in Eastern Europe" (14) during the 1950s, as Street points out.

Obviously influenced by Marxist thinking, the Italian Neorealist movement, which emerged out of the end of Fascist rule in Italy in the mid-1940s, and lasted in its classical phase from 1945 to 1949, emphasized the following points. Overall, Neorealist films should show a realistic "slice of life" and should not flinch from looking at war, conflict, poverty, hunger, abuse, and so forth. Neorealist films should emphasize the everyday experiences of ordinary men, women, and children rather than the exceptional, supernatural, or magical happenings of extraordinary heroes and heroines. Settings in Neorealist films should be plain, local, above all real. Lighting and dialogue should be approriately natural, not enhanced by studio lights (wherever possible), formal scripts, or studio speech coaches. Regional and local dialects should be used rather than any standard English or American. In the Marxist tradition, Neorealist films should reveal how adverse environments adversely affect the daily lives of people.

Economic and legal matters brought the classic Neorealist period to a close. As in the United States, there was an economic recovery in Italy after World War II. The Andreotti Law of 1949 took a decidedly protectionist stance, threatening to withhold state subsidies from those Italian film companies that did not show Italy recovering from the war. As Parkinson remarks: "Increasingly formal, psychological, and stereotypical, Neo-realism ultimately fell victim to the economic recovery which eroded its ideological basis and thematic resources and which financed the resumption of studio production" (154).

Rossellini's 1945 *Roma Città Aperta* (*Rome Open City)* is generally considered the first Italian Neorealist film, though in "Italian neo-realism" (191–194), Susan Hayward argues that Luchino Visconti's *Ossessione* (1942) in fact initiated the Neorealist movement. Regardless, other Neorealist films would be Rossellini's *Paisan* (1946), De Sica's *Shoeshine* (1946), Rossellini's *Germany Year Zero* (1947), and the famous *The Bicycle Thief* (1948) (see Figure 6).

Since the post-World War II era, Italian films such as Antonioni's *The Red Desert* (1964), Olmi's *The Sound of Trumpets* (1961), Bertolucci's *1900* (1976), and the Taviani Brothers' *The Night of the Shooting Stars* (1982) are considered Neorealist. Outside of Italy, the 1973 film from Spain, *The Spirit of the Beehive* (*El Espiritu de la Colmena*) contains Neorealist elements.

To take one example from the preceeding list: *La Notte di San Lorenzo* (*The Night of the Shooting Stars*) is a story about the heartbreaking events that happen to ordinary villagers—hence the Neorealist term—in San Martino, Italy as World War II grinds to a close. The villagers are awaiting the liberating American armed forces. In a series of last-minute, vindictive reprisals, the German and Fascist soldiers occupying San Martino mark several houses with single green crosses. The marked houses are then mined. The occupying armies threaten to explode the mines at 3 A.M. All the villagers are ordered into the local cathedral, warning that anyone found outside the cathedral after 3 A.M. will be summarily shot. Not unsurprisingly, many villagers don't trust the German and Fascist soldiers. Under the cover of night, one group strikes out in search of the advancing American soldiers whose bombs can be heard in the distance. A second group remains, knowing full well

Figure 6. Vittorio De Sica's *The Bicycle Thief*. Photo courtesy of the Museum of Modern Art/Film Stills Archive, New York.

their homes will be destroyed but otherwise trusting the orders of the occupying German and Fascist armies because those orders are passed down through the local religious leaders. Narrated by Cecilia, a survivor who experienced the traumatic events as a six-year-old, the film shows what happened to both groups of villagers.

Befitting a film in the Italian Neorealist tradition, *La Notte di San Lorenzo* does not glorify the struggles between the indigenous villagers and the occupying armies. In complete contrast to the way corporate Hollywood often glorifies war in general and World War II in particular, *The Night of the Shooting Stars* makes war mundane and thus all the more horribly real by concentrating on the very ordinary ways in which the villagers, all of whom know one another well, cope with the loss of their village, the tragic deaths of their friends and family, their sense of hopelessness, isolation, community spirit, and eventual liberation. Settings include the village square, wheat fields, forests, unlit basements, and rooms lit only by moonlight or candle. Natural lighting here works to great effect. When the fleeing villagers rest in a bombed-out crater, they are bathed in moonlight and look uncannily like dead bodies executed and dumped into mass graves, the allusion to the genocide of World War II quite clear. At other times, when we see characters lost in thought, voice-overs indeed show them remembering the sheets, matresses, clothes, and pots and pans they left behind-the minute details of their daily lives. Neorealist to the very end, the film largely refuses the heroic, fairy tale ending common to corporate Hollywood films. Instead of having, say, the liberating American forces arrive just in time to prevent the departing German and Italian soldiers from destroying the cathedral, the film in fact shows the cathedral being blow up with the villagers who stayed behind still inside. The flailing and mutilated bodies of those who barely survive spill out into the village square, a deadly reminder to audiences that in real life the cavalry more often than not arrives late.

French Classicism

Whilst Italian Neorealist films from 1945 to 1949 showed ordinary men and women and children struggling against inhumane social conditions, the major French directors from this immediate postwar period were René Clair, Jean Renoir, Jean Cocteau, René Clément, and Marcel Carné. Cocteau's *Beauty and the Beast* (1946) perfectly expresses French Classicist ideas.

Not all French films in the immediate postwar period concerned themselves with questions of style and form. Other films examined World War II through the eyes of children and young adults. Clément's 1952 *Leus Jeux Interdits* (*Forbidden Games*), considered by Goldstein and Zornow a "classic of children in war and of the gap between children and adults" (211), is a case in point.

Summary

World War II and the years immediately following obviously affected children's cinema and film in more ways that just commercially successful adaptations and images of the child. The Disney Company consolidated both its profit and power base by working tirelessly in conjunction with various government agencies. American hegemony in the realm of global economics and politics was matched by Disney's hegemony in animation. Even so, at least five non-Disney film classics from this period that starred children (four from Europe) were popular among audiences: *The Window, Shoeshine, The Bicycle Thief, Beauty and the Beast* and *Forbidden Games.* By the late 1940s and 1950s, child stars from the 1930s such as Shirley Temple and Jane Withers had grown up and been replaced by Elizabeth Taylor and others. Temple's famous films, for example, were all from the 1930s and mostly produced by 20th Century Fox. By the 1940s, she was making films for studios such as MGM, United Artists, Columbia, RKO-Radio, Warner Brothers/First National, and the like. According to her autobiography, *Child Star,* Temple's last film was *A Kiss for Corliss* in 1949. Temple, Withers, and Taylor had themselves replaced the child stars of the silent era. In *Capital,* Marx writes that the commodity is the "elementary" (125) form of capitalism. Given the way Hollywood employs and then makes redundant a few years later its child stars, it's not far-fetched to see the child star as a commodity, an "elementary form" (125) both of corporate Hollywood and American capitalism.

Many of the major themes that flower in post-World War II children's films from corporate Hollywood took root in the political soil of the 1940s and 1950s. During the Cold War, the Soviet Union was presented as a major threat to the American way of life, the "American Century." The threat of the Soviet Union, the "Red Scare," legitimated the emergence of the military-industrial complex and the emphasis on technology. Of course, Soviet Union technology was presented as bad technology, relentlessly ridiculed as out of date, inefficient, dangerous because it was in the wrong hands. By comparison, American technology was presented as good technology because it was in the right hands, those working for capitalism and democracy rather than communism and socialism, the free market and private property rather than the command economy and shared property. That the Cold War was really a way for the United States and the Soviet Union as imperial powers to dominate an emerging Third World is rarely mentioned.

1960s CHILDREN'S CINEMA AND FILM HISTORY: FEMINIST POLITICS AND THE DEATH OF A CHILD STAR

Goldstein and Zornow say about 1960s children's film history that "When the "generation gap" was a cult word, we got a clinker called *The Impossible Years* (1968), which demonstrated how helpless a college professor could be in the toils of adolescent daughters" (xviii). According to Street, "Possibly as a way to outdo the [popularity] of television . . . the sixties brought to the theaters a trio of high budget, musical adaptations led by Julie Andrews and the *Mary Poppins* crew" ("Overview" 16). Street refers here to two issues: the rise of television and the response of the studios to the concomitant decline in movie attendance with films such as 20th Century Fox's *Doctor Dolittle,* an adaptation of the Hugh Lofting story (remade in the 1990s with Eddie Murphy), United Artists' *Chitty Chitty Bang Bang,* and, of course, the 1964 Walt Disney film *Mary Poppins,* described as "One of the greatest children's films ever [and] a timeless story" (*Movie Guide* 426). Jackson argues that the screen image of the child in 1960s films reflects a growing ambiguity in the United States toward children. Thus, on the one hand a number of films continue to reflect the belief that children are innocent. Dramas such as *To Kill a Mockingbird,* musicals such as *Oliver,* and filmmakers such as Disney "colored their portrayals of children with a natural innocence" (127). On the other hand, Jackson claims, "By the 1960s, several new images of children in American films had taken hold" (126). Films such as *The Innocents* (1961),[6] *The Miracle Worker* (1962), *The Children's Hour* (1962), and *Rosemary's Baby* (1968) suggest a quite different attitude toward children, one that stems from the fact that during the 1960s "Americans were bombarded with threats from all sides—the Cuban Missile Crisis; the assassinations of a president, a presidential hopeful, and a noted civil-rights leader; and the Vietnam war, the first time United States military involvement in a major war was not perceived by the public as clearly in the right" (126).

Studios

No doubt as a result of the antitrust legislation, the rise of television, the temporary decline in movie attendance, and other socioeconomic factors, the ownership of the major Hollywood studios during the 1960s began to change. Thus, in 1962, Universal Pictures, originally founded in 1912 when Carl Laemmle merged his IMP company with corporations such as Bison 101, Nestor, and Powers, became a subsidiary of MCA

Inc., a worldwide entertainment conglomerate that owned, among other things, Decca Records. Universal became part of Universal City Studios Incorporated in 1966. Before it became a wholly owned subsidiary of Viacom in 1994, Paramount was bought by Gulf and Western, also in 1966. In 1967, Warner Brothers was acquired by Seven Arts Production, a Canadian corporation. Again in 1967, United Artists became a subsidiary of TransAmerican Corporation. Columbia Pictures became Columbia Pictures Industries in 1968. A year later, in 1969, the ownership of Warner Brothers again changed: This time it was sold to Kinney National Service.

Literary Adaptations

The studios continued to make expensive, blockbuster productions. MGM made *Mutiny on the Bounty* with Marlon Brando. 20th Century Fox made *Cleopatra* with Richard Burton and Elisabeth Taylor and *The Sound of Music.* Warner Brothers made *My Fair Lady.* Other films from the 1960s would include historical epics such as *Dr. Zhivago,* and dramas such as *The Longest Day, Guess Who's Coming to Dinner,* and *The Planet of the Apes.* MGM/Hawk produced Kubrick's 1968 *2001: A Space Odyssey* (from Arthur C. Clarke's *The Sentinel*). Popular musicals included *Funny Girl, Can-Can* (1960), and *West Side Story* (1961).

Whilst several of these films—*The Sound of Music,* for example—made money, many, such as *Cleopatra,* did not.

Other than the "trio of high budget, musical adaptations" cited by Street, the studios adapted and produced many films for younger viewers. At the beginning of the decade, in 1960, Columbia adapted Swift's *Gulliver's Travels* to make *The Three Worlds of Gulliver.* Known for its (then) clever trick photography and special effects, *The Three Worlds of Gulliver* mostly ignores the biting satire of Swift's 1726 masterpiece. In 1961, Columbia turned to an 1874 Jules Verne story, *The Mysterious Island.* In 1962, 20th Century Fox adapted Jules Verne's 1863 novel *Five Weeks in a Balloon.* MGM adapted H. Rider Haggard's 1887 tale *She* in 1965 and Universal adapted Percival Christopher Wren's 1924 book *Beau Geste* in 1966. It was originally released by Universal in 1939. The 1966 version starred Guy Stockwell, Doug Mclure, Telly Savalas, and Leslie Nielsen. Savalas, after Kojak (1973–78), also acted in *The Muppet Movie* (1979). Nielsen starred in comedies such as *Airplane* (1980), *The Naked Gun* (1988), *The Naked Gun 2 1/2,* and *Repossessed* (1990), a spoof on *The Exorcist* starring a much older Linda Blair.

Hollywood's studios also produced films starring children and young adults that were not commercially successful but literary adaptations nonetheless. Warners-Seven Arts Productions released *Up the Down Staircase* (1967), *The Heart is a Lonely Hunter* (1968), *The Learning Tree* (1969), and a version of *Heidi* (Johanna Spyri's 1880 classic). MGM produced *Two Loves* (1961). Universal made *And Now Miguel* (1966). Based on William Faulkner's novel of the same name, National General produced *The Reivers* (1969) starring Mitch Vogel as eleven-year-old Lucius.

Child Stars

In the 1960s, Mitch Vogel, Hayley Mills, Brandon de Wilde, Michael Kearney, Patty Duke, Mary Badham, Mark Lester, Jack Wild, and others were among the popular child stars.

Whilst Brandon de Wilde is perhaps most famous for his role as Joey Starrett in the Paramount Pictures/George Stevens production of *Shane* (1953)—Joey is the young boy who idolizes the mysterious ex-gunslinger Shane, played by Alan Ladd—de Wilde also made two films in the 1960s: *All Fall Down* in 1962 for MGM and *Hud* in 1963 for Paramount. Of these, *Hud,* directed by Martin Ritt (who in 1972 would direct Paul Winfield and Cicely Tyson in *Sounder*) is probably the most famous. Cast to type, de Wilde again plays a young boy attracted to an antihero, this time Hud Bannon rather than Shane. Also, just as Mary Pickford in the silent era was cast to play young girls long after she had grown up—she played a girl of twelve in *Pollyanna* as a twenty-seven-year-old—similarly de Wilde in *Hud* played the fifteen-year-old role of Lon Bannon when he was himself twenty.

Starring opposite Anne Bancroft as Anne Sullivan, Patty Duke played seven-year-old Helen Keller in *The Miracle Worker* (1962). As a reflection of the rise of television, Patty Duke is perhaps best known for the success of her television show "The Patty Duke Show." However, she also did a remake of *The Miracle Worker* in 1979. Her personal life was less of a success. The "youngest child of an alcoholic father and an emotionally unstable mother" (Chandler 18), Duke suffered after her show from depression, anorexia, drugs, and alcohol abuse. She was eventually diagnosed as a manic depressive. Married four times, Patty Duke had two children. Sean, her eldest, has acted in films such as *The Goonies* (1985), *Toy Soldiers* (1991), and *Encino Man* (1992).

Social and Political Issues

In relation to the image of the child, whilst Jackson's idea—that the screen image of the child reflected the ambiguous attitudes Americans held at the time toward children—rests upon a solid enough foundation, Fredric Jameson's essay "Periodizing the 60s" provides a more detailed account of what happened in the 1960s. What Jackson sees as ambiguous was in fact a radical split.

Jameson writes that "The simplest yet most universal formulation surely remains the widely shared feeling that in the 60s, for a time, everything was possible; that this period, in other words, was a moment of a universal liberation, a global unbinding of energies" ("Periodizing" 207). Indeed, the period is generally known by a number of famous movements—the women's movement, the civil rights movement, the student and antiwar demonstrations—on the defensive today but on the offensive in the 1960s and 1970s. There also were the hippies, flower-power, love, and peace, The Beatles and the Rolling Stones, drugs and rock 'n' roll, Woodstock, and other First World countercultural changes that all erupted during the 1960s. Kennedy's election in 1961 as the thirty-fifth President of the United States inaugurated what Giannetti and Eyman call an era of "romantic idealism, best typified by the youthful [president] and his glamorous wife" (*Flashback* 309).

Yet if the social, cultural, and political changes of the 1960s are traditionally seen as leading to a era of hope and freedom, they are also seen as leading to a period of despair and repression. JFK admitted responsibility for the Bay of Pigs fiasco in 1961. The Cuban Missile crisis threatened to plunge the world into a nuclear holocaust in 1962. In 1963 and 1965, people watched the race riots in Alabama and Los Angeles on television. JFK was assasinated in 1963. Immediately afterward, JFK's assassin Lee Harvey Oswald was shot and killed on television by Jack Ruby. In 1965, Malcolm X was assassinated. In 1968, Martin Luther King was assassinated by James Earl Ray. Robert F. Kennedy was assassinated in 1968, the same year the former Soviet Union invaded Czechoslovakia. With JFK and Robert F. Kennedy dead, Nixon became president in 1968, promising to end the war in Vietnam. As the promises grew, so did the number of dead soldiers. Janis Joplin, Jimi Hendrix, and Jim Morrison all died from drug overdoses. Woodstock, a love-in, stands in stark contrast to the Vietnam War, a death-in. No wonder Giannetti and Eyman call "The 1960s . . . a schizoid decade in the American cinema" (309).

A general glance at the films released during the 1960s suggests precisely how "schizoid" rather than "ambiguous" the decade was in terms of its images of the child. In 1960 and 1961, for example, utterly different images of the child could be found in classic horror films such as *Village of the Damned* or children's animated musicals such as Disney's *One Hundred and One Dalmations.* Two years, later, in 1962, audiences could again see completely divergent images of the child in films as dissimiliar and incongruous as *The Miracle Worker, The Children's Hour, Lolita,* or *To Kill a Mockingbird.* Toward the end of the decade, in 1968, viewers could see almost diametrically opposed images of the child in two very successful films: Paramount's infamous horror movie *Rosemary's Baby,* directed by Roman Polanski from the novel by Ira Levin, or Warwick's celebrated musical *Oliver*!, directed by Carol Reed from Dickens's *Oliver Twist.*

A comparison between *Island of the Blue Dolphins* and *Mary Poppins* suggests how "schizoid" the decade was in terms of its images of the child. *Island of the Blue Dolphins* (1964) reflects Jameson's assessment of the sixties as a period of "universal liberation" (Jameson, "Periodizing" 207). Other critics agree. Ellen Seiter's comment in *Children's Novels and the Movies* that the 1964 filmed version of Scott O'Dell's 1960 *Island of the Blue Dolphins* is a feminist parable, because it shows diaries as a form of "women's self-expression," and because its heroine, Karana, offers "an exceptionally positive role model for girls," reflects precisely the kind of liberational developments taking place within the women's movement throughout the 1960s. In particular, as Toril Moi points out, "Images of Women" criticism, which began with Mary Ellmann's *Thinking about Women* in 1968 and became part of the curriculum of "American colleges in the early 1970s" (Moi 42), demanded the "representation of [impressive] female role-models in literature" (47). Of course, in subsequent decades, feminist theory evolved and developed in multiple directions, as Mills et al. note in their introduction to *Feminist Readings/Feminists Readings* (1989). Nonetheless, Seiter's observations are appropriate. Universal's 1964 filmed version of *Island of the Blue Dolphins* reflects the ideals of feminist groups in the 1960s, who were "increasingly starting to form their own liberation groups, both as a supplement and an alternative to the other forms of political struggle in which they were involved" (Moi 22).

In complete contrast to films such as *Islands of the Blue Dolphins* are films such as *Mary Poppins,* Disney's adaptation of the children's classic by P. L. Travers.

The "schizoid" aspects of children's cinema and film in the 1960s is reflected in the rise and fall of two Disney stars: Hayley Mills from London, England and Bobby Driscoll from Cedar Rapids, Iowa. Hayley Mills was one of the most popular child stars of the 1960s. She was signed as a child star by the Walt Disney Corporation and made films such as *Pollyanna* (1960), *The Parent Trap* (1962), *In Search of the Castaways* (1962), and *That Darn Cat* (1965). She won an Oscar for her performance in *Pollyanna,* a remake of a 1920s film starring Mary Pickford. Bobby Driscoll had also been a popular Disney child star during the 1940s and 1950s. He acted in films such as *Song of the South* (1946), *So Dear to My Heart* (1948), *The Window* (1949), and *Treasure Island* (1950). He was the voice of Peter in the Walt Disney Productions version of *Peter Pan* (1953). Like Mills, Driscoll won an Oscar, this time for his performance in *The Window,* a film considered a perfect example of American film noir. But the utopian images of childhood represented in the Disney films by Hayley Mills stands in complete "schizoid" contrast to the dystopian realities of Driscoll's later years. In 1968 he was found dead, apparently from a drug-induced heart attack, in an abandoned New York City tenement building. It was a year before his dead body was identified through dental records.

European Children's Cinema

In Europe, the British and French moving picture industries in particular made significant films concerning children and childhood. Some have since become classics. United Kingdom productions such as *Loneliness of the Long Distance Runner* (1962), *Lord of the Flies* (1963), *Born Free* (1966), *To Sir With Love* (1967), and *If . . .* (1968), UK/Italy productions such as *Romeo and Juliet* (1968), and French films such as *L'Enfant Sauvage* (1969), all require inclusion in any comprehensive global history of children's cinema and film.

Overall in the 1960s, British cinema enjoyed what Giannetti and Eyman call "a golden age . . . not only at home but abroad" (353). For example, films such as David Lean's *Lawrence of Arabia* (1962), Tony Richardson's *Tom Jones* (1963), and Carol Reed's *Oliver!* (1968) all won Oscars. Films such as *A Man for All Seasons* (1966) were also extremely popular. I remember *A Man for All Seasons,* because it was one of many films during the 1960s my mother took me to see, but also because of the abrupt ending: The end of Moore's life coincides with the end of the film. The 1960s saw the beginning of the James Bond series. Despite, or because, the Cold War has ended, the James Bond franchise, now starring Pierce Brosnan rather than Sean Connery, remains as profitable and popular with audiences as ever. *GoldenEye* (1995) and *Tomorrow Never Dies* (1997) are two of the top grossing movies of all time worldwide, earning $350,900,000 and $336,300,000 respectively.

From that golden age of British cinema, two quite opposite film movements have emerged as important to an understanding of the history of children's cinema and film: the Angry Young Men (1958–63) and the Swinging London (1963–70) movement. The former emerged out of three sets of conditions: John Osborne's 1956 play *Look Back in Anger,* which was directed by Tony Richardson, the Free Cinema movement in 1950s England, which was started by Lindsay Anderson, Karel Reisz, and Tony Richardson, and the 1958 release of Jack Clayton's *Room at the Top* and Richardson's adaptation of *Look Back in Anger.* Lindsay Anderson made *If . . .* and *O Lucky Man.* As well as *Look Back in Anger,* Tony Richardson also made *The Loneliness of the Long Distance Runner* and *Tom Jones.* Another Angry Young Man director, Jack Clayton, made *Room at the Top* (1958) but also *The Innocents* (1961) and *Our Mother's House* (1967).

Whilst the Angry Young Man movement strongly emphasized social realism, the Swinging London movement tended to emphasize what Giannetti and Eyman call the "prosperity and trendy stylishness of the era" (354). The former was all seriousness, the latter all fun. Other than James Bond films such as Terence Young's *From Russia With Love* (1963), Swinging London films included *A Hard Day's Night* and *Help* (1965). Both starred The Beatles. Contemporary films such as *The Avengers, Austin Powers: International Man of Mystery,* and *Austin Powers: The Spy Who Shagged Me* (1999), films most kids have heard about if not seen, poke fun not at the social realism of the Angry Young Man movement but the Swinging London movement.

Other important films from the 1960s relevant to a history of children's or youth cinema and film would include James Clavell's 1967 *To Sir With Love,* based upon E. R. Braithwaite's real experiences as a black teacher discriminated against because of his color. The film introduced Sidney Poitier as a firm but sensitive teacher who, against all odds, believes that his otherwise drop-out students can beat the system. A prototype for numerous 1970s, 1980s, and 1990s films that place a young, relatively naive teacher in the classroom with a group of tough but eventually generous high-school deadbeats, a recent example of *To Sir With Love* would be *Dangerous Minds.* [7]

Finally, as mentioned previously, the screenplay for British Lion/

Columbia's *Born Free,* a 1966 movie starring Virginia McKenna and Bill Travers, was written by Lester Cole, one of the famous "Hollywood Ten" blacklisted and imprisoned by the HUAC in 1947 for his Communist sympathies. British director Carol Reed's 1968 *Oliver!*, a Warwick/ Romulus Production, won Oscars and produced two child stars: Mark Lester and Jack Wild.

If the major filmmakers in America and Europe at this time were Sidney Lumet, John Frankenheimer, John Cassavetes, Mike Nichols, Sam Peckinpah, Stanley Kubrick, and others, nouvelle vague (New Wave) directors in France included François Truffaut, Jean-Luc Goddard, Louis Malle, and Claude Chabrol. Of these, Louis Malle and François Truffaut are perhaps most relevant here for both have made lasting contributions to children's cinema by making films that concentrate on children themselves. Malle's contribution consists of films such as *Zazie dans le Metro* (1960), *Murmur of the Heart* (1971), *Black Moon* (1975), which was inspired by Carroll's *Alice's Adventures in Wonderland, Pretty Baby* (1978), and *Au Revoir les Enfants* (1987). Truffaut established himself as a director of children with a film called *The 400 Blows* (1959). This was followed with *The Wild Child* (1969/70) and *Small Change* (1976). *The Wild Child* introduced into children's cinema the image of the feral child, an image that remains popular today in films from America and Iran such as *Aliens* and *The Apple,* respectively.[8] Though both Malle and Truffault are now dead, their filmmaking style and thematic concerns can be found in French directors like Jacques Doillon, whose most recent film was *Ponette*.

International

At least two important films starring kids were released in Japan during the 1960s: *Bad Boys* (1960) and *Boy* (1969). *Bad Boys* concerns the lives of delinquent kids in a reform school. Particularly, *Bad Boys* focuses on Asai (Yukio Amada) as he deals with life inside Akehama Reformatory. Director Susumu Hani was inspired to make the semidocumentary *Bad Boys* after reading *Pinioned Wings,* a true account of life inside a reform school in Kurihama, Tokyo Bay written by the inmates themselves.

Bad Boys is similar to films such as *Dead End* (1937), *Shoeshine* (1946), *Los Olvidados* (1950), and *Pixote* (1981). Generally, like these films, *Bad Boys* works within the Italian Neorealist tradtion: shooting took place in the "actual haunts of juvenile delinquents . . . in downtown Tokyo" (Goldstein and Zornow 231). There was no formal script. The cast were all nonprofessionals encouraged to improvise and respond to circumstances as they otherwise would do in real life. Contentwise, each of these films deals with social issues such as crime, poverty, juvenile delinquency, and the general deprivation suffered by children at the hands of uncaring adults and their faceless institutions.

Summary

The 1960s are an important decade in the history of children's cinema and film. The ownership of the studios passes from individuals to individual corporations. Blockbuster hits continue to make money: think here of *My Fair Lady* and *Mary Poppins.* But also in children's cinema, there are the release of films such as Paramount's *All the Way Home* (1963), which deals with death, a French/Italian production, *The Christmas Tree* (1969), which deals with the way a child confronts his own death through leukemia, *Ivan's Childhood* (*My Name Is Ivan*), a 1962 USSR film by Andrei Tarkovsky about a twelve-year-old boy Ivan, who works as an intelligence spy for the Soviet army until he is caught, and Robert Bresson's 1966 *Mouchette,* from Georges Bernanos's *La Nouvelle Histoire de Mouchette,* a French film about the suicide of an utterly downtrodden fourteen-year-old peasant girl, Mouchette. The difference between, say, *Mary Poppins* and *Mouchette* surely captures the "schizoid" nature of the image of the child in the 1960s. Other films from the 1960s that should be included in a history of children's cinema and film would be *The Children's Hour, Lolita,* and *The Killing of Sister George,* early precursors of 1990s films dealing with sexuality as different as *The Cement Garden, The Incredibly True Adventure of Two Girls In Love, Mulan, Harriet the Spy,* and of course, the 1998 remake of *Lolita* starring Dominique Swain. The contributions of European nations such as England and France are critical to the world history of children's cinema: think here of *L'Enfant Sauvage.* Finally, whilst a minority of child stars survive the pressures of Hollywood (one thinks of Shirley Temple, Deanna Durbin, Elizabeth Taylor, and, more recently, Ron Howard, and Jodie Foster), beginning in the 1960s more and more child stars seem unable to cope with the pressures of Hollywood: One thinks of Bobby Driscoll, and also all the other child stars listed in Suzanne Chandler's 1993 *Children of Babylon*—Rebecca Schaeffer, Heather O'Rourke, Dominique Dunne, Rusty Hammer, Brandon de Wilde, Patty Duke, and so forth. Run by corporations, it is hard to see Hollywood's studios as anything but exploiters of cheap child labor.

FIRST AND THIRD WORLD CHILDREN'S CINEMA: THE 1970s AND 1980s

Goldstein and Zornow's assessment of the 1970s is confined to one paragraph, in which they note how "Producers continue to sell . . . late models of the old styles" (xviii). They suggest that after *The Cowboys* and *Bad Company,* we get *Jory* (1974), a pubescent Western about a boy who takes a blood bath to become a man. After the trendy characters in *American Graffiti* and *Paper Moon,* we get *Rafferty and the Gold Dust Twins*" (xviii).

In relation to the commercially successful adaptation of children's literature texts, Street devotes a paragraph to a discussion of animation in the 1970s and a paragraph to a discussion of the live-action feature. Noting that "The 1970s sparked a rebirth of interest in the animated feature in America" (14), Street lists films such as *The Phantom Tollbooth* (1970), *Charlotte's Web* (1973), *The Rescuers* (1977), *The Hobbit* (1977) and *The Lion, the Witch, and the Wardrobe* (1979) as examples of how "anxious producers" ("Overview" 14) turned yet again to children's literature for their story lines and their profits. In relation to the live-action feature, Street notes that there were a number of "nicely executed, unpretentious films during this time" (16). As examples, he lists *Willy Wonka and the Chocolate Factory* (1971), *Sounder* (1972), *The Railway Children* (1971), *From the Mixed-Up Files of Mrs. Basil E. Frankweiler* (1973), *Tuck Everlasting* (1976), *Sounder Part 2* (1976) and *A Hero Ain't Nothin' but a Sandwich* (1978).

Literary Adaptations and Race: *Sounder*

Because neither Goldstein and Zorno, Street, or Jackson focus on questions of race it is worth looking closer at *Sounder. Sounder* grossed $9.5 million for 20th Century Fox in 1972, just ahead of *Bednobs and Broomsticks* (Disney, $8.3 million). But it represents more than just a 1970s example of what would become in the 1980s and 1990s a lucrative source of income for the corporate studios, the commercially successful adaptation of a classic work of children's literature: Think here of *The Little Mermaid, Beauty and the Beast, Matilda, Harriet the Spy, James and the Giant Peach, Madeline,* and so forth. Nor can *Sounder*'s secure position within the history of children's cinema and film be explained away merely as a simple reflection of the modern Civil Rights movement. *Sounder*'s importance in the history of children's cinema and film emerges out of a complex amalgam of personal, political, and filmic contexts.

For example, director Martin Ritt's career, which had begun in the 1930s when he acted as a young man in socially conscious plays such as

Golden Boy (1937), came to a grinding halt in the 1950s when he was blacklisted because of his Communist affiliations. No doubt the blacklisting was on his mind when he directed not just *Sounder,* which deals with questions of race, but also *Norma Rae* (1979), which deals with questions of class. Furthermore, just as *Sounder* reflects one man's personal commitment to social justice, so it also reflects the broader racial and sociopolitical issues of the day. By 1969 twenty-eight Black Panthers had been killed by police. As the Civil Rights movement shifted from "nonviolence to strident militancy" (Giannetti and Eyman 377), a new genre emerged to mirror the urban warfare between whites and blacks in America's cities. The blaxploitation genre, parodied most recently by Keenan Ivory Wayan's *I'm Gonna Git You Sucka* (1988), produced two famous films: *Shaft* (1971) and *Superfly* (1972). Ritt's *Sounder,* released in the same year as *Superfly,* is clearly a response to, rather than an example of, the blaxploitation genre.

Sounder emerges, then, out of various historical contexts. First, to be sure, it was for the 1970s a commercially sucessful adaptation of a classic work of children's literature. Second, from a biographical point of view, the film is clearly marked by Ritt's own personal experiences and subsequent committment to the use of film as a tool for social change. Third, from the point of view of race, politics, and cinema, it is a response to the evolution of the Civil Rights movement during the 1960s but also the appearance of Black Cinema, particularly the blaxploitation genre, in the early to mid-1970s. The commercial success of *Sounder* is only one reason why it is relevant to the history of children's cinema and film.

Three important films from the 1970s that starred children, but which were hardly children's films, were *Pretty Baby, Taxi Driver,* and *The Exorcist.*

Child Stars

Three famous child stars whose careers began in the 1970s were Brooke Shields, Jodie Foster, and Linda Blair. Robert Downey, Jr. also began his career in the 1970s in a film called *Pound* (1970).

European and International Children's Cinema and Film: the 1970s

France, Britain, Spain, Canada, and Australia all produced important films during the 1970s, some of which, though not all, were adaptations from classic works of children's literature. The contribution of French directors Malle and Truffaut to world children's cinema in the 1970s I have already discussed. In Britain, Joseph Losey produced *The Go-Between* (1971), whilst Lionel Jeffries directed *The Railway Children* (1970), an adaptation of E. Nesbitt's novel. In Spain, Victor Erice's first directorial effort was the acclaimed 1973 drama *The Spirit of the Beehive* (*El Espiritu de la Colmena*). Nicholas Roeg's *Walkabout* (1971), a combined Britain/Australia production, that was adapted from the novel by James Vance Marshall and starred Jenny Agutter, Lucien John, and David Gumpilil, was also well received.

Each of these films has historical significance. Though British cinema according to critics was on the decline during the 1970s, *The Go-Between* and *The Railway Children* were surely two notable exceptions, if only because they produced such excellent performances from their respective child stars.

Spain's contribution to 1970s children's cinema and film history is a film called *The Spirit of the Beehive.* Not adapted from a work of children's literature, but instead developed from an idea by director Victor Erice and Angel Fernandos Santos, *Spirit of the Beehive* is nonetheless described by Goldstein and Zornow as one of the "most haunting [films] ever made about children" (274). All image, the film contains little dialog. Erice's story of a young girl's obsession with the Frankenstein monster is told visually. *Spirit of the Beehive* is not so much a children's moving picture as it is a children's moving picture book that speaks volumes in images even as it says nothing in words.

Spirit tells us immediately that the drama we are about to see is set in a mostly deserted village somewhere in Castile, circa 1940. One day, a man in a truck delivers a movie, the 1931 James Whale-Boris Karloff version of *Frankenstein,* which the village kids and adults gather to watch later that evening. After the show, Ana (Ana Torrent) asks her sister Isabel (Isabel Telleria) why the little girl was killed by the monster and why the monster was killed by the people. In one of the great ironic statements of children's cinema, Isabel tells Ana that in fact movies always lie, that monsters do exist, and that Frankenstein, Isabel continues in hushed whispers, is alive and well in a local barn. Enchanted by this tale and believing it to be true, Ana begins to play in and around the local barn and, when an escaped convict arrives, thinks that movies do indeed lie and that Frankenstein is in fact alive. The strange and eerie encounter between Ana and the convict takes place at night, the shadows in the moonlight making Ana's dreams appear real enough.

Like so many European films that deal with children, Erice's *Spirit of the Beehive* exists on multiple levels, its significance to children's cinema not just the stunning performances from its two child stars (hardly known today) but precisely the fact that it weaves together historical and symbolic meanings virtually out of thin air. Set in the 1940s, *Beehive* clearly situates itself within the post-World War II, Spanish Civil War period. As such the monster Frankenstein clearly alludes to Franco. The film also situates itself in the Italian Neorealist tradition, one whose classical phase had ended in the late 1940s but whose poetic phase—gritty realism romanticized—obviously continued into the 1970s and beyond as *Spirit* attests. Thus, whilst the film deals realistically with a group of ordinary people living sparsely in Castile in the 1940s—the children go to school, the father keeps bees, the mother writes letters, trains pull into the station and then leave—the camerawork is richly symbolic rather than socially probing. We know that Ana, Isabel, and their parents are relatively poor, but the film focuses on their harsh dreams as well as their harsh environment. The camerawork, the low lighting, and the allusions to Frankenstein and the monster lend to the film symbolic as well as realistic power.

Reacting against the fact that so many films seen by Australians during the 1960s were American, it was decided that an Australian Film Development Corporation (AFDC) would have to be created in order to challenge the importation of American movies: American cinematic imperialism could be resisted but only with government legislative and financial help. Accordingly, the Australian Parliament passed the Australian Film Development Corporation Act in 1970 and, as Zonn and Aitken, note: "the AFDC became functional in 1971" (141). Like other fledgling cinemas in Europe, notably in Denmark and Iran,[9] money would come through "direct grants" or "tax incentives" (141).

Walkabout, Peter Weir's 1975 *Picnic at Hanging Rock,* H. Safran's *Storm Boy* (1976), and George Miller's *Mad Max* (1979) reflect the renaissance of Australian cinema in the 1970s, in particular its use of children to "subvert a series of myths of male dominance in Australian culture" (137).

In relation to the 1980s, Street's essay concludes with a statement that foreshadows precisely the direction in which corporate children's films have since developed. Street writes, "If 1982's eagerly awaited [children's films] are indications, the medium [of children's cinema] is in for a commercially successful and an artistically satisfying future" ("Overview" 17). The profitability of children's films in the 1980s is easily demonstrated. Setting aside for the moment Ingmar Bergman's *Fanny and Alexander,* Truffaut's *Au Revoir les Enfants,* August's *Pelle the Conqueror,* and Hector

Babenco's *Pixote,* the "1980s variant" (Wood, *Hollywood* 163) of American children's films has surely been commercially successful. Chronologically, the decade begins with Paramount's *Popeye* (1980). Starring Robin Williams, *Popeye* earned $24.5 million. In 1981, Disney's *The Fox and the Hound* grossed $29.8 million. In the same year, United Artists' *The Great Muppet Caper* earned $16.6 million. *E.T.* grossed $228 million in 1982. MGM's *WarGames* made $38.6 million in 1983, whilst *The Karate Kid* grossed $43.2 million when released in 1984. In 1985 *The Goonies* and *Pee Wee's Big Adventure* earned $29.9 and $18.1 million respectively for Warner Brothers. United Artists's *The Land Before Time* grossed $23.0 million when first released in 1988. Disney's *Honey, I Shrunk the Kids* grossed $72.0 million when released in 1989. Disney's *The Little Mermaid* made $40.2 million, also in 1989. In sum, these films earned $563.9 million, clearly a profitable decade for the moving picture industry.

Many of the films mentioned above are important to the history of children's cinema and film, because they have achieved a significance beyond the merely commercial. Directed by Clements and Musker, the financial success of *The Little Mermaid* in 1989 symbolized the return to economic prosperity of the Disney Corporation as a whole under new CEO Michael Eisner. *WarGames* is one of a number of acclaimed 1980s films dealing with the issue of nuclear war: think here of Spielberg's *Empire of the Sun* (1988), *Fat Man and Little Boy* (1989), *The Manhattan Project* (1986), *Silkwood* (1983), and others. Paramount's *Pee-Wee's Big Adventure* (1985) and the sequel *Big Top Pee-Wee* (1988) starred the controversial figure Paul Reubens, whose two television shows, the strange, anarchic, and yet fascinating *The Pee-Wee Herman Show* (1981) and *Pee-Wee's Playhouse* (1986), were immensely popular with adults and children until Reubens was arrested on July 28, 1991 "at an adult porno theater in Sarasota, Florida" (Bronski 64).

Studios

In the 1980s, as in the 1960s, the contours of the National Entertainment State continued to take shape. In 1981, 20th Century Fox was sold to billionaire Marvin Davis and then Rupert Murdoch in 1985. In 1981, MGM bought United Artists from TransAmerica Corporation and became MGM/UA. TriStar merged with Columbia Pictures owned then by the Coca-Cola Company. In 1989, TriStar/Columbia merged with Sony Pictures Entertainment. In 1989, Warner Brothers became part of Time-Warner, one of the four media giants Miller thinks defines the National Entertainment State.

Two new companies, both of which have since made highly successful children's films, started in the 1980s: Steven Spielberg's Amblim Entertainment in 1984 and Steven P. Jobs' Pixar Productions in 1986. Amblin, in conjunction with Universal, made two of the top grossing films worldwide to date: *E.T.: The Extra-Terrestrial* (1982), which has so far grossed $704,800,000 and *Jurassic Park* (1993), which has so far grossed $919,700,000. Purchased from Lucasfilm, Ltd. by Steve Jobs, Pixar, in conjunction with Disney, produced *Toy Story* in 1995.

Directors

Who were the important directors of the 1980s? According to Jackson, "one cannot consider the portrayals of children in contemporary movies without focusing on the contributions of one particular filmmaker: Steven Spielberg" (165). Spielberg's portrayals of innocent children have established him "as one of Hollywood's premier directors and producers" (165). Thus, on the one hand, in *Close Encounters of the Third Kind* (Columbia Pictures 1977), for example, audiences are invited to see the alien visitors through the innocent eyes of Barry Guiler (Cary Guffey). Other Spielberg-inspired films such as *Annie* (1982), *Six Weeks* (1982), *Raggedy Man* (1982), *Something Wicked This Way Comes* (1983), and *The Neverending Story* (*Die Unendliche Geschichte*) (1984) by Wolfgang Petersen "all hinge on traditional portraits of innocent children" (170). According to Jackson, "This is the message of Steven Spielberg and perhaps his greatest contribution to the developing image of children on the popular American movie screen" (173). Spielberg's children are not entirely innocent, naive, and devoid of knowledge, Jackson argues. Like children in real life, Spielberg's screen children must always cope with real life issues. According to Jackson, even Spielbergian films such as *Raiders of the Lost Ark* (1981) and *Indiana Jones and the Temple of Doom* (1984) all in some way mirror the real world. Jackson notes that, whereas 1970s films showed "abnormal children" (172–3) inhabiting a "seemingly happy, secure, normal world, 1980s films suggest the opposite: Normal children must cope with an abnormal world" (173). In other words, Spielberg's portrayal of children is not "overidealised" (173) but, relatively speaking, "real" (173).

Other influential directors appeared in the 1980s and made important films relevant to a history of children's cinema and film. The 1980s is the era of Spielberg and Lucas but also John Hughes, Christopher Columbus, Tim Burton, Don Bluth, John Musker and Ron Clements, John Badham, Bob Balaban, and others. Hughes's films include *Sixteen*

Candles (1984), *The Breakfast Club* (1985), *Ferris Bueller's Day Off* (1986), and *Curly Sue* (1991). Along with *Risky Business* (1983) and *Pretty in Pink* (1986), *The Breakfast Club* is generally considered one of the better teen movies of the 1980s. Hughes and Columbus would later collaborate on *Home Alone* (1990). After having won a Disney fellowship to study animation at the California Institute of the Arts, and subsequently produced *Frankenweenie,* a parody of *Frankenstein* that the Disney Corporation deemed too scary for children, Tim Burton was hired by Warner Brothers to make *Pee-Wee's Big Adventure* (1985), starring Paul Reubens (Paul Rubenfeld) and co-written by Reubens and (now deceased) Phil Hartman. Described by one critic as "one of the only geniuses working in American cinema" (Stephens 1) and "one of a handful of visionary directors whose style is instantly recognizable" (1), Burton's other credits include *Beetlejuice* (1988), *Batman* (1989), *Edward Scissorhands* (1990), and *Mars Attacks* (1996). Educated at Brigham Young University, ex-Disney animator Don Bluth made films such as *The Researcher* (1977), *The Secret of NIMH* (1982), *The Land Before Time* (1988), and *All Dogs Go to Heaven* (1989). To lower production costs and thus improve profits, Bluth moved his company to Ireland. Musker and Clements worked on *The Little Mermaid* (1989) and *Aladdin* (1992). John Badham, who is perhaps more famous for directing *Saturday Night Fever* in 1977 and *Stakeout* in 1987, also made *WarGames* in 1983. Bob Balaban's contribution to children's cinema in the 1980s is *Parents* (1989).

Child Stars

Particular periods in film history produce films that in turn produce a new crop of child stars. One thinks of *Bright Eyes* and Shirley Temple in the 1930s, *National Velvet* and Elizabeth Taylor in the 1940s, *The Parent Trap* and Hayley Mills in the 1960s. In the 1970s, *Pretty Baby, Taxi Driver,* and *The Exorcist* produced Brooke Shields, Jodi Foster, and Linda Blair, respectively. In the 1980s, successful films such as Spielberg's *E.T.* (1982), John Badham's *WarGames* (1983), Richard Donner's *The Goonies* (1985),[10] John Hughes's *The Breakfast Club* (1985), and Reiner's *Stand By Me* (1986) introduced child stars such as Drew Barrymore, Henry Thomas, and Robert MacNaughton (*E.T.*), Matthew Broderick and Ally Sheedy (*WarGames*), Corey Feldman (*The Goonies*), Emilio Estevez, Judd Nelson, and Molly Ringwald (*The Breakfast Club*), and River Phoenix, Wil Wheaton, and Jerry O'Connell (*Stand By Me*).

The lives of the child stars from the 1980s have varied tremendously. Often called a 1980s version of Shirley Temple, Drew Barrymore's career began when she played Gertie in Spielberg's *E.T.* (1982).[11] Interestingly, Barrymore, whose great uncle, Lionel Barrymore, played opposite Shirley Temple in *The Little Colonel* (1934), refers to Spielberg as "the Dad I never had" (quoted in Cawley 34). After *E.T.,* Barrymore starred in *Irreconcilable Differences* (1984) and *Firestarter* (1984). As she grew older, though, her film career temporarily ended. She took drugs (marijuana and cocaine), ended up in various rehabilitation centers, and had a failed suicide attempt. Her marriage ended in divorce when she was nineteen years old. At twenty, she posed for *Playboy.* [12] More recently, Barrymore has starred in *Batman Forever, Bad Girls, Cinderella, Ever After: A Cinderella Story,* and *Never Been Kissed.* By comparison, Henry Thomas, Elliott in *E.T.,* quickly faded into relative obscurity, as did Robert MacNaughton (*I Am the Cheese*) who played Elliott's older brother, Michael. After *The Breakfast Club,* Judd Nelson's career went stale. Recently, he landed a role as a magazine editor in a television sitcom starring Brooke Shields, called *Suddenly Susan.* The life and times of these and other child stars from the 1970s and 1980s, such as Brandon de Wilde (who died in a car accident in 1972) Edward Furlong, Traci Lords (who starred in many XXX-rated movies during the 1980s), Dana Plato (died of a drug overdose in 1999), Ally Sheedy, and Melanie Griffith, are more fully told in Suzanne Chandler's *Children of Babylon: The Untold Stories of Hollywood's Youngest and Brightest Stars* (1993).

Of course, there were many child stars in the 1980s from overseas. *Pelle the Conqueror* (1987) starred Pelle Hvenegaard as Pelle, the son of Pappa Lasse (played by Max von Sydow). *Au Revoir Les Enfants* (1987) starred Gaspard Menesse as Julien. These two child actors—Hvenegaard and Menesse—did not become popular with American audiences, although they were well known in their respective countries. Yet, along with Sweden's Anton Glanzelius, who played Ingemar Johansson in Lasse Hallström's 1985 comedy *My Life as a Dog,* and Shafiq Syed, who played Chaipau in Mira Nair's *Salaam Bombay,* they acted in acclaimed pictures.[13]

Social and Political Issues

In *Hollywood from Vietnam to Reagan,* Robin Wood writes that "Reassurance is the keynote and one immediately reflects that this is the era of sequels and repetitions" (162), the function of which is to "diminish, defuse, and render safe all the major radical movements that gained so much impetus, became so threatening, in the 1970s: radical feminism, black militancy, gay liberation, the assault on patriarchy" (164). Because of this, Wood argues, 1980s films, especially those from Lucas and Spielberg, reconstruct "the adult spectator as a child, or more precisely, as a childish adult, an adult who would like to be a child" (163). For Wood, this reconstruction of the adult as a child is achieved in six ways. First, the Spielberg-Lucas films are childish, because they are "intellectually undemanding" (165). Second, the special effects of these films prevents audiences from thinking too deeply about what they are watching. Special effects distract audiences from thinking about political spectacles such as the possibility of the end of capitalism brought about through a "series of escalating economic crises prophesied by Marx well over a century ago . . ." (166). Third, special effects make films such as *Star Wars* and so forth seem imaginative, original, unique, exciting, whereas in fact they are utterly banal and often derivative. Fourth, Wood suggests that the threat of nuclear war "is certainly one of the main sources of our desire to be constructed as children, to be reassured, to evade responsibility and thought" (168). The happy endings of *Star Wars, The Empire Strikes Back, Raiders of the Lost Ark,* and others might be seen as a failure to confront the realities of nuclear war—there is no happy ending—and thus a perpetuation of nuclear war and the way films invite audiences to indulge in the childish fantasy that nuclear war is winnable. Wood argues that many 1980s fantasy films center "on the struggle for possession of an ultimate weapon or power" (168). Implied here is the simplistic notion that technology in the right hands (First World, USA, dominant powers) is good, whilst technology in the wrong hands (Third World, USSR, emergent powers) is bad. Fifth, according to Wood, the Lucas-Spielberg films are not Fascist films, but they are "precisely the kinds of entertainment that a potentially Fascist culture would be expected to produce and enjoy" (170). Sixth, perhaps the kind of reassurances these sequels and repetitions most offer is the restoration of the father "which assigns all other elements to their correct, subordinate, allotted roles [and thus guarantees] the perpetuation of the nuclear family and social stability" (172).

Before discussing Wood's argument further, that 1980s films from corporate Hollywood defused 1970s radical politics and made adult viewers childish, it is worth noting something of the extent to which 1970s films were made into sequels. *Star Wars* (1977) begat *The Empire*

Strikes Back (1980), and *Return of the Jedi* (1983). *Star Wars Episode 1: The Phantom Menace* (1999) can now be seen all over the world. *Star Trek* was released in 1979. This gave birth to sequels in 1982 (*Star Trek II*), 1984 (*Star Trek III*), 1986 (*Star Trek IV*), 1989 (*Star Trek V*), and 1991 (*Star Trek VI*). *Superman II* and *Superman III* arrived in 1981 and 1983 respectively. *Jaws* came in 1975 and was followed by *Jaws II* (1978) and *Jaws 3-D* (1983). John Avildsen's 1976 *Rocky* was followed by *Rocky II* in 1979, *Rocky III* in 1982, *Rocky IV* in 1985, and *Rocky V* in 1990. *Beverly Hills Cop* was first made in 1984: Sequels include *Beverly Hills Cop 2* in 1987. *Lethal Weapon* first appeared in 1987. *Lethal Weapon 2* followed soon after in 1989. *Lethal Weapon 3* was released in 1992. *The Muppet Movie* was released in 1979. *The Great Muppet Caper* followed in 1981, *The Muppets Take Manhattan* in 1984, and *A Muppet Christmas Carol* in 1992. Amy Heckerling's *Look Who's Talking* was first released in 1989: Sequels were made in 1990 and 1993. Robert Zemeckis's *Back to the Future* was released in 1985 with sequels in 1989 (*Back to the Future II*) and 1990 (*Back to the Future III*). *The Karate Kid,* made in 1984, had sequels in 1986 (*The Karate Kid 2*) and 1989 (*Karate Kid 3*). The 1980s also was the decade for sequels to films such as *Police Academy, Crocodile Dundee, A Nightmare on Elm Street, Friday the Thirteenth,* and so forth.

We can now return to Wood's argument and ask: To what extent do these 1980s sequels "reconstruct adults as children" and in the process "diminish, defuse and render safe" (164) 1970s radical movements such as feminism, black militancy, and so forth? Stated slightly differently, the issue here is perhaps less about the degree to which these 1980s films from corporate Hollywood contain images of innocent children (they obviously do), but the *function* of the repetition of the image of the innocent child? Let us take one example, that of the relationship between women and feminism and children.

During the 1970s, feminist theory turned its gaze directly on the oppressive nature of patriarchal capitalism, in particular the role of women within the home and society at large. In this regard, two important publications are *The Dialectic of Sex: The Case for Feminist Revolution* and *Women and Revolution: A Discussion of the Unhappy Marriage of Marxism and Feminism.* The first book, by Shulamith Firestone, was published in 1970. The second book, a collection of essays written throughout the 1970s, was published in 1981 and edited by Lydia Sargent. Both works are concerned with the degree to which patriarchal capitalism oppresses women in the areas of family, motherhood, labor, and children as well as sexuality, race, and class. Shulamith Firestone's closing comments in her chapter on childhood summarizes what was a generally held sentiment among radical feminists from the 1970s. She writes: "So it is up to feminist . . . revolutionaries . . . We must include the oppression of children in any program for feminist revolution . . ." (104). Revolution, the liberation of women from the enslaving practices of patriarchal capitalism, includes the freedom of children.

Out on the streets rather than in the halls of academia, the 1970s began with women marching on Washington in favor of the Equal Rights Amendment act and New York adopting a liberal abortion bill. In 1973, Roe vs. Wade was passed. Thoughout the 1970s, record numbers of divorces meant record numbers of divorced children living in one-parent homes: As is well known, *Kramer vs. Kramer* popularizes the issue of divorce and child custody. At the First National Women's Conference, participants demanded sex-education at all grade levels and flexible-hour child care. In 1972, *Ms.* magazine began publishing.

If *Star Wars, Raiders of the Lost Ark, The Empire Strikes Back,* and so forth in the 1980s lessen the social impact of 1970s radical feminism, and so on, then arguably *Close Encounters of the Third Kind, E.T., The Little Mermaid,* and all the other 1980s films and sequels from corporate Hollywood function similarly. To take one obvious example, admittedly not a sequel, in *E.T.* the alien visitor is at first neither asexual or bisexual: There is no logical reason to assume that E.T. is a boy or a girl. Nonetheless, E.T.'s evolution from asexual being to sexual child, from an "it" to either a "boy" or a "girl," these latter two sexual identities long since established in society as dominant, occurs as the film unfolds. In a particularly telling scene, Gertie dresses E.T. in women's clothes and accessories and teaches E.T. to speak his name. What to Gertie seems natural, seems to Elliot unnatural because the masculine identity he has already established with E.T. is suddenly and visibly usurped. Elliot cries out: "You should give him his dignity. This is the most ridiculous thing I've ever seen."

Consider also the role of home in *E.T.* Images of home are invariably placed alongside images of homelessness. In the opening scenes of *E.T.,* for example, Elliott's home and the domestic calm within is set rather obviously against the turmoil that exists outside caused by E.T.'s untimely arrival. Spielberg cuts back and forth between E.T. landing in a dangerous environment where he is hunted like an animal and Elliott living in a safe house. E.T. is alone in the dark forest. Elliott is surrounded by friends and family in the brightly lit kitchen. E.T. is hunted by men, Elliott is watched over by his mother.

When seen in terms of the social and political demands of radical groups from the 1960s and 1970s, *E.T.* assumes a tremendous historical and ideological importance. Elliott's degrading and humiliating comment about E.T. being dressed in women's clothes, and the film's heavy-handed use of the home as a place of sanctuary against the outside world, completely defuses the demands made by 1960s and 1970s feminists such as Shulamith Firestone for freedom and liberation from the restrictive domestic roles placed upon women and children by the forces of patriarchal capitalism in the 1980s. Arguably, *E.T.* is an early precursor of what Susan Faludi would later call the backlash against women.

In relation to questions of race rather than gender, another example of how 1980s films diffused the radical politics of the 1970s is a PG-15 film called *White Dog* (1982). Adapted by director Samuel Fuller from Romain Gary's novella, *White Dog* is about a white, stray dog that has been trained to attack black people. A black dog-trainer called Keys (played by Paul Winfield from Ritt's 1972 *Sounder*), attempts to retrain the white dog. Though the film was considered by critics in Europe to be a masterpiece, Paramount Studios felt that the subject of race relations was too volatile and controversial and insisted upon revisions before allowing the film to be released on cable for American audiences in 1984.

Third World Children's Cinema

Third World cinema, or Third Cinema, first emerges out of the 1950s with the films of young Indian director Satyajit Ray who was deeply influenced by De Sica's *The Bicycle Thief.* Ray himself became famous for The Apu Trilogy. The trilogy consists of *Pather Panchali* (1955), *Aparajito* (1956), and *The World of Apu* (1959). The first film, adapted from a book Ray was initially commissioned to illustrate for children, deals with the lives of a poor Bengali family whilst the father is away seeking work in the city. The second and third films in the trilogy follow the son, Apu, as he grows from a child to a man and a father.

Given its oppositional, counterinsurgent nature, Third World cinema inevitably draws inspiration from Marxism. Generally, Third World cinema emphasizes a realistic approach to the production of films (echoing the Italian Neorealists), the use of nonprofessional actors (again Italian Neorealism, but also the Angry Young Man movement in London and the realism of Japanese films in the 1960s), and local, actual settings. Further, Third World cinema assumes that art can be used as a tool for social and political change. Powerful films that uncompromisingly reveal to audiences the actual realities of poor people's lives will make audiences demand reforms at the local, national, and international level of government. Third World cinema reflects other basic Marxist beliefs: a rejection of religion in favor of historical materialism and a belief in the dialectics of history. Generally, Third World cinema shows the injustices of the world as those injustices affect the world's poor, particularly the world's poor children. In this regard, Third World cinema is invariably critical of how the world's imperial powers exploit children.

The 1980s produced at least two famous examples of Third World cinema starring children: *Pixote* (1981) and *Salaam Bombay* (1988). Ignored by Street and Jackson, both films offer brutally frank depictions of adult cruelty toward children (see Figure 7). In this they offer a perfect counterpoint to films such as *E.T.* and *The Little Mermaid* and the image of the child offered by the "Disberg stables" (Bazalgette and Staples 93).

1990s UNITED STATES AND EUROPEAN CHILDREN'S CINEMA AND FILM: *THE BICYCLE THIEF, TOY STORY,* AND THE END OF CHILDREN'S CINEMA

Douglas Street foresaw in 1982 what has since come to pass in the 1990s, corporate Hollywood's commercially successful adaptation of classic works of children's literature (*The Indian in the Cupboard*). Beyond adaptation, corporate Hollywood in the 1990s has made billions of dollars from films starring children and the merchandizing of related products—collectables—to young consumers: Witness the case of *Jurassic Park* (1993). The major studios continued to change ownership in the 1990s but also an entirely new studio was formed in 1994: DreamWorks SKG (*The Peacemaker, Mouse Hunt*). Despite the immense resources of corporate Hollywood, its children's films such as *Home Alone* continued to ignore the pressing social problems that face children actually left home alone. Fortunately, independent companies continued to produce films that dealt seriously with child-related issues: one thinks of *Kids, Lolita, The Secret of Roan Inish, Smila's Sense of Snow, Life Is Beautiful, Polish Wedding,* and so forth. Outside mainstream and independent Hollywood, the 1990s saw a relatively new development in the history of world children's cinema, that of children's film festivals.

If all this cinematic activity—adaptations, blockbuster hits, studio changes, independent films, festivals, and so forth—seem to celebrate the appearance of children's cinema and film in history, a confirmation of

Figure 7. The impoverished children of Bombay in Mira Nair's *Salaam Bombay* make a perfect counterpoint to the image of children in most Hollywood and Disney movies. Photo: Museum of Modern Art/Film Stills Archive, New York. Courtesy of Mirabai Pictures.

the economic importance of children's cinema to Hollywood and the economy as a whole, the 1990s is also witness to the disappearance of children's cinema and film: What the Neorealist *The Bicycle Thief* was to the 1940s and the end of cinema, for example, arguably the animated *Toy Story* is to the 1990s and the end of children's cinema. Thus, if I had to choose a phrase that summarized this and other aspects of children's cinema and film in the 1990s, I would look no further than Marx's prophetic 1856 comment that "In our days everything seems pregnant with its contrary" ("Speech" 134).

Literary Adaptations

The adaptation of classic works of children's literature remained a commercially successful venture for the corporate studios in the 1990s. Disney's revival, begun when Michael Eisner assumed control of the studio in the 1980s, continued in 1991, for example, with *Beauty and the Beast,* which grossed $69.4 million. In 1992, *Aladdin* grossed $82.5 million for Disney. Considered a financial flop by some, Spielberg's 1991 *Hook,* a version of Barrie's *Peter Pan* starring Robin Williams, grossed $65 million. In 1993, *Dennis the Menace* made $24.2 for Warner Brothers. In the same year, yet another version of Frances Hodgson Burnett's classic children's tale *The Secret Garden,* this time by acclaimed Polish director Agnieszka Holland and starring Kate Maberly as Mary Lennox, Heydon Prowse as Colin, and Andrew Knott as Dickon, grossed $13.5 million for Warner Brothers. *Mulan, James and the Giant Peach, The Indian in the Cupboard, Harriet the Spy, The Matrix* (loosely based upon *Alice's Adventures in Wonderland*): As Douglas Street foresaw in 1982, classic works of children's literature have continued to make Hollywood profitable.

Indeed, overall, kid's films, though not a film called *Kids* (1995), were big business in the 1990s. *USA Today* recently printed a list of the highest-grossing animated films of the past five years (in millions of dollars). From top to bottom, the list reads as follows: *The Lion King* ($312), *Toy Story* ($191.8), *Pocahontas* ($141.6), *Mulan* ($120.5), *The Hunchback of Notre Dame* ($100.1), *Hercules* ($99.1), *Antz* ($81.1), *Beavis and Butthead Do America* ($63.1), *Anastasia* ($56.5), and *The Nightmare Before Christmas* ($50).[14]

Beyond literary adaptation and animation, *Home Alone* and *Jurassic Park* are good examples of films from corporate Hollywood that were highly profitable but historically important for the wrong reasons. *Home Alone* (1990) has grossed $533.8 million worldwide so far (in Sweden it has grossed SEK 26,634,867 from 514,219 admissions) and taken $140.099 million in rentals in the United States alone. Two years later, *Home Alone 2: Lost in New York,* took $103.377 million in U.S. rentals and has so far grossed $279.6 million. Five years later, *Home Alone 3* took $5.085m on its opening weekend in the United States and has since bought in $30.672 million.

The vast sums of money these three *Home Alone* films have generated, and the image of the happy, upper-middle-class family with which they conclude, utterly contradicts the reality for many children today. As the comic abandonment of children on-screen reels in the money, the tragic abandonment off-screen continues. Thus, in 1990, a dramatic *Time* editorial asked, "Do We Care About Our Kids? The Sorry Plight of America's Most Disadvantaged Minority: Its Children." In 1991, a *Mother Jones* headline declared, "America's Dirty Little Secret: We Hate Kids." A 1994 *Newsweek* headline declared, "Growing Up Scared: How Our Kids Are Robbed of Their Childhood." Joe L. Kincheloe's "The New Childhood: Home Alone as a Way of Life" is only the latest in a long line of editorials and articles drawing attention to the gulf between America's *Home Alone* movies and America's "Home Alone" kids. The gap between the affluence in the films and the poverty on the streets is a stark reminder that the economic gap that began to widen under Ronald Reagan's presidency continues under the presidency of Bill Clinton.

A similar point might be made in relation to young girls and Girl Power. A *USA Today* cover story by Claudia Puig, entitled "Little Girl Power in Hollywood," refers to the way "girl films" in particular, rather than children's films in general, have recently become economically successful. Puig cites films such as *Paulie, Madeline, Parent Trap, Ever After, Matilda,* and *Harriet the Spy* as examples of "Little Girl Power" in Hollywood. We could add to the list films such as *Fly Away Home.* At any rate, *Matilda* and *Harriet the Spy,* both from 1996, are credited with making "girl films," or "little girl movies," those boys wouldn't otherwise watch, worth seeing and thus financially lucrative for the corporate studios. *Matilda* grossed $33.6 million. *Harriet* grossed $26.6 (Puig DI).

If anything in children's cinema and film in the 1990s seems "pregnant with its contrary" (Marx, "Speech" 135), it must be the contradictory term "Girl Power." Whilst there are a mere handful of "little girl films" from corporate studios such as 20th Century Fox, MGM, Paramount, and Disney there are hundreds of thousands of little girls abroad who are also child prostitutes. The lives of these young girls are described in books such as *Children of the Cities* (1991), by Jo Boyden, and articles such as "The Last Commodity: Child Prostitution in the Developing World" (1994), by Aaron Sachs, and "Prostitution: Child Chattel Lure Tourists for Sex" (1995), by Christopher P. Baker. In "Prostitution: Child Chattel," Baker cites the example of Veronica who is "just one of more than a million young victims lured, sold, or forced into prostitution worldwide every year . . ." (8). According to Baker, "Brazil now has more than 250,000 child prostitutes; Moscow more than 1,000 . . . Studies suggest that there are at least 300,000 child prostitutes in India" (8). Child prostitution, of young girls though also of young boys, has now reached epidemic proportions.

Surely there is a contradiction here, an uncomfortable paradox: At the time when a minority of children's films from corporate Hollywood show empowered heroines outwitting their oppressors, vast numbers of young girls around the world are disempowered. The schizoid aspect of children's cinema and film that structured children's cinema and film in the 1960s remains firmly in place in the 1990s.

Studios

During the 1990s, the history of the studios continued to evolve in at least three ways. First, in general, they became more corporate. In 1990, the Matsushita Electrical Industrial Company purchased MCA Inc and Universal for $6.6 billion. In 1990 also, MGM/UA was taken over by Pathé Communications. In 1992, Credit Lyonnaise, a French bank, bought a controlling interest in MGM/Pathé. In other developments, Paramount was bought by Viacom in 1994 for $9.5 billion. Viacom also owns MTV, Showtime, Nickelodeon, Nick Jr., and other media companies. In the same year, Seagram bought an 80 percent controlling interest in MCA Inc for $5.7 billion. In 1995, Disney CEO Eisner signed a deal with Capital Cities/ABC worth $19 billion (Boroughs 32). Second, in the 1990s, a new studio, no less corporate than the others, was created. In 1994 Jeffrey Katzenberg, Steven Spielberg, and David Geffen formed DreamWorks SKG, the first major new studio in Hollywood since the 1930s. Some of the films released by DreamWorks SKG include *The Peacemaker* but also *Mouse Hunt, Prince of Egypt,* and *Antz.* Third, in "Tomorrow's Media Today," Warren Cohen and Katia Hetter note that the media giants and their studios have also developed "video games and multimedia computing" (49) divisions. Disney/Capital Cities, Viacom, Time Warner, DreamWorks, and Pixar have all developed divisions in or related to film, television, music, animation, Pay-Per-View TV, syndication, merchandising, distrubution, marketing, and so forth. Children's culture in general and children's cinema and film from Hollywood has truly become part of the National Entertainment State.

Independents

Whilst corporate Hollywood in the 1990s attempted but largely failed to deal with serious themes (*Boyz N The Hood, Jungle Fever, Amistad*), this was certainly not true of independent studios and directors in the United States, who made films as different as *Welcome to the Dollhouse, Closet Land, The Secret of Roan Inish, Smilla's Sense of Snow, Kids, The Incredibly True Adventure of Two Girls In Love, Lolita,* and so forth.

Like other juvenile delinquent genre films such as *Rebel Without a Cause* or *River's Edge, Kids* concerns a day in the life of a group of lost, wayward, and thrill-seeking young teenagers who live in a completely immoral world. In particular, *Kids* focuses on the sexual exploits of sixteen-year-old Telly (Leo Fitzpatrick) who, as a self-proclaimed "virgin surgeon," likes to deflower young virgins. Essentially, he rapes young girls. Indeed, *Kids* begins with a long, graphic scene in which Telly coerces an obviously unwilling young girl (Sarah Hendersen) to have sex with him. Later, we learn that another of Telly's previous conquests—Jenny—has contracted HIV-AIDS from him. Jenny (Chloe Sevigny) decides she must warn Telly. Telly is oblivious to the fact that he is a walking timebomb. Utterly immersed in their own nihilistic world, he and his close friend Casper walk around town urinating in the street, stealing money, getting stoned, fighting, drinking, and puking. At a party that evening, Telly and Casper get drunk, take drugs, vomit and pass out. When Jenny finally catches up with Telly, he is about to have unprotected sex with yet another young girl. Jenny simply turns and walks away. In an amoral world, why take a moral stand.

In the history of children's cinema and film, or more properly young adult cinema and film, *Kids* is important for at least two reasons. First, *Kids* stands as a realistic corrective to the usual fantasy coming-of-age movies from corporate Hollywood such as *She's All That.* Given an NC-17 rating, *Kids* contains graphic scenes of young teenagers having unprotected sex with multiple partners, taking drugs and sharing obviously infected needles, drinking heavily and indiscriminately, swearing crudely at strangers, parents, and other kids. Night turns to day and day to night in an everlasting orgy of violent sex, deathly drugs, misogyny and immorality. Given a PG-13 rating, *She's All That* is the complete opposite. Drugs and the use of shared needles are missing. Whilst the kids in the school go out with many partners, the film emphasizes monogamy and heterosexuality. There is almost no swearing. Whereas Telly and Casper are both repulsive in their physical appearance and their emotional outlook on life, Zak, from *She's All That,* epitomizes the handsome, clean-cut, successful, white Anglo-Saxon Protestant, graduating high school senior whose life choices consist of deciding between Harvard, Yale, and Dartmouth rather than more drugs, more booze, and more unprotected sex. The girls in *Kids* are shown as infected either with HIV or as having a careless and carefree attitude toward love, romance, pregnancy, marriage, and motherhood. The girls in *She's All That* are compulsively romantic and dream of precisely that which the girls from *Kids* reject: Mr. Right.

Second, films such as *Kids* (and *Lolita,* though in different ways) raise other issues about children's cinema and film that have existed since the beginning of the twentieth century, but which are becoming increasingly urgent today: the relationship between child actors and controversial dramas. Should children be allowed to or prevented from acting in films such as *Kids* and *Lolita,* those that deal seriously, graphically, and explicitly with drugs, HIV, and other important social issues such as race and gender discrimination?

For example, should children be allowed to act in war films? Whilst the example of *Kids* is perhaps clearcut—children probably should not have been allowed to act in it—the same debate arose in France in the 1940s when child actor Brigitte Fossey starred in the René Clément's *Forbidden Games,* a film about the horrors of war and its effect on children. Critics at the time asked whether or not children should be allowed to star in such films. It seems to me that a more relevant question might be: Why should children have to live through such events as World War II? Adults critiquing films that use kids to reflect back to adults the horrors of the world adults themselves have created is hypocritical.

From an historical point of view, children have clearly acted in serious dramas since at least the 1940s. Still, a disturbing feature of children's cinema and film in the 1990s is not just the increased use of children in grave, earnest, and thoughtful dramas such as *Kids, Lolita, The Professional, A Time to Kill* (1996), *Dracula,* or *Face-Off,* but the visual intensity of such films. Unbearably real, they are almost unbearably watchable.

There are few easy answers to these issues. In the past, there were once laws against children acting in films that tackle themes like war, sexuality, drug abuse, and so forth. Talking about 1930s children's cinema and film in England, Terry Staples reports that "Most importantly, there was a limitation imposed by the Children and Young Persons Act of 1933 which made it illegal to emply children of school age in filmmaking . . . School age at that time meant under fourteen . . ." (92). Today, there is the Child Pornography Prevention Act of 1996, which, according to Rachel Abramowitz, who is actually talking about Lyne's *Lolita,* makes it "now illegal not only to show a child having sex but to even make it look as if a child is engaging in sexual conduct" (98).

But, on the other hand, federal legislation can only be half of the solution and is very often part of the problem. Indeed, legislation merely raises another question: Who defines and decides whether *Kids, Lolita, A Time to Kill,* are examples of child pornography or art? Government reviewers? Corporations? Parents? Hollywood?

Graphic and shocking, *Kids, Lolita, A Time to Kill,* and so forth are important reminders in the history of children's cinema and film that many of the world's directors work outside the National Entertainment State and the dream factory that is Hollywood and that art and life can coexist, albeit uncomfortably, within a film that revolves around children or young adults. As one critic put it at the time, *Kids* is a movie that "isn't all that good but contains a message of burning importance and that's enough" (Cannon 2). The "Indies," as they are often known, make a vital contribution to children's cinema in the 1990s.

Child Stars

As in previous decades, corporate Hollywood in the 1990s has employed a new crop of child stars. Today's child stars include Ashley and Mary Kate Olsen (twins in *The Little Rascals*), Michelle Trachtenberg (*Harriet the Spy*), Mara Wilson (*Matilda*), Natalie Portman (Mathilda in *The Professional* and Queen Amidala in *Star Wars Episode 1*), Victoire Thivisol (*Ponette*), Dominique Swain (*Lolita*), Rae'ven Kelly (*A Time to Kill*), Haley Joel Osment (*The Sixth Sense,* 1999), and so forth. Natalie Portman turned down the title role of *Lolita* before it went to Dominique Swain.

Many child stars today, of course, are not children but toys: Think here of Simba, Woody, Buzz Lightyear, Hercules, and Mulan from films such as *The Lion King, Toy Story, Hercules,* and *Mulan*.

European Children's Cinema: Russia, France, and Iran

Russia, France, and Iran continue to make important contributions to the history of children's cinema and film. For example, Gorbachev's 1980s policies of Glasnost (openness) and Perestroika (restructuring) led to the Fifth Congress of Soviet Filmmakers who decided to make films that would finally explore the otherwise hidden history of Russia. In the process, films starring children such as *Burnt by the Sun* (1994) and *The Thief* (1997) are important correctives to the usual stereotyping of Russians in corporate Hollywood films such as *You Lucky Dog. Burnt by the Sun* and *The Thief* are both set in postrevolutionary (1917) Russia and, in their different ways, confront the Stalinist Purges of the 1930s and 1940s, what became known as Stalin's "Great Terror."

In Mikhalkov's 1994 *Burnt by the Sun,* ex-Revolutionary hero Colonel Kotov (a friend to Stalin himself) has retired to the country with his young and attractive wife Marussia and their six-year-old daughter Nadya (played by Mikhalkov's real-life daughter Nadezhda) to enjoy the fruits of his revolutionary labor and the leadership of Stalin. However, the film is set in 1936, as Stalin's purges of the Communist Party were getting under way: Stalin ordered the assassination of fellow revolutionary leader Leon Trotsky, for example, in 1940. Thus, when Dimitri, an ex-lover of Kotov's much younger wife Marussia, arrives, it is not so much to rekindle an old romantic flame as it is to extinguish a bright revolutionary light: that of Kotov. In the context of Stalin's purges, the chilling climax is inevitable.

Much of the film revolves around Kotov's daughter, Nadya, and her survival of course symbolically represents the possibility of a better future—one that eventually arrived only after the Reign of Terror gave way to the Cold War, which itself gave way to Glasnost, Perestroika, and a better understanding of twentieth-century Russian history.

From France, the films of Jacques Doillon, like those of François Truffaut between 1959 and 1976, continue to explore the world of children, "their behavior, their language, their psychology, and their potential as screen actors and objects of cinematic scrutiny" (Temple 51). Doillon's latest film is *Ponette.* In a car crash, four-year-old Ponette, played by four-year-old Victoire Thivisol, suffers a broken arm. Her mother dies (think here of *Fly Away Home*). Ponette's father has to go away on a business trip and she is sent to stay with her aunt and cousins. As in Truffaut's 1976 *Small Change, Ponette* concerns itself with the emotional effect and psychological consequences of children living without parental love and care.

In recent months, a number of articles and reviews have focused on Iranian children's cinema and film. For example, in "The Kids Are Alright," Richard Corliss extolls the virtue of contemporary Iranian children's cinema. Pointing out that "To most Americans, the Islamic Republic of Iran is known for denouncing the Great Satan U.S., swearing out fatwas . . . and defining women's rights as the privilege of wearing a chador" (85), Corliss argues that in fact "Children's films—by which is meant movies about the young but not necessarily for them—have an honorable pedigree in Iran" (85). As examples, Corliss cites how the Shahrina sponsored several children's film festivals before her husband was overthrown in 1979 and how an Iranian film, Majid Majidi's *Children of Heaven* was recently nominated for an Academy Award as best foreign film. Other Iranian children's films of note are *The Mirror* and *The Apple*.

Situating itself directly with the Italian Neorealist tradition that began in the 1940s with Vittorio de Sica's *The Bicycle Thief* (of which more momentarily), Corliss writes that *Children of Heaven* is about an eight-year-old boy who loses his younger sister's shoes. Without the shoes, she cannot attend school. Ali (Mir Farrokh Hashemian), who was taking care of the shoes when they were stolen, must search for them (just as Antonio and his son Bruno searched for the stolen bicycle in *The Bicycle Thief*). Eventually, Ali enters a local race and wins a pair of shoes for his sister.

More recently still, Richard Pena's review of the 17th International Fajr Film Festival in Tehran cites several films from the festival that star children and were critically received. Majidi's *Color of God* is a story of a "blind boy and his frustrated, widowed father" (71). Pena reports that one of the winners of the children's film competition was *Son of Mary* by Hamid Jebeli. Set in Azerbaijan, the film is about the relationship "between a young Muslim boy and an older Armenian priest" (71). Citing *Son of Mary*—a children's film—as an example, Pena considers that "the film points to a possible new direction [in history] for one of the most fertile national cinemas today" (71).

The Bicycle Thief, Toy Story, and the End of Children's Cinema and Film

Recently, I was reading Andre Bazin's *What Is Cinema?* I was struck by his comments on Vittorio De Sica's *Ladri di Biciclette* (*The Bicycle Thief,* Italy, 1948). I wanted to discuss the film here rather than in an earlier section on Italian Neorealism, because Bazin's ideas seem strangely relevant to a discussion of an important development in 1990s children's cinema: that of computer generated images and animation.

Bazin notes how more than any other Italian film in the post-World War II era, *The Bicycle Thief* reflects the fundamental ideas of Italian Neorealism. Bazin writes: "*Ladri di Biciclette* certainly is Neorealist, by all the principles one can deduce from the best Italian films since 1946. The story is from the lower classes, almost populist: an incident in the daily life of a worker" (49). The incident in question is the theft of Antonio's (Lamberto Maggiorani) bicycle. The theft is critical to Antonio's survival because it is the means by which he makes a living. As Gerald Mast puts it: "Without the bicycle he has no job; without a job his family starves" (319). Essentially, the film concerns the trials and tribulations that befall Antonio's search for the stolen bicycle, an "epic" quest through the streets of Rome made all the more poignant because of the presence of Antonio's son Bruno (Enzo Staiola). (See figure 6.)

The Bicycle Thief is a classic Neorealist film, Bazin argues, because the plot "would not deserve two lines in a stray-dog column" (50) and because "Not one scene [is] shot in a studio. Everything is filmed in the streets" (51). The city becomes the set, the street the mise-en-scène. Also, none of the actors had "the slightest experience in theater or film" (50). In keeping with the Neorealist aesthetic, that films should reflect the life of ordinary people, nonprofessional actors star in *The Bicycle Thief.* Enzo Staiola was a newsboy.

Particularly interesting about Bazin's essay is not just the argument that *The Bicycle Thief* reflects post-World War II Italian Neorealism. Bazin concludes his discussion with the following comment: "For this reason, *Ladri di Biciclette* is one of the first examples of pure cinema. No more actors, no more story, no more sets, which is to say that in the perfect aesthetic illusion of reality there is no more cinema" (60). Bazin is not arguing that cinema ends after *The Bicycle Thief.* Clearly, that would be nonsensical, like saying that there is no such thing as children's literature, because children's literature is an impossible fiction—not the point Jacqueline Rose was trying to make. Bazin argues that as an exemplary example of Neorealism, *The Bicycle Thief* literally and symbolically represents the end of the production, distribution, and reception of cinema "in the acceptance we now give this word" (Metz 95). *The Bicycle Thief* makes redundant corporate studios, expensive sets, wealthy producers and directors, highly paid actors and actresses, and the illusion of reality films from corporate Hollywood construct to interpellate audiences. In short, *The Bicycle Thief* represents the appearance of Neorealism—it is the supreme achivement of Neorealism—but also the disappearance of cinema and thus, ironically, Neorealism.

Bazin's comments concerning De Sica's *The Bicycle Thief* struck me as surprisingly relevant to a discussion of John Lasseter's *Toy Story,* one of the most successful computer generated movies of the 1990s. *Toy Story* is clearly a children's film, "by all the principles one can deduce" (Bazin 49). Characters such as Little Bo Peep inhabit the world of children's nursery rhymes. Several characters are well-known children's toys: Mr. Potato Head, Slinky, Mr. Spell, and so forth. These and other toys are examples of what Woody, Andy's favorite toy until replaced by Buzz Lightyear, calls a "child's plaything." *Toy Story* contains several children, principally the boys Andy and Sid, but also their respective sisters Molly and Hannah. Parents, actually only Andy's mother, make brief appearances, mostly at the beginning and the end. By any definition, *Toy Story* is a children's film.

Bazin argues, we recall, that *The Bicycle Thief,* a supreme example of Neorealism, represents the end of cinema because it contains "No more actors, no more story, no more sets . . ." (60). Similarly, *Toy Story,* a supreme example perhaps not so much of American animation but of the vast resources corporate animation studios in America can command, represents something similar, the end of children's cinema. I don't mean literally, of course. That would make no sense, as Jacqueline Rose says in a different, though related, context. Still, *Toy Story,* like *The Bicycle Thief,* contains no live professional actors and no sets. *Toy Story*'s principal actors, the toys and the boys, are computer generated images. The dialogue in *Toy Story* is voiced by adult actors such as Tom Hanks (Woody), Tim Allen (Buzz Lightyear), John Ratzenberger (Piggy), and Annie Potts (Little Bo Peep). Furthermore, though the action of the movie takes place mostly in the bedrooms of Andy and Sid, a deserted garage, a combined amusement arcade/pizza parlor, and Sid's backyard, these and other suburban settings exist only as computer images. Though set in cyberspace, *Toy Story* ironically has no settings.

Furthermore, one year after *Toy Story* was released, movie magazines such as *Cinescape* were asking "Is *James and the Giant Peach* the next *Toy Story?*" And Pixar has just released *Toy Story 2.* In other words, *Toy Story* undoubtedly represents a moment of supreme technological progression, a synthesis of corporate, economic, technological, and aesthetic ideals a marvel to behold. The making of *Toy Story,* for example, required Pixar to register several new patents. But, as the *Cinescape* quote implies, *Toy Story* is at one and the same time a moment of supreme regression as it makes obsolete and is in turn made obsolete by the very historical and technological conditions from which it initially emerged. 1895 saw the beginning of children's cinema. *Toy Story* in 1995 represents the end of children's cinema.

Of course, children's cinema and film has not literally ended. Indeed, one important development is the continued growth of American and European children's cinema and film festivals. In October 1999, the National Children's Film Festival (NCFF), in conjunction with the Miami Children's Museum, held its third annual not-for-profit festival in Indianapolis. The mission of the NCFF is to "sponsor an international program that encourages the making of films and videos written, directed and produced by youth ages 9–18, and creating annual international and local festivals to honor the achievements of young filmmakers in order to promote [greater] communications and understanding between adults and young people" (quoted in *Oak Ridger* 1).

There is a thriving European Children's Film Association. Founded in 1988 in Belgium, the ECFA supports "the cinema for children in its cultural, economical, esthetic, social, political and educational aspects" (http://www.euronet.com). Connected to the ECFA are associations such as the *Cinema for Juniors* in Belgium, *Cinekid* in Italy, and *Iranian Young Cinema.* The latter society was founded in 1974, contains fifty film centers through Iran, and this year (1999) held the Children and Junior Film Festival in Tehran. In England, there is a Children's London Film Festival. The festival, held in 1991 at the National Film Theatre in London, resulted in films but also scholarly books such as Cary Bazalgette and David Buckingham's *In Front of the Children: Screen Entertainment and Young Audiences* (1995). Clearly there exists today an emergent children's cinema and film industry—production facilities, young directors, budding stars, films, critical studies, reviews, and so forth—around the world that in the future will no doubt challenge and contest the hegemony of corporate Hollywood.

CONCLUSION

The history of children's cinema and film just presented organizes for students of children's cinema different periods, films, styles and genres, and critical issues from the 1890s to the 1990s. We see the important periods in children's film history. We can see which films have stood the proverbial test of time (*Pinocchio, The Wizard of Oz, M, The Night of the Hunter, Aladdin, Searching for Bobby Fischer, Toy Story,* etc.), which directors played an important role in a history of children's films (Méliès, De Sica, Reed, Fleming, Burton, Bluth, Spheeris, etc.), and what styles (Neorealism, Disneyfication, Ozification, etc.) and technological developments (silent to talkies, black-and-white to color, animation to claymation and computer generated images, film reel to digital film) have significantly affected the cinematic experiences of children (and adults). We can see who the child stars have been (Shirley Temple and Jane Withers) and are today (Macaulay Culkin and Anna Paquin). In short, we can write a history of children's cinema and film that goes some way to explaining both without simplifying either.

NOTES

[1]There are other histories of children's films. For example, see Jack Zipes, "Toward a Theory of the Fairy-tale Film: The Case of *Pinocchio,*" *Lion and the Unicorn* 20 (1996): 124, or Terry Staples, *All Pals Together: The Story of Children's Cinema* (Edinburgh: Edinburgh University Press, 1997). But the histories in these works specifically pertain to their topic: in the case of Zipes, Disney's

Pinocchio, and in the case of Staples, children's cinema in England. What I have tried to do in Part Three: History is set out a comprehensive overview of world children's cinema and film.

[2]In another instance of this, Phyllis Bixler writes thus about Pickford's role in the 1921 production of *Little Lord Fauntleroy*: "In 1921, audiences marveled as Mary Pickford, playing both mother and child, kissed a miniature version of herself on the silent screen" (69). See Phyllis Bixler, "Continuity and Change in Popular Entertainment," *Children's Novels and the Movies,* ed. Douglas Street (New York: Fred Ungar Publishing, 1983): 69–80. More recently, in the 1980s and 1990s, there have been several films such as *Big,* in which adults take over the body of a child or vice versa.

[3]For a discussion of Mary Pickford's career, see Richard Corliss, "Queen of the Movies," *Film Comment* Mar.–Apr. 1998: 53–62.

[4]Both Gary Cooper and Ronald Reagan starred in movies with Shirley Temple. Temple and Cooper starred in Paramount's 1934 *Now and Forever.* Temple starred with Reagan in a 1947 Warner Brothers production called *That Hagen Girl.*

[5]Despite the fact that Disney had some of the most brilliant animators working for him, he would not allow their names on the credits. For a discussion of this, see Leonard Mosley, *Disney's World: A Biography* (Lanham, MD: Scarborough House, 1985), 188–189.

[6]For a particularly interesting review of *The Innocents,* see Donald Chase, "Romancing the Stones: Jack Clayton's *The Innocents,*" *Film Comment* Jan.–Feb. 1998: 68–73.

[7]See Henry Giroux, "Race, Pedagogy, and Whiteness in *Dangerous Minds,*" *Cinéaste,* 22:4 1997: 46–49.

[8]John Hart refers to Carrie Henn, who plays Rebecca "Newt" Jorden in *Aliens* (1986) as "almost a feral child" (2), whilst Richard Corliss, in an article on contemporary Iranian children's cinema, situates *The Apple* in the context of a "fable of the Wild Child civilized" (85). Not all feral child images are in serious drama. Comedy films such as *Jungle 2 Jungle,* starring Tim Allen, play with the idea of the feral child.

[9]Bazalgette and Staples note: "Because there is such a small home market, Danish films cannot hope for a massive return, so virtually all of them are subsidised . . . by the state-funded Danish Film Institute. In Iran . . . films for children are regularly made by the Institute for the Intellectual Development of Children and Young Adults" (97).

[10]Corey Feldman starred first in *The Gremlins* (1984) and then in *The Goonies.* In this latter film, he played Clarke "Mouth" Devereux, one of several kids who go on an adventure in search of stolen treasure. After *The Goonies,* Feldman starred in *Stand By Me* (1986). In 1990, he was the voice of Donatello in *Teenage Mutant Ninja Turtles.*

[11]Lionel Barrymore starred alongside Shirley Temple in the Fox Film Corporation 1933 *Carolina* and Fox's 1934 *The Little Colonel.*

[12]Traci Lords posed for *Playboy* at fifteen.

[13]Max von Sydow (Pelle's father, Pappa Lasse) is more familiar to American audiences for two other films, one from the 1970s and one from the 1950s. Sydow was Father Merrin in William Friedkin's 1973 horror film *The Exorcist* and Antonius Block in Ingmar Bergman's 1957 drama *The Seventh Seal.* Lasse Hallström is perhaps more famous for *Abba—The Movie* and *What's Eating Gilbert Grape?* (1993). The latter film starred not only Johnny Depp and Juliette Lewis (before she starred in Oliver Stone's 1994 *Natural Born Killers*), but also Leonardo DiCaprio as Arnie Grape. After *Salaam Bombay,* Mira Nair directed *Mississippi Masala* (1992) and *Kama Sutra: A Tale of Love* ((1996).

[14]See Josh Chetwynd and Andy Seiler, "Top 10 'toons," *USA Today* November 20, 1998, E1.

PART FOUR

Ideology

The ideas of the ruling class are in every epoch the ruling ideas.

—MARX & ENGELS,
The German Ideology 44

Part Four: Ideology examines questions of ideology in general and then specifically in relation to the representation of class and gender in children's films. I first consider some aspects of Marxist theories of ideology and how they might apply to children's cinema and film. Second, I look at the representation of class in a 1930s film called *Bright Eyes,* starring Shirley Temple, and then some more recent children's films such as *Stand By Me* and *Harriet the Spy.* Third, as critics have pointed out, discussions about class ideologies in film gave way to discussions about gender ideologies. I want to sketch in the evolution of these changes and consider their connection to feminist children's film criticism and children's films. Stated another way: Overall, I want to bring out further the ideologies of class and gender that were beginning to emerge from the general historical conditions set forth in Part Three: History, in particular the production of children's films by a few giant media conglomerates (rather than an aristocratic family) who own the factories (studios) that make the products (movies) that sell ruling class ideologies to (un)suspecting young viewers. As a result, children's films are works of art that entertain but also sites of ideology that indoctrinate young viewers into traditional class and gender roles.

MARX, ALTHUSSER, COMOLLI AND NARBONI: DISNEY, *HOME ALONE,* AND *FERNGULLY*

During the 1960s and 1970s, the Estates General of Cinema in Paris, and French and British film journals like *Cahiers du Cinéma, Cinéthique,* and *Screen,* rejected aesthetic, generic, and auteurist forms of criticism for the poststructuralist theories of Althusser, Foucault, and others. These journals wanted "To establish how cinema functioned ideologically, how meaning was produced, and how it involved the spectator . . . in a project that would draw on an unprecedented combination of Marxism, semiotics, and psychoanalysis" (Lapsley & Westlake 2). By common consent, at the outset of this "project the single greatest influence was the Marxist philosopher Louis Althusser" (2). Althusser's intervention in the 1960s and 1970s represented a significant development in the history of Marxist theories of ideology and twentieth-century film studies.

A basic classical Marxian belief is that ideology is the propaganda of the ruling classes. This idea is expressed most famously by Marx and Engels in *The German Ideology:* "The ideas of the ruling class are in every epoch the ruling ideas: i.e., the class which is the ruling material force of society, is at the same time its ruling intellectual force" (44). Those who control the means of production, those Marx and Engels call "the ruling material force of society," control the production of society's ideas—its ruling ideology. The ruling classes then, according to Marx, make their ideas appear "as the common interest of all the members of society" (45). In this way, the dominant ideas of society are produced and imposed upon the masses by the ruling classes of society.

Implied here also is a second basic Marxist belief, what Raymond Williams calls the concept of a "determining base and a determined superstructure" (75), initially discussed in Marx's 1859 Preface to *A Contribution to the Critique of Political Economy.*

In contrast to the classical Marxian approach to ideology, that in any given epoch or era a single, all-embracing ruling-class ideology—a master narrative—imposes itself upon the oppressed masses, Althusser argued in his seminal 1969 article "Ideology and Ideological State Apparatuses" that "Ideology represents the imaginary relationship of individuals to their real conditions of existence" (162). Althusser suggests that "What is represented in ideology is therefore not the system of real relations which govern the existence of individuals, but the imaginary relation of those individuals to the real relations in which they live" (165). Ideology is the imaginary relationship by which individuals live in society, an imaginary produced and subsequently cemented in place not so much by the overarching ideas of an elite ruling class such as the British Royal Family but by the concrete ideologies of state apparatuses like the church, the armed forces, education, the media, and so forth, each of which hails the always already constituted individual to behave in certain ways, including the correct way to read or see a film. As John Mepham, in says: "Ideology is not a collection of discreet falsehoods [as in Marx] but a matrix of thought firmly grounded in the forms of our social life and organized within a set of interdependent categories" (227), including those of the media in general and films in particular. There is no blanket ideology covering all people, adults and children alike. There are only a number of relatively autonomous ideological state apparatuses such as Hollywood cinema whose ideological discourses construct realities, including the reality of the individual, that appear real but which are imaginary. Ideology does not descend from above. Ideology walks among us. Ideologies 'R' Us!

Influenced no doubt by the revolutionary politics of the era, 1960s French film theorists looking for a more rigorous, scientific, rational explanation for commercial film's ability to reinforce the ideological status quo, turned to what became known as Althusserian Marxism. As Lapsley and Westlake write: "The film journals *Cahiers du Cinéma* and *Cinéthique* both adopted an Althusserian Marxist perspective . . ." (8). A combination of classical Marxist theory and Althusserian Marxism echoes throughout the work of French film theorists Jean-Luc Comolli and Jean Narboni, editors of the *Cahiers du Cinéma.* Published the same year as Althusser's essay on ideological state apparatuses, Comolli and Narboni's 1969 "Cinema, Ideology, Criticism," a radical film manifesto that emerged out of the equally radical student politics of the era, draws on Marx and Althusser to make three overlapping points: 1. Hollywood films are commodities. 2. Film is often ideologically conservative and reactionary even when it seems ideologically liberal and progressive. 3. Films can subsequently be classified according to their degree of conservatism (they support the status quo) or their degree of liberalism (they contest the status quo). Combined, these three points of attack dethrone the formalist (auterist, generic, and aesthetic) approaches to film criticism that had reigned throughout the first part of the twentieth century.

1. Film as Commodity

Comolli and Narboni begin by asking "What is a film?" (683). They reject the humanist, idealist notion derived from the history of bourgeois aesthetics that films are timeless expressions of the human condition. Instead, Comolli and Narboni adopt a historical, materialist position derived from Marx who wrote: "The wealth of societies in which the capitalist mode of production prevails appears as an 'immense collection of commodities'; the individual commodity appears as its elementary form. Our investigation therefore begins with the analysis of the commodity" (*Das Capital* 125). In other words, Comolli and Narboni argue that films are in fact commodities, forms of private property specific to the world historical development of capitalism and its ruling classes but made to appear as what Marx and Engels in *The German Ideology* call "the common interest of all the members of society" (45) by the workings of ideology, in particular the ideology of Hollywood's ruling classes. Put another way, Comolli and Narboni suggest that films do not just magically appear on the screen. Films are manufactured within a mode of production that is historically specific—capitalist rather than tribal, communal, or feudalist—and thus designed to transform raw material (technology, film stock, labor, etc.) into finished products (movies) for sale in stores as commodities to be consumed around the world.

Let us explore the idea of children's films as commodity further. To take one obvious example: In general, the Disney Corporation's animated feature-length films begin as raw material (ink, pencils, paper, sketches, film stock, etc.), which are worked upon by labor (animators, etc.) and capital (producers, financiers, etc.) and eventually transformed into finished products—*The Little Mermaid, Beauty and the Beast, Aladdin*—otherwise known as commodities. Grounded in 1930s Taylorist and Fordist production values,[1] these finished products or commodities then circulate like all commodities throughout the economy (exchange-value) generating wealth for Disney (and other dream factories like MGM or 20th Century Fox) and their shareholders. Corporations like Taco Bell, Burger King, McDonalds, and Sears also profit from the circulation of what A. Waller Hastings calls "Product spin-offs" (89), in the case of *The Little Mermaid* commodities such as "dolls, clothing, books, tapes, records, bath toys, etc." (89). In fact, Disney/Capital Cities' annual profits are huge. Hastings notes that *The Little Mermaid* "grossed $76 million in its initial phase" (89). Taking a broader, macroeconomic view, Henry Giroux notes: "Influencing large facets of cultural life, Disney ranks 48th in the Forbes 500 and controls ABC Network News, numerous TV and cable stations, five motion picture studios, 429 Disney stores, multimedia companies, and two major publishing houses. In 1996, Disney pulled in a record $21 billion in revenues from all of its divisions" ("Disney, Southern Baptists" 47). Given these figures, defining Disney's studios as factories that manufacture commodities rather than films, is not that surprising. As Althusser writes: "[M]arx said, every child knows that a social formation which did not reproduce the conditions of reproduction . . . would not last a year"

(127). Disney's films—or commodities—are designed to reproduce the micro- and macroeconomic conditions that enable Disney/Capital Cities to survive capitalism.

The degree to which corporate children's films function generally within capitalism as an "elementary" commodity form is reflected most obviously in how commodities function within specific films both as advertisements for capitalism (and thus expressions of capitalism) and narrative devices that legitimate the alliance of patriarchy, capitalism, and democracy. *Armageddon* functions as an advertisement for cars (BMWs and Volkswagens), insurance companies (Metropolitan Life), soft drinks (Coca Cola), and other films (*Star Wars, The Right Stuff, Pulp Fiction*). Similarly, *Home Alone, Richie Rich,* and *Blank Check* function as extended messages or advertisements that sell to upscale young consumers toys, televisions, computer software, electronic games, music, and so forth. But these films and the commodities they sell did not just spring forth: They contain within them not just raw material but also the labor of individual workers under capitalism. Thus, they are a visible expression (a commodity) of that which they render invisible (commodity production).

What narrative function does the commodity fulfill and how is that narrative function linked to patriachal, capitalist democracies? Films like *E.T., Aladdin, Star Kid, The Secret Kingdom, Quest for Camelot,* and so forth revolve around a particular thing, or commodity. In *E.T.* it is an alien pet, in *Aladdin* a lamp and a genie, in *Star Kid* and *Terminator 2: Judgment Day* a robot (the selling of tomorrow's technology to today's youngsters). As the narrative develops, the commodity changes (disruption) the stable environment in which it finds itelf placed until its true value has been realized at which point the film's various conflicts are resolved (resolution). Over the course of the narrative, the commodity facilitates certain events: The central (usually) male protagonist can own (private property) the commodity, use it to bargain with (exchange-value) and acquire more wealth in either literal or symbolic terms (girl, family, house, visible signs of upper-class status, etc.). Commodity consumption among young viewers is thereby legitimated, naturalized, made "the common interest of all the members of society," because it brings about that which capitalist cultures privilege: heterosexuality, monogamous marital relations, cultural capital, private property, class status, financial wealth, success, democracy, and so forth.

What commodities also reproduce among the young are vast inequalities of wealth. In "Boom Times for Billionaires, Bust for Workers and

Children," Holly Sklar cites examples of the extreme differences between CEO and worker pay. In 1997, Bill Gates, for example, was worth $39.8 billion net, whilst in 1994 the average wage for a married couple was $29,190.00. Sklar reports that "The average U.S. CEO made 209 times the pay of factory workers in 1996. That's way up from 1980, when CEOs made 42 times as much as U.S. factory workers" (34).

This inequality is replicated throughout Hollywood in general and Disney in particular. The economic gulf between Disney CEO and worker is most dramatically seen in the following comparison. Sklar reports in "Upsized CEOS" that Michael Eisner's unexercised stock options for 1996 were $317 million (33). By any definition, Marxist or otherwise, Eisner belongs to an economic elite, a financial ruling class. On the other side of what appears to be an unbridgeable economic and ideological class chasm, the Disney Corporation's Haiti workers earn approximately 28 to 39 cents per hour or $11.20 to $15.60 per week" (*Industrial Worker* 9). Ironically, four workers were fired attempting to improve their working conditions (9). Nike workers in Vietnam earn 20¢ an hour or $1.60 in eight hours (Sklar, "Upsized" 34). Sklar reports also that "Unions in the United States and abroad . . . are leading campaigns for living wages and decent conditions for the workers making products for Nike . . . Disney, and others" (34). In short, within the Disney/Capital Cities organization, a global organization that has evolved from a "$1.5 billion theme-park-dependent relic to a $10.1 billion entertainment giant" (Streisand 46), there exists a vast, unequal distribution of wealth.

2. Film as Ideology

The National Entertainment State giants such as General Electric, Disney/Cap Cities, Viacom, Pixar, and so forth, rarely declare that the corporate children's films they produce are about capitalism: Given the fantastic inequalities that exist in Hollywood and the world at large, this is not surprising. Corporate films cannot celebrate the poverty they produce. Corporate Hollywood cannot openly acknowledge the incredible inequalities of wealth it perpetuates with each and every film.

Ideology functions to mask these inequalities. Just as ideology never declares itself to be ideological (Althusser 175), so Viacom, and its corporate subsidiary studios such as Paramount or Nickelodeon, never declare their children's films to be anything other than "pure," "simple," "entertainment," "fun for the whole family," a movie "kids will love the world over," a "movie the whole family can watch." But this moment of denial, or masking, is surely also a moment of admittance, of unmasking. The corporate world's insistence upon a film's aesthetics, and a cor-ressponding disavowal of the film's politics, surely draws our attention to the film's status as a site of profound ideological struggle.

***Home Alone* (1990).** Capitalism appears in the shape of the commodity and the most attractive shape in which the commodity appears today is a blockbuster kid's film: At the heart of *Home Alone,* a 20th Century Fox/John Hughes production rated PG, is the commodity, the elementary form of capitalism. Though much has been written about *Home Alone,* the presence in the film of various commodities has largely been ignored. For example, *Home Alone* begins inside an enormous house in an affluent Chicago suburb with the McCallister family and assorted relations hustling to prepare for a vacation trip to Paris, France over Christmas. Inside the house, separate, linked, or open bedrooms, dining rooms, and games rooms are spacious, carpeted, and decorated with matching accessories. Other rooms are similarly decorated. The kitchen, large enough to accommodate separate dining, cooking, and washing areas also has at least one microwave, a television, and a full set of overhanging pots and pans. Kitchen appliances are clearly new. In general, the house contains what Harry, one of the crooks, calls "top-flight goods, stereos, vcrs, marketable securities, toys, fine jewelry, and a possible cash horde." Indeed, in one sense, *Home Alone* is less a film and more an advertizement for capitalism. The film is merely a vehicle for delivering images of desirable commodities to viewers young and old. Marv learns that the McCallister house is empty through a message on a SONY answering machine. Put another way, *Home Alone* is not so much a movie we enjoy as it is an economic system we experience. The setting, the characters, the plot: These are simply ways of visibly transforming for the young consumer the anarchy that is capitalism into the democracy that is capitalism. *Home Alone* is an expression of the acceptable face of capitalism. Produced by the National Entertainment State, how could it be anything else?

If *Home Alone* is part of the capitalist economic system and is thus procapitalist, it is just as surely part of a complimentary ideological system: In this instance, *Home Alone*'s ideology is profamily. Historically, the rise of capitalism is linked to the rise of the nuclear family, the state, and the emphasis on private property. There is capitalism, which generates surplus goods and profits. Capitalism requires families to buy these consumer goods—usually at inflated prices. Capitalist institutions such as the media giants like Disney/Cap Cities, Viacom, and so forth that own the studios that produce children's films must therefore make films that legitimate family values and the value of family—precisely what happens in *Home Alone*.

Althusser sees the nuclear family as an ideological state apparatus that universalizes what is actually a specific historical construct: the white Anglo-Saxon Protestant nuclear family and the hierarchical relations of gender and class, sexuality and labor, said nuclear family normalizes, that is, makes appear real, natural, inevitable, and desirable. The closing scenes of *Home Alone* play out quite dramatically this script, firing out ideological answers to ideologically loaded questions. Having been accidentally left home alone in Chicago by his mother when the family flies to Paris for a Christmas vacation, Kevin comically gets on with the job of defending his home (private property) against Marv and Harry, the two inept burgulars. On the airplane (an advert for American Airlines), Kevin's guilt-stricken mother suddenly remembers she has forgotten Kevin and asks "What kind of a mother am I?" The film answers itself. First, it assumes that she must be the one to return for Kevin. Second, in order to do so, she must relinquish the visible signs of her economic independence. Frantically, she tries to buy a plane ticket for the return trip to Chicago by selling her expensive watch, jewels, and so forth, an allegorical stripping of the economic gains of feminism before the court of conservatism (another example of Susan Faludi's "backlash"). Third, eventually the family returns home. Kevin's mother arrives first, the film symbolically reestablishing her role as primary caregiver inside the home. The "natural" bond between mother and child, so important to the historical rise of the middle classes and middle-class ideology—idealized images of motherhood, domesticity, childrearing as woman's work, and so forth—is put firmly back in place. Fourth, the happy ending, the intimate mother and child reunion (Kevin and his mother), takes place under the watchful eye of the father, the family patriarch who returns with the other family members. With all the questions answered, the film ends.

3. Films classified according to their ideology

Comolli and Narboni make a third point about how films can be placed in several categories that either unthinkingly reproduce or deliberately contest bourgeois ideology. Category A consists of films that are "imbued through and through with the dominant ideology in pure and unadulterated form, and give no indication that their makers were even aware of the fact" (685). This category includes the majority of films, not just the typical commercial films from corporate Hollywood in particular and the National Entertainment State in general. In Category A one would place feature-length animated films from Disney/Cap Cities and feature-length live-action films from Rupert Murdoch's 20th Century Fox Film Corporation, such as *Home Alone.* These films show "The [dominant] ideology . . . talking to itself [with] all the answers ready before it asks the questions" (685). Films belonging to categories B and C "deal with a directly political subject." Films from these categories do not just reflect a politically current issue but "reiterate it, paraphrase it . . . use it to attack the ideology" (686) in terms of both form and content. Categories B and C, the most important for the Cahiers editors, might contain films like *Alsino and the Condor, City of Lost Children, Kids,* or *The Incredibly True Adventure of Two Girls in Love.* The avant-garde films of Stan Brakhage such as *Scenes from under Childhood* (1970) and *A Child's Garden and the Serious Sea* (1991) are relevant to categories B or C.

From the point of view of ideology and children's films, a particularly interesting category is Category D. For Comolli and Narboni, Category D films have a political content but do not "effectively criticize the ideological system in which they are embedded because they unquestioningly adopt its language and its imagery" (687). To rephrase this: Category D films appear liberal but are actually conservative, appear progressive but are actually reactionary, appear full of meaning but are actually empty of meaning. Films like *Ferngully* contain political content that challenges accepted ways of thinking about particular issues such as environmentalism. Comolli and Narboni argue, however, that the language and imagery of films in this category negate their positive messages. Witness the ahistorical, apolitical politics of *Ferngully.*

***Ferngully* (1992).** What William Johnson calls a "message movie" (39), *Ferngully*'s oftenstated political agenda, its message or theme, is that life will end unless corporations stop destroying the environment. Various characters repeat the film's central point, that saving Ferngully, synechdochially the natural environment as a whole, is crucial for human and planetary survival. First, Ferngully's surviving matriarch, Crysta's grandmother and magic fairy Magi Lune (Grace Zabriskie), tells Crysta about the last time Hexxus, a "spirit of destruction," rose up from the "bowels of the earth." Then humans "fled in fear." The second warning about environmental destruction follows soon after Magi's lecture to Crysta. Having just flown in from a "biology lab" where human technicians conduct animal research, Batty Koda (Robin Williams), delirious, exhausted, and out of control careens through the canopy and crashes below in Ferngully. Batty subsequently recounts his gruesome experiences in order to warn Crysta and her nonhuman community that human beings will likely destroy Ferngully just as they almost destroyed him. "Exercise a little prudence when dealing with humans," Batty impresses upon them. Ironically, a third warning comes from Hexxus himself, the evil "spirit of destruction." Inadvertantly set free by Zak, Hexxus (voiced by Tim Curry) gleefully recognizes that "human beings will always lend a hand with the destruction of this worthless jungle land." Human greed makes humans complicit in their own destruction. The film's closing dedication—"For our children and our children's children"—reiterates the message a fourth time, that unless caring human beings save the rainforests from corporate destruction today, future generations of humans (children) and nonhumans (species) will die. Global environmental ecocide equals mass human and species suicide, a worthy political message repeatedly championed by *Ferngully.*

But *Ferngully*'s proenvironmental message fails as a critique of that "ideological system" in which it finds itself embedded. Except when Hexxus speaks, Ferngully's inhabitants talk about their environment using cliches rather than the contestatory language of environmental politics. Rather than instruct Crysta in the history of environmental activism, from Justus von Liebeg's Law of the Minimum to Ronald Reagan's deregulating of environmental legislation and UNESCO's 1992 *Warning to Humanity,* Magi Lune teaches Crysta that only her "magical powers" will defeat Hexxus. Shamanlike, though nothing like a shaman, Magi completely romanticizes the interconnectedness of the world's ecosystems when she mystically chants that "everything in our world is connected by the delicate strands in the web of life." Magi acts as though recognizing the interconnectedness of all things will automatically prevent the destruction of all things interconnected, including life itself! As sparkling streams and waterfalls gush forth, so do the cliches. Magi reiterates that there is a "simple harmony to life" and that the "air we breathe is a magic thing." Rafti sings: "It's raining like magic. It's falling like starlight. It's raining life. The forest is rejoicing. The trees are all singing. It's raining life."

As Hexxus creeps ever closer, Magi Lune's solution is for Crysta to discover the "good and loving heart" in others because "we all have the power when it is shared." However, what stops water and air pollution, "acid rain pouring down," environmental racism, and "toxic love" is green politics not green aesthetics, collective forms of political organisation rather than individualist forms of heroic self-sacrifice.

Ferngully is a disturbing film, because the words and images it uses to discuss the destruction of the environment do not actually critique the ideological systems causing the environmental destruction. The language and imagery of *Ferngully* makes the film's unpalatable politics easy to stomach and thus prevents it from critiquing the "ideological system" in which it is embedded—Hollywood in particular and world bourgeois capitalism in general. The film ends by concealing that which it starts out to reveal: the need to prevent the destruction of the world's ecosystems by the world's transnational corporations.

Other solutions *Ferngully* offers to environmental destruction are equally apolitical, equally capitulatory. In full control of the leveler, a huge logging machine destroying the forests, Hexxus steers a course toward Ferngully. Led by Magi Lune, Ferngully's humans and nonhumans gather themselves within a circle for protection. The leveler, symbolizing rampant, out-of-control technology,[2] continues on its path of (self) destruction until Zak, aided by Pips and Batty, frantically climbs into the leveler's cockpit and switches it off. The engine dies, technology stops, deforestation ends. The very presence of *Ferngully,* of course, suggests that technology can't be stopped. The same technology killing the environment is the same technology bringing the film to life. Unable or unwilling to critique its own "eminently reactionary" (685) ideology, *Ferngully* finds itself complicit with the very ideology it seeks to contest. All politics, *Ferngully* is nonetheless apolitical, "caught in the system" it wishes to "break down" (687).

Generally, in these and other categories, Comolli and Narboni argue that criticism's function is to reveal how some films are completely wedded to the dominant ideology (category A), whilst others divorce themselves (categories B and C) or partially divorce themselves (categories D, E, F, G) from the dominant ideology at the level of both form and content. I want to turn now away from a general discussion of ideology to a more detailed discussion of the representation of class ideology in some children's films.

CLASS AND CHILDREN'S FILMS: *BRIGHT EYES, STAND BY ME,* AND *HARRIET THE SPY*

In "Wage Labour and Capital," Marx theorized that within the historical development of mankind as a whole, specific societies arose that had "peculiar, distinctive" (103) characteristics. According to Marx, the general history of man indeed corresponds to the specific development of three kinds of societies: ancient, feudal, and bourgeois. In turn, each of these corresponds to a particular form of ownership, social and familial relations and modes of production. In bourgeois society, the mode of production is capitalist and the most elementary form of capitalism is the commodity, that is, commodity production. For Marx, capitalist modes of production set up a class conflict between capital and labor, between those who finance and own the mode of production and those who work for the owners, those who give up their labor for wages, the proletariat.

In relation to children's cinema and child labor, several silent-era movies such as *Children Who Labor* (1912), *Why?* (1913), *Child Labor* (1913), *The Cry of the Children* (1913), and *The Blood of the Children* (1915) all dramatized the conflict between labor, capital, and class. *Children Who Labor,* which featured Viola Dana and Shirley Mason, otherwise known as the Flugrath sisters, shows an image of Uncle Sam hovering over several lines of poor children as they enter a factory. The word "Greed" appears over the factory, the implication being that greedy capitalists exploit working-class children in the workplace. Beginning by quoting the opening lines of Elizabeth Barrett Browning's poem of the same name, *The Cry of the Children* similarly portrays capitalism as heartless and corrupt. According to Kevin Brownlow, the millworkers in *The Cry of the Children* strike against their wealthy employers but are defeated. The film, which also stars Thanhouser kidlet Marie Eline as little Alice, shows the millowners as quite happy that the workers and their children are starving to death.

In relation to class issues in the 1930s, Michael Parenti in *Make-Believe Media* notes that: "To gladden the troubled spirits of people gripped in the Great Depression, Hollywood in the thirties also created Shirley Temple, the adorable song-and-dance imp . . . In *Bright Eyes* . . . and *Poor Little Rich Girl,* Shirley . . . teaches us not to hate the rich [and that] the Depression is just a silly thing that should not be taken seriously" (93). Parenti's point is that although *Bright Eyes* appears to have nothing to do with class, the opposite is in fact true.

Talking about *Bright Eyes* and other films starring Shirley Temple in *Images of Children in American Film: A Sociocultural Analysis* (1986), Kathy Jackson argues that Shirley Temple's enormous popularity in the 1930s can be explained not just in terms of her "cuteness" and her "remarkable talent" (62), but because the problems she fixed in her films were akin to the problems that needed fixing in society. In Parenti's terms, she smoothed "the troubled spirits of people trapped in the Great Depression." Indeed, Jackson states that, "Coming as it did after the prosperous 1920s, Depression America seemed to be a world gone wrong" (63). Jackson notes that the New Deal solutions to the failed economy were hard work, industriousness, belief in a better future, patriotism, and nationalism. Similarly, in *Franklin D. Roosevelt and the New Deal* (1963), historian William E. Leuchtenburg writes that Roosevelt had "discipline, and action demonstrated he was a man confident in his powers as leader of the nation. [He installed] hope and courage in the people. [He] knew how to lead and had faith in the future" (42). Hard work, industriousness, hope, optimism, faith—these are precisely the solutions Shirley Temple applies to the various problems she encounters in films like *New Deal Rhythm* (1933), *Stand Up and Cheer* (1934), and *Bright Eyes* (1934).

Jackson further notes that Temple's popularity during the Great Depression suggests an interesting contradiction. "At precisely the time when Americans professed to be taking an interest in the institution of childhood, many real children lived in misery. In view of this, the exalted on-screen image of Shirley Temple suggests a societal conflict" (65). Temple signifies both hope and despair. She represents "Depression Americans" hope that youth will bring about a better world but also a "subconscious guilt" that through no fault of their own, Americans were unable to provide fully for those children who suffered through the Depression.

Whilst Jackson's brief gesture toward the language of psychoanalysis ("subconscious") as a way of showing that the mixed emotional responses ("guilt," "conflict") of Americans during the Great Depression are reflected in the films of Shirley Temple is useful, I want to talk about how a rather more ideological reading of *Bright Eyes* begins not with the presence of Shirley Temple but with the absence of U.S. history.

The Great Depression made millions of Americans unemployed. Leuchtenburg comments: "By 1932, the unemployed numbered upward of thirteen million" (1). A common sight, therefore, in the 1930s was "At least a million, perhaps as many as two million [Americans] wandering the country in a fruitless quest for work or adventure or just a sense of movement" (2). Not just unemployed workers wandered the roads. After the Bonus Army marched on Washington, many World War I veterans, "homeless, jobless, and aimless, stayed on in Washington" (14). Disgruntled union workers took to the streets. Children themselves took to the road. Jackson herself notes that: "Some of those [children] who could not find work near their homes simply took to the road to avoid being burdens on their impoverished families, so that by 1932 the United States Children's Bureau reported that a quarter of a million youths were roaming the country—hopping freight trains, bumming food, and living among hoboes" (65). Robert Cantwell sums the situation up when he writes in *The Land of Plenty* that "Christ, there are thousands of people on the roads, thousands, men looking for work—sometimes whole families—all up and down the country—thousands! You see the poor devils hiking along the highways . . . everywhere you go" (quoted in Leuchtenburg 94).

Despite the millions of children, women, and men walking the highways and byways of America in search of work and food, capitalism, the system that put them there in the first place, remainded largely intact. A Senate investigation into Wall Street during the spring of 1932 "revealed that the most respected men on Wall Street had rigged pools, had profited by pegging bond prices artifically high, and had lined their pockets with fantastic bonuses . . . At a time when millions of Americans . . . had to scavenge for food [corporate executives] drew astronomical salaries . . ." (Leuchtenburg 20–21). Even Roosevelt's New Deal program of relief, recovery, and reform—the National Recovery Administration (NRA) and the Social Security Act, for example—did not so much save the working man from unemployment as it did the capitalist from capitalism.

The New Deal saved capitalism from self-destruction by regulating the mechanisms by which capitalism had traditionally operated. The trickle-down, free-market theories of the economy, in which wealthy individuals and families "regulated" the "free" market, were replaced by a planned economy in which Roosevelt's Brains Trust reconstructed and regulated the economy on behalf of the people at large. An emphasis on corporate greed was replaced by an emphasis on worker need as the Roosevelt Administration created what became known as the social contract. Under the social contract, since replaced by the Contract With America, capital and labor, both regulated by NRA codes of fair practices, worked together for the common good.

Perhaps because the millions of people out on the streets of America represented a real revolutionary threat, "The word that appears most frequently in the writings of New Deal theorists is 'balance'" (Leutchenburg 35), and in this regard, *Bright Eyes* is particularly interesting. First, the opening scenes foreground and foreshadow the kind of class issues the film generally articulates. Second, they foreground those class issues so obviously (editing and cross-cutting are all important) that seeing the film any other way is virtually impossible. In "Image and Voice: Approaches to Marxist-feminist Criticism," Christine Gledhill writes that "A film includes in its structure the positions from which it must be understood and viewed" (117). To paraphrase Gledhill, the way the child spectator sees *Bright Eyes* is understood to be class.

The film's opening scenes have Shirley cheerfully hitchhiking along a straight, tree-lined road. Two drivers stop. The first person who offers Shirley a ride is an old man dressed in threadbare work clothes. He drives a slow-moving, noisy, dirty, beaten-up truck. Shirley rejects his offer. By comparison, a young man dressed in fashionable clothes recognizes Shirley and offers her a ride. He drives a fast, quiet, smooth, expensive car. Shirley jumps in and speeds away toward the airport to meet the aviator-friend of her dead father, Loop Merrit.

None too subtly, the first lesson in class difference—physical appearance—has begun. Peter Hollindale's observations about ideology in children's books are useful. Hollindale suggests that teachers of children's literature should note which characters embody "desirable" and undesirable traits (39).[3] Shirley's choice, the expensively dressed man in his equally expensive car over the poorly dressed man in his equally poor truck, signifies the former attributes as desirable and the latter attributes as undesirable. On the one hand, Shirley (and audience) are offered a life of relative poverty, a life of manal labor. On the other hand, Shirley (and audience) are offered a life of relative wealth. A life of luxury or a life of toil? On behalf of the audience, Shirley chooses wealth and comfort over poverty and hardship, upper class over lower class.

Taking sides with labor, capital, or state ideologies is not the film's function. Recall that the key word in the New Deal vocabulary was "balance." Thesis, antithesis, synthesis: these opening scenes function dialectically. They show emerging out of the historical conflicts between wealth and poverty, labor and capital, employers and employees, the kind of ideal child that will take the country down the road to economic growth and emotional recovery but also the kind of ideal parents necessary to look after her. *Bright Eyes* shows the ideal family unit required to reproduce the ruling social order. From the spectator's point of view, this opening sequence from *Bright Eyes* interpellates the audience to conceptualize themselves as a new and emergent class that through the institution of the nuclear family will achieve a balance between work (labor) and money (capital) and thus put the country back on the road to economic prosperity.

In this regard, Loop is particularly important. A symbol of adulthood experience, whilst Shirley is a symbol of childhood innocence, Loop is neither particularly poor nor wealthy, young nor old. Rather, Loop is a hard-working aviator, a middle-aged man struggling to make ends meet whilst affectionately caring for his (dead) best friend's daughter (he symbolizes a 1930s version of the 1990s sensitive man). He takes financial risks when necessary. To afford lawyers for his custody battle with Uncle Ned Smith over Shirley, he tries to earn $1,000 by delivering mail by airplane even as a raging storm makes flying immensely dangerous. Generally, though, his financial and moral feet are planted firmly on the ground: Loop sternly warns Shirley to "Think the right thoughts [and] do the right thing." This moral position—be fair to others if you would have them be fair unto you—is later rewarded. On behalf of the state, the presiding judge, impressed by Loop's constant declarations of affection for Shirley, decrees that Shirley will live with Loop.

In other words, the film overall offers the audience neither an undesirable poor old man (the truck driver) or a desirable wealthy young man (the car driver). The film offers the audience a third alternative, a working man in his prime who fuses commonsense with passion and who embodies a range of "desirable," that is to say socially acceptable features, including the desire to marry, settle down, start a family, and raise children. Such a man will live in a "Swell house, be educated, and refined." Loop represents upward mobility. He represents not just an economic solution to the Great Depression but a particular kind of middle-class solution, a union of money and morality, Protestantism and capitalism. In this way, the film erases class difference even as it pencils in the outlines of a new and emergent class.

That the film's project is to get the audience to conceptualize and identify themselves as a stable, middle-class family unit emerging intact out of the historically determined struggles between capital and labor is suggested in the way the film sets up the rather obvious class differences and struggles between the Smythes and their employees. The Smythes are wealthy and cultured, able to live a life of relative comfort and ease. Their large house accommodates the live-in servants and Uncle Ned. They buy Joy, their daughter, expensive gifts and enroll her in costly piano lessons. They can afford a psychoanalyst for Joy (and presumably medical expenses for the wheelchair-ridden Uncle Ned). Parents and child dress fashionably. They confidently hire several expensive lawyers to fight Loop over the custody of Shirley. Given their wealth, they expect to win.

However, though the Smythes are wealthy, *Bright Eyes* makes it quite clear that money has only made them superficial, hypocritical, egotistical, cold, and friendless, concerned more with surface appearances than deeper realities. Wealth, the film makes clear, has transformed them into heartless human beings, weak and ineffective parents, harsh and uncaring employers. Neurotic and fastidious, they appear as snobbish bores, 1930s caricatures of the 1920s monied classes. They symbolize a set of social relations—a class—largely out of touch with Depression-era problems. The Smythes, for example, obviously represent Herbert Hoover and the Republican monied classes out of touch with the needs of working people. Historian Thomas Bailey describes Hoover as "standoffish, and stiff . . . colorless, accustomed during much of his life to giving orders to subordinates not to soliciting votes" (807), a description perfectly befitting the Smythes who throughout *Bright Eyes* unfeelingly order their servants and generally come across as indifferent to the suffering of others. Just as Hoover lost the sympathy of the people in 1932, the Smythes would have lost the sympathy of the audience in 1934. Like the Republicans, they might have had money, but they would have had no morality and were thus not the right kind of family to put America on the road to economic recovery. A family, they had no family values. Desirable in the 1920s, they are undesirable in the 1930s.

In a telling scene, Anita Smythe visits the kitchen to inform her staff of her cousin's visit. The camera positions itself so that just before Anita enters the kitchen the audience sees the servants sitting together around the kitchen table joking and laughing with a sense of easy familiarity and affection. Loop, Shirley, Mary, Mr. and Mrs. Higgins (cook and butler) and Thomas (chaueffeur) exude warmth and friendliness. Moving easily around the small and crowded kitchen, they make space for themselves even as they come into contact with one another. Smiling and talking, they good-naturedly interact. Food has been prepared and a pot boils on the stove. Throughout the film, and particularly in this scene, Shirley is the center of everyone's attention (see Figure 8).

When Anita Smythe enters the kitchen, however, the temperature in the kitchen rapidly cools. A cold formality—a great depression—descends upon the gathering's warm informality as Anita, obviously used to giving orders, instructs the servants how to prepare for her cousin's impending visit. Thomas is dispatched to the airport. Everyone else is ordered to behave with the utmost propriety. Undesirable visitors and phone calls are precisely that, undesirable and unwanted. Turning her back on the disgruntled servants, Anita leaves the room.

Other scenes from *Bright Eyes* might be deconstructed to show how the film represents the Smythes as cruel, heartless, and, ironically, unable to manipulate the courts despite their obvious wealth and ostentatious displays of class privilege. After Shirley Blake's father died in an aviation accident, the Smythes somewhat reluctantly adopted Shirley and her mother, Mary. After Mary's death (she is killed by a car), the Smythes

Figure 8. Shirley Temple in *Bright Eyes* (1934). Photo: The Museum of Modern Art/Film Stills Archive, New York. Courtesy of Fox.

consider Shirley a financial burden. Inhumanly, they refuse to care for the "child of a servant." However, Uncle Ned Smith, who befriends Shirley partly because he so vehemently dislikes his granddaughter Joy Smythe, overhears the Smythes abdicating responsibility for Shirley, heartlessly rationalizing her economic and emotional welfare as none of their business. Bemoaning the fact that she actually hired Mary Blake, Anita Smythe, for example, states that "There are no legal and moral reasons why we should care for her [Shirley]." Overhearing Anita and J. Wellington speak so coldly and cruelly about the fate of Shirley, Uncle Ned Smith accuses them of gross hypocrisy, reminding them that their name is Smith not Smythe, that their parents were originally lowly retail butchers (working class, in other words), and that "sanitary engineering," their current source of wealth, is a thoroughly pretentious term for "sewage." Uncle Ned loudly warns Anita and J. Wellington that if they ever want to inherit his fortune they will remember their own lowly class beginnings. Clearly echoing the sentiments of Roosevelt, he states that they will be "human and decent enough" to care for Shirley, a young orphaned girl (echoes of orphans Oliver Twist, Jane Eyre, etc.) who through no fault of her own finds herself at the bottom of the social scale. Thus threatened, the Smythes go to court to win the custody battle for Shirley. Immediately after learning from the judge that she is not to be awarded custody of Shirley, Anita Smythe viciously slaps her spoilt bratish daughter Joy on the cheek. Beneath the "civilized" appearances of the monied middle classes lie their "savage" realities.

In conclusion: Like the history from which it emerges, *Bright Eyes* begins and ends with class issues. We see five-year-old Shirley Blake choose between poverty and wealth and, in Marxist terms, the two classes (proletariat and bourgeois, ruling class and ruled class) these economic conditions historically represent. But to understand *Bright Eyes* merely in terms of these historical and economic conditions is to simplify Marxist theory and the way the film interpellates adults and children alike and thus functions as a form of social control. A third class appears out of the dialectic between the film's poor characters (the servants as employees) and the film's wealthy characters (the Smythes as owners and employers). That third class is the nuclear, middle-class family consisting of Loop Merritt, Adele Martin, and Shirley Blake, a poor flier, a wealthy socialite, and an orphan girl.

• • •

The Goonies (1985), *Stand By Me* (1986), *The Sandlot* (1993), *North* (1994), *Blank Check* (1994), *Richie Rich* (1994), *The Lion King* (1994), *The Big Green* (1995), *Toy Story* (1995), *Matilda* (1996), and *Harriet the Spy* (1996): In their various ways, contemporary children's films from corporate Hollywood, like those from the 1930s such as *Bright Eyes,* are thoroughly class conscious even when they deny their own class consciousness. What we find in the late twentieth century is not so much the disappearance of class, impossible in a centralized political system ruled by wealthy Democrats and Republicans. In "Liberal and Marxist Conceptions of the Class Struggle," Lenin writes that the liberals want to "narrow down, to curtail and emasculate the concept of class struggle" (458). In other words, arguably, under late capitalism, children's films do not make class disappear: They simply narrow it down and conceal it wherever possible behind all those traditional humanist themes of friendship, family, romance, innocence, and so forth. Arguably, children's films in recent years no longer blatantly expose the conditions of class exploitation as they so graphically did in the silent era. Nor are they so specifically concerned to construct classbound images of the nuclear family as way of uniting labor and capital under the social contract, that socioeconomic arrangement that served from the 1930s through to the 1980s. To further penetrate the children's culture market, to erase the class conditions the commodity-based culture market produces, contemporary children's films from corporate Hollywood are where Edward Herman's "low-intensity class war" (Herman) is currently fought. Class is everywhere in children's films, though not everywhere in children's films is it expressed in quite the same manner.

For example, *Stand By Me*'s many themes—childhood, friendship, the power of memory, storytelling, religion, war, life and death, time, and so forth—are all grounded fairly openly in images of social class. Framed as a series of childhood memories, *Stand By Me* shows how Gordie, the introspective and sensitive storyteller from the middle classes, and Chris, the tough kid from a "bad family," that is, the working classes, stand by one another despite their class differences (Vern is "the fat kid" and Teddy DuChamp is "the crazy kid"). Whilst out looking for the dead body of Ray Braur, Chris remarks to Gordie that when they attend junior high in the fall he, "Teddy, and Vern will be in the shop courses with the rest of the retards," whilst Gordie will take "college courses." Disturbed that class threatens his relationship with his friends, especially Chris, Gordie screams, "Fuck the writing, it's stupid." Always the surrogate father, Chris tells Gordie that "stories are not stupid" and that without college courses he will end up "another wise-guy with shit for brains." Ironically, it is Gordie, the child endowed with many of the verbal and storytelling abilities valued in middle-class cultures, who denies his class background. Adopting a classic middle-class, humanist point of view, Gordie believes that friendship can transcend class. Chris, from a less privileged background, is fully conscious of his own class position and how it will affect his friendship with Gordie when they enter Junior High in the Fall. Chris has no illusions about the illusion of class.

Rob Reiner's *North,* a PG-rated comedy, pokes fun at the idea of social class and children. *North* is about a young boy—North (Elijah Wood)—who feels completely unappreciated by his busy, self-obsessed, class-driven, yuppie parents. Whilst sitting in what the narrator/guardian angel character (Bruce Willis) calls his private place, an easy chair in an upscale mall furniture store, North decides he will divorce his parents, become a free agent (baseball is the film's sport and controlling metaphor), and travel the world in search of parents who appreciate his good grades, his politeness, his athletic skills, and his acting abilities. North is hailed as a leader, a champion of children's rights, one whose actions, according to the narrator, "challenge the entire concept of the family as we know it!" Once the plan is printed in the school newspaper by the Machiavellian journalist/editor Winchell (Mathew McCurley), who sees North's actions as his own "Watergate," North duly sets off around the world searching for the perfect parents watched over by his wise-cracking guardian angel (disguised as the Easter Bunny, Gabby, Joey Fingers, the Fed Express driver, and so forth). Everywhere North is hailed a hero.

Gradually, though, the potentially comic and enlightening idea of North as an Everychild and a leader of children-as-a-class overturning the dictatorship of the parents becomes less and less funny and is eventually dropped. Abroad, the perfect parents turn out to be offensive caricatures of ethnic minorities and in the end the perfect family is North's workaholic, white Anglo-Saxon, middle-class parents. Meanwhile, at home, Winchell and his corrupt lawyer Belt (played by Jon Lovitz parodying opportunistic, ambulance-chasing lawyers) seize the day and start a political movement out of North's heroism. With what the Narrator calls "inspirational speeches," Winchell works the young crowd: "How much longer do we have to put up with this indignity? How much longer must we tolerate these injustices?" he asks. "This is the era of our liberation," he tells the children. As the children's revolution gathers momentum, the kids unite as a social class behind their fearless, globe-trotting leader. In the park, the kids as one cheer "Viva El Norte!" Viva El Norte!" But when things go wrong and North decides to return to his own parents, Winchell says to his lawyer that there is "one catalyst that can give a political movement true cohesion: a martyr." The kids turn on North who is nonetheless finally reunited with his parents in the mall. The idea of children as a social class making demands on those directly in power (the parents) is let go, the issue of class subsumed beneath the issue of class.

Harriet the Spy (1996), starring Michelle Trachtenberg as Harriet, seems to be merely a "Little Girl Power" film from corporate Hollywood about the transcendent trials and tribulations of a young writer—Harriet—rather than a discussion about the visible presence in contemporary urban America of social class. Indeed, in the context of a postradical 1970s feminism, that coincided with the Children's Rights Movement, what better way of continuing to diffuse the presence of class conflict and struggle within America and among children in the 1990s than to make films that privilege women and young girls, that is, the social group stereotypically most likely to disavow class relations in part because, as numerous feminists have quite rightly pointed out, class oppression and patriarchal oppression are often synonymous. Categorized a PG children's comedy (how innocuous) and starring Michelle Trachtenberg, previously from Nickelodeon's *The Adventures of Pete and Pete* (even more innocuous), as Harriet M. Welsch, how could *Harriet the Spy* have anything to do with the representation of class in contemporary children's cinema and film?

Charming, pretty, articulate, and witty, Harriet, rather "obsessively" (1) according to Christine James, spys on the local people in her neighbourhood as well as her 6th grade school friends and writes down in her private notebook—marked PRIVATE—everything she sees. Often her musings are candid, cruel, and potentially hurtful. Indeed, the spying and writing eventually land the relatively precocious Harriet into trouble when her classmates accidentally discover her notebook and read aloud (they are in the park) what Harriet has written about them. Harriet's closest friends, Sport and Jamie, are particularly distressed that Harriet should so furtively betray their confidences and, as a result, their friendship. Behind the mask of friendship all along lay the face of betrayal. At any rate, rather than accept that a private diary consisting of intimate details about one's supposedly closest friends is likely to destroy rather than foster that friendship, Harriet reveals to the whole school even more personal secrets about Sport and Jamie, posting, for example, Xerox copies of Sport dressed as a housewife doing housework. This, of course, completely backfires. Sport, Jamie, and the others end their friendship with Harriet. Harriet's self-obsessed parents force her to relinquish the notebook writing and send her, appropriately enough, to a psychiatrist. Harriet insists that her writing cannot be given up: it's who she is. In the end, Harriet's ex-nanny, Gully (Rosie O'Donnell), deus ex machina, returns and sternly informs Harriet that she must apologize to her friends but also keep writing. By way of apology, Harriet suggests sharing the coveted editorship of the sixth-grade newspaper with her once sworn enemy, Marian Hawthorne. The girls end up as friends.

The themes of writing, friendship, identity, and individuality—Gully tells Harriet: "You're an individual and that makes people nervous"—all of which revolve around humanist-type questions of gender (they revolve around Harriet) are surely grounded in materialist images of social class. Though it seems to have nothing to do with class difference, class difference is in fact everywhere. For example, Sport's father, a would-be writer, is poor. A particularly effective scene in *Harriet the Spy* occurs when relatively wealthy Harriet, a would-be writer, accidentally bumps into Sport, who is shopping. He is embarrassed because he lacks the money to pay the store clerk for the basic groceries his father has, presumably, sent him to buy. In other ways, *Harriet the Spy* distinguishes between wealth and poverty and thus makes us aware of how class issues intersect with children. Sport does all the housekeeping, whilst Harriet has a nanny because her father has a "high-pressure job." Other parents drive their kids to school in Range Rovers. Jeanie wants to win the Nobel Peace Prize and Sport (not unsurprisingly) wants to be "filthy rich." At the park, just before Harriet's incriminating diary is discovered by Sport and made public by Marian, Marian actually suggests they play a game called "Buy the Volvo" with her as the dealer selling affordable cars to young couples. The comic effect of this only barely disguises the seriousness of the issue. Last but not least, Gully speaks to Harriet using middle-class maxims rather than working-class rhetoric. Indeed, Gully completely betrays her working-class position—she is a servant—by talking to Harriet using meaningless phrases rather than the language of class privilege.

But then Gully's class betrayal is unsurprising given the film's corporate origins. *The Adventures of Pete and Pete* and *Harriet the Spy* were produced by Nickelodeon and Paramount respectively. Both Nickelodeon and Paramount are owned by Viacom.

FEMINIST FILM THEORY, FEMINIST CHILDREN'S FILM CRITICISM, AND CHILDREN'S FILMS

Marx, Althusser, Comolli, Narboni, and others are solid theoretical contexts for discussing how capitalist cultures use children's films to interpellate children into the class hierarchies of bourgeois society. Heidi Hartmann's 1981 essay, "The Unhappy Marriage of Marxism and Feminism: Towards a More Progressive Union," though, argues that Marxism, Althusserian or otherwise, remains gender-blind. Hartmann writes that "To continue our simile further, either we need a healthier marriage or we need a divorce" (2). Michèle Barrett echoes Hartmann's sentiments: "In charity, it [women's oppression] should be seen in the context of a history of Marxist thought in which questions of gender relations and male dominance have long been ignored and marginalized" (23). Hartmann and Barrett argue that Marxist theory privileges class analysis over gender analysis.

In *Film Theory: An Introduction,* Lapsley and Westlake note that within the history of film theory, questions of gender eventually "displaced" (23) questions of class. The contemporary women's movement recognized that "economic exploitation, political exclusion and cultural disadvantaging" (23) took place in society but also in film. Sexism existed in the workplace as well as in the theater, on the streets but also on the screen. Feminist theorists argued that deconstructing the oppressive representation of women on-screen would help bring down the forms of sexual exploitation experienced by women off-screen. Consequently, as Kuhn writes: "[F]eminist textual analysis inserted a feminist perspective into procedures of ideological reading by raising as their central concern the question of the specifically patriarchal character of the ideological operations of the classic Hollywood film" (85).

Susan Haywood's *Key Concepts in Cinema Studies* (1996) divides the history of feminist film theory into three phases: 1968–74, 1975–83, and 1984–90s. The first phase, 1968–74, examined the stereotypical representation of women in Hollywood as a reflection of women in society. The three leading feminist critics writing about images of women in early 1970s dominant cinema were Molly Haskell, Marjorie Rose, and Joan Mellen in books such as *From Reverence to Rape: The Treatment of Women in the Movies* (1974), *Popcorn Venus: Women, Movies, and the American Dream* (1973), and *Women and Their Sexuality in the New Film* (1974), respectively. Writing about Mae West, for example, Joan Mellen notes that "The stereotyped image [of West] thus draws upon a partial truth" (646). Mellen and others examined how the images of women in films reflected certain stereotypical images of women in society. During the second phase of feminist film theory, 1975–83, the reflectionist position of Haskell and Mellen, illustrated by Mellen's quote about West's sexuality, was critiqued by feminists Claire Johnston, Laura Mulvey, and Annette Kuhn as essentialist and reductionist. Haskell and Mellen's "sociological and empiricial" (100) approach "presumed a predetermined sexual identity, difference" (100) and generally ignored the nuances of spectatorial relations, Haywood notes in her history of feminist film theory. As a result of these critiques, Johnston, Mulvey, Kuhn et al., more closely examined the stereotpyical images of women in film, not just as a reflection of society, but as a construction of a particular film's narrative, its story line, camera angles, lighting, clothes (or lack thereof), positioning of the body, spectator response, and so forth: Ideology was seen to be an integral component part of the cinematic framework rather than something merely imposed from without. The emphasis shifted from examining what the images supposedly reflected about women in society to examining how images of women were constructed by films (not so much the logic of capitalism but the logic of narrative), filmmakers (straight, gay) and audiences (the pleasure of looking, for example). In this and other ways, Laura Mulvey's seminal "Visual Pleasure and Narrative Cinema" (1975) remains extremely important and influential. Judith Mayne cites Laura Mulvey as a filmmaker and theorist whose "Visual Pleasure" drew on the insights of semiotics and psychoanalysis to deconstruct the way classical cinema uses codes and conventions to privilege the male gaze and thus the (ideological) way women in film narratives (and girls in children's film narratives) are positioned as objects of patriarchal desire. 1970s feminist film theorists could now show how patriarchal ideologies of sexual difference sutured women into the text as silent objects of male desire and exchange. In the third phase, 1984–90s, feminist film analysis continued to discuss the "patriarchal character" of Hollywood film, but textual forms of analysis began to once more include contextual forms of analysis. Mulvey's male gaze was replaced by Tania Modleski's bisexual gaze. Teresa De Lauretis situated women's ability to watch films from multiple points of view in the context of Foucault's theories of discourse, power, and resistance. Black, Asian, and Latin American film scholars and theorists insisted that feminist film theory in the 1990s situate gender in the contexts of race and, once again, class.

Annette Kuhn writes that, "While feminist perspectives in film theory and criticism have generated a substantial body of work on film texts, other potentially productive areas remain virtually unexplored" (106). Kuhn goes on to discuss the intersections between feminist theory, pornography, and women in film, arguing that,

> In these [pornographic representations] women are frequently portrayed in particular ways: either unclothed or, if not strategically clad in garments or accessories which represent anything from slight states of undress to various fetishes and sexual perversions-unbuttoned blouses . . . and so on . . . In an address to male spectators, the body of the woman is constructed as . . . spectacle and the mise-en-scène of representations of women's bodies coded in various ways both to be looked at by the spectator and, in the process, to evoke sexual arousal in him. These codes include the way in which the body is posed, lit, the overall composition of the image—including props, gestures, clothes, accessories—and the nature of the direction of the gaze of the model. This is what is implied by the notion of the 'objectification' in certain representations of the female body. (110)

Kuhn is arguing here that feminist theorists have noted how women in mainstream movies are often presented in varying states of dress and undress. Drawing on the theories of Laura Mulvey and others, Kuhn is arguing that women are presented this way to appeal to the male gaze and men's desires. Camera position, clothing (or lack thereof), accessories, the woman's gaze, and so forth: in these coded ways, the woman's body is constructed for the viewing pleasure of men. Women's bodies are objectified, much like they are in softcore pornography. The representation of women in mainstream films is not unlike the representation of women in softcore pornography. We will return to these issues momentarily.

• • •

Like feminist film theory, the history of feminist children's film criticism can be divided into three overlapping periods. The first period, "Images of Children," extends approximately from 1965 to 1980. As discussed in Part Two: Criticism, Frances Clark Sayers' "Walt Disney Accused" makes an important contribution to feminist children's film criticism in this first period by discussing the image of the heroine in the work of Disney.

The second period in feminist children's film criticism extends from 1980 to 1993. Overlapping with the first period, this second period remains concerned with "Images of Children" criticism. However, there is a marked interest in adaptation and pedagogical issues, as well as the incorporation of different critical theories into the analysis of particular texts. Ellen Seiter's discussion of Scott O'Dell's *Island of the Blue Dolphins* and Virginia L. Wolf's discussion of Frances Hodgson Burnett's *The Secret Garden* raise feminist and psychoanalytic theories respectively. Kathy Merlock Jackson's book *Images of Children in American Film* takes a sociocultural approach. Largely ignoring the work of Johnston, Mulvey, and Kuhn, nonetheless these critical studies in this second period represent important stages in the development of feminist children's film criticism.

Reworking the title of Lissa Paul's seminal essay, we might call the third phase of feminist children's film criticism, "What Feminist Film Theory Knows about Children's Cinema and Films." In "Enigma Variations: What Feminist Theory Knows about Children's Literature," Lissa Paul argues that "There is good reason for appropriating feminist theory to children's literature. Both women's literature and children's literature are devalued and regarded as marginal or peripheral by the literary and educational communities" (149). Paul notes, however, that this marginalization of women's literature is changing because feminist critics are "tracing the history of women's writing" and are "giving definition and value to women in literature and literature by women" (150). Feminist theory is relevant to children's literature because "As it happens, the forms of physical, economic, and linguistic entrapment that feminist critics have been revealing in women's literature match the images of entrapment in children's literature" (150). For example, whereas men go on "technicolor epic adventures" (151) women's literature and children's literature tend to focus on "the minute and mundane features of everyday life around which their lives revolve: household effects, food, clothes, sewing, interior decorating, and nuances of social relationships" (151). To discuss these and other differences, Paul states, feminist critics have drawn on "a host of disciplines: semiotic theory to make the signs of otherness visible; linguistic theory to identify the differences between male language and female language; [and] Marxist theory . . ." (155).

Feminist children's film criticism in the third phase, 1993 to the present, foregrounds a similar interdisciplinarity. Just as feminist film theory turned to cinema's "historical and social contexts" (Hayward 107) that included "The voices of Latin American women, Asian women and Asiatic women as well as those of Black and White women" (115), so feminist children's film criticism has similarly developed. Relevant essays would be James Snead's "Shirley Temple" in his 1994 *White Screens, Black Images: Hollywood from the Dark Side,* Poonam Arora's 1994 "The Production of Third World Subjects for First World Consumption: *Salaam Bombay* and *Parama*" and D. Soyini Madison's 1995 "*Pretty Woman* through the Triple Lens of Black Feminist Spectatorship."

A final note in this brief overview: As important as it is to situate films in the historical and social contexts of gender, race, and class essays such as Janet Wondra's "A Gaze Unbecoming: Schooling the Child for Femininity in *Days of Heaven*" and Patricia Erens' "A Childhood at the Cinema: Latent Fantasies, the Family, and Juvenile Spectatorship" continue to make substantial contributions to children's film criticism. Looking back to the work of Laura Mulvey, for example, Wondra argues for a child's gaze, a "third kind of looking . . . a gathering gaze" (6). In "Split Skins: Female Agency and Bodily Mutilation in *The Little Mermaid,*" Susan White draws on "Psychoanalysis, as a branch of psychology dealing specifically with sexuality and with the unconscious . . ." (186) to discuss what constitutes a woman's—that is to say, Ariel's—story. Like modern children's literature and children's literature criticism, feminist children's film criticism draws deeply from the well of interdisciplinary studies.

• • •

Barbara Quart's 1988 *Women Directors: The Emergence of a New Cinema* brings into focus many of the issues just discussed concerning the relationship between feminist film theory, the history of feminist children's film criticism, and children's films. Quart begins by noting that from 1949 to 1979, "one-fifth of 1 percent of all films released by American major studios were directed by women" (1). This amounts to a "virtual exclusion from directorial ranks" (6) for women. However, Quart argues, this situation of women being marginalised within the very industry that insists upon centering them, is slowly changing. More women directors have appeared on the scene, as it were. In the process, a new cinema has emerged.

How is this new cinema defined and what is its relation to children's cinema? There are four main areas of discussion. First, endings in films by women do not always conclude with the restoration of the traditional heterosexual couple and, by implication, the image of the traditional nuclear family (parent/child). Second, there is often the absence of a controlling male gaze in films by women. Men play a role within such films but the power of looking is not ascribed to them as in classical Hollywood narratives such as *Home Alone.* Third, indeed, in female-centered films, male bonding is displaced by female bonding: think here of *Matilda* or *Harriet the Spy.* Fourth, films by women do not often subscribe to the same realist paradigms constructed by men. In this regard, women's films are antirealist.

Of particular interest in Quart's book for questions of children's cinema, ideology, and gender, is the presence of more girls' coming-of-age stories such as Diane Kury's *Peppermint Soda,* Mart Meszaro's *Diary for my Children,* Margaretha von Trotta's *Marianne and Julianne,* and Joyce Chopra's *Smooth Talk.* In these films, audiences will find "girlhoods of a kind not represented before on film" (4).

To illustrate these issues, we might turn to *The Incredibly True Adventure of Two Girls in Love.* Quart's belief that women directors now make commercially successful films that do not necessarily capitulate to the traditional Hollywood narrative pattern of disruption and closure is perfectly exemplified by writer and director Maria Maggenti's *The Incredibly True Adventure.* Set in and around Wallace High School, *The Incredibly True Adventure* primarily concerns the coming-out of Evie and her subsequent relationship with girlfriend Randy. There is no controlling male gaze in the film. Randy works in a garage with another woman, lives in a lesbian commune, and hangs out at school with her gay friends. Evie lives with her divorced mother and mostly hangs out at school with three not very understanding or sympathetic girlfriends. Most of the film's gazes and looks are done by other women and female bonding rather than male bonding is at the film's heart. Finally, the film's insistence on presenting relationships, school, work, and life from the perspectives of homosexual women suggests that there are ways of seeing the world other than through the eyes of heterosexual men.

• • •

Just as Kuhn notes that there remains "potentially productive areas" (106) for feminist critics to explore, so there remain equally valuable areas for children's feminist film critics to discuss, in particular the issue of children's cinema and film and pornography.

Feminist theorists such as Linda Williams have provided an historical context for understanding how women's bodies are objectified, a context that has a direct bearing on the relation between children's cinema, film, and pornography. In *Hard Core: Power, Pleasure, and the "Frenzy of the Visible"* (1989), Williams provocatively places Eadweard Muybridge's nude and seminude photographs of women at the beginning not just of cinema but of modern pornography and film. Williams argues that whilst Muybridge's photographs facilitate a certain kind of scientific curiosity about the human body, that scientific knowledge is intimately related to questions of plesure and sexual difference. Williams argues that whilst "Naked and semi-naked men . . . walk, run, jump, throw, catch . . . and perform simple trades" (39), the women "blow kisses, narcissistically twirls about, endlessly flirt fans, and wear transparent drapery that emphasizes the nudity underneath" (40). In short, Williams argues that these early nude and seminude photographs of the male and female anatomy are not just part of the technological prehistory of the cinema but the early use of the camera to encode women's bodies as sexual objects, the early stirrings of pornography and dominant Hollywood cinema.

What's rarely mentioned by any critic, feminist or otherwise, is that Muybridge's book contains numerous photographs of nude and seminude children. When film historians like Mast, Shipman, Street, and/or Jackson write about film and history, Eadweard Muybridge's photographs of nude and seminude children, from his *Complete Human and Animal Locomotion,* are usually ignored. About the silent era, for example, Shipman writes: "Photography was invented in 1835 but the cinema did not become possible until 1888, when George Eastman devised . . . the celluloid roll film. In the meantime, English-born photographer, Eadweard Muybridge had been commissioned by the Governor of California to take action pictures of a favorite race-horse [using] his zoopraxiscope, by which . . . his photographs were projected" (17).

Mast describes how Muybridge used multiplane cameras to shoot "motion sequences of horses and elephants and tigers [of] nude ladies and wrestling men and dancing couples" (*A Short History* 12) which he then projected through his zoopraxiscope. Mast concludes that "Continuous motion had been divided into distinct frames, but it had not yet been photographed by a single camera" (13). Substantial detail about the various histories behind the invention of cinematography—photography, celluloid film, and projection—but nothing much about the appropriate or inappropriate use of naked children as cinematic subjects, nothing at all about the history of sexuality and children's cinema such nakedness implies.

In fact, the presence of these photographs, taken at precisely the same time the cinema appears in history, raise a set of questions similar to those raised by Linda Williams. Do the often extremely explicit photographs of the nude boys and girls reflect a genuinely disinterested scientist using a child's body to consider questions of cinematography and human locomotion? Are the pictures about science or sexuality, the observed or the observer, that which is looked at or that which does the looking, the child in the image or the adult behind the camera? Perhaps only the reader can judge?

In a sense, these questions have already been raised and to some extent answered, though not specifically in relation to Muybridge's photographs. In the final pages of his 1992 cultural studies book *Child-Loving: The Erotic Child and Victorian Culture,* James Kincaid argues that the seminude images of child stars Patty McCormack, Jay North, Mark Lester, and Macaulay Culkin in films like *The Bad Seed* (1956), *Maya* (1965), *Oliver!* (1968), and *Home Alone* (1990), respectively, are recent examples of the "perfect erotic child" (365), the kind that reaches back throughout the twentieth century. Indeed, Kincaid argues that this image of the "perfect erotic child" is particularly noticeable in Shirley Temple. "The image of Shirley Temple is perhaps most suggestive, as she flirted and seduced and sashayed her way through movie after movie . . . swishing her short skirt around above a camera positioned at a remarkably low level" (371). Kincaid also argues that "Defining the child as an object of desire, we create the pedophile as the one who desires, as a complex image of projection and denial: the pedophile acts out the range of attitudes and behaviors made compulsory by the role we have given the child" (5). Society defines the child as an object of desire. Defining the child as desirable produces the pedophile and the kind of pornography considerable socially acceptable.

This is not the place for a full analysis of Kincaid's book and the controversies books like it inevitably generate when discussing the representation of childhood sexuality in children's and adult culture. Still, I want to suggest that just as Muybridge's photographs of nude and semi-nude women are perhaps early examples of what, according to Williams became soft/hardcore pornography, Muybridge's cinematic experiments with naked children might be seen as early cinematic examples of Kincaid's "essentially genderless" (364) and "perfect erotic child" (365), the child who regularly appears and reappears in children's films throughout the twentieth century, from *Bright Eyes* in the 1930s all the way through to *Milk Money, Lolita, Exotica,* and *Mulan* in the 1990s. These films and others like them position female children and young kids in the narrative in ways that are consistent with Kuhn and Kincaid's observations. In other words, whilst feminist theorists like Kuhn note that mainstream films and soft/hardcore films from corporate Hollywood both narrativize women as sexual objects for men's viewing pleasure as a function of the patriarchal nature of capitalism, a similar argument might be used in relation to children's films.

PG13-rated *Milk Money,* for example, situates women and young girls in the narrative as sexual objects of desire for male gaze in a variety of ways. There are discussions of women's body parts and functions, boys staring at young girls, a pornographic movie, naked girls for "$100 a day" in the city, prostitution, a striptease in a 7th grader's biology class, and so forth.

In the beginning of the film, we are introduced to three young likely lads: Frank, whose mother has died, Kevin, the cute punk with the black leather jacket, and Brad, the slightly neurotic, nervous, nerdy type. In Frank's treehouse one night, Frank shows Kevin and Brad a diaphragm and an eyelash curler hidden in his shoebox. An excrutiatingly embarassing discussion ensues concerning the diaphragm's sexual function. Matter-of-factly, Frank informs Brad and Kevin that diaphragms prevent "the passage of sperm into the uterus." As the scene ends, the boys wonder why girls don't fart or spit and acknowledge that, in the battle of the sexes, they—the boys—are losing.

Next, the three boys, self-declared "virgins," are in Brad's bedroom.[4] They watch a hardcore porn movie on television. Eventually Kevin switches off the porn movie only to declare the twenty-four-hours-a-day availability of naked girls for $100 in the city. With the need to "see a woman naked," the boys get their money together, ride their bicycles to the city, and buy sex from Vee (Melanie Griffith), who poses for them on a bed in the Fort Washington Hotel. Once the money is handed over, she drops her top, exposing her breasts.

Later in the film, Vee helps Frank with his homework. Frank has been told by his teacher that because his knowledge of the female reproductive system is woefully inadequate he must complete in class an "oral presentation of the material with footnotes and visual aids." Enlisting Vee as a visual aid, Frank uses her body to point out (he draws on her) the different parts of the female reproductive system: the breasts (at which point all the young girls in the class look at theirs), the ovaries, the uterus, and the fallopian tube. As Frank's presentation ends, Vee escapes through a window, the teacher returns from answering a fake telephone call in the school office, and order in the classroom is restored. Vee eventually falls in love with Frank's dad, and turns from a life of prostitution in the city to a life of domesticity in the suburbs.

Whilst *Milk Money* is not necessarily pornographic, however, it is arguably an example of what Kincaid calls "allowable cultural pornography, managed by power's most savage agents: legislators, lawyers, and cops" (383). The emphasis is on the physical beauty of the women, not the men. Vee is mostly dressed in short skirts, high heels, and tight, revealing blouses in an address to male spectators designed to evoke sexual arousal. Throughout the film, the body of Vee is constructed as sexual spectacle, an object of sexual desire at first for the boys and then for the father. There is an emphasis on girls' body parts. All the looks and gazes within the film are controlled by the boys and men and directed at the women (though admittedly Frank won't look when Vee undresses because he wants to be a gentleman) and the pubescent girls. In general, the bodies of the film's women and young girls are objectified either by the clothes, the accessories, the gazes, the camera angles, and, of course, the money. Obviously, given the theme of prostitution, money is the medium that facilitiates the exchange of women between the two men, the son (Frank) who is the father-and-husband to be and the father himself.

In other classical Hollywood films, young girls are similarly positioned as sexual objects to be gazed at. In *Star Kid,* twelve-year-old Spenser (Joseph Mazzello) is continually bullied at school until an alien lifeform, a robot Spenser nicknames Cy, lands from outer space. Stepping inside Cy's half human/computer body, Spenser finds a newly found confidence and, after beating up a bully named Turbo Bruntley, visits a local carnival searching for his girlfriend, a pretty girl whose beauty silences him (he is tongue-tied when she adresses him) even as it makes him want to talk to her. Hidden within Cy's technologically sophisticated suit, but able to see outside through Cy's eyes, Spenser locates his girlfriend at the carnival and follows her around.

As with *Milk Money, Star Kid* in general and the carnival scene in particular is not so much pornographic, but it does offer viewers an example of how young girls are often situated within the narrative as sexual objects to be stared at. For example, as Spenser follows the girls around at the carnival, he obviously becomes the voyeur, the peeping tom staring at the girls, watching them as they have fun on the rides. When their carnival ride breaks and the cage in which they are sitting falls to earth, they are rescued by Spenser in a scene that reinforces their status as dependent, submissive objects of desire.

Like *Milk Money,* no doubt *Star Kid* did not set out to situate the young girls within the narrative in ways that imitate softcore pornography. Yet in a sense, the relations of power between the sexes that exist within the film—Spenser looks at Michelle, Michelle is looked at, Spenser rescues Michelle, Michelle is rescued, he is active, she is passive, he is controlling, she is controlled, he spys on her, she is spied upon by him—suggests that it has everything to do with pornography and thus with children's feminist film criticism.

NOTES

[1]In this regard, see Charles Musser, "Work, Ideology, and Chaplin's Tramp," *Resisting Images: Essays on Cinema and History,* ed. Robert Sklar and Charles Musser (Philadelphia: Temple University Press, 1990), 36–67. Musser situates Chaplin's *The Tramp, The Idle Class, The Pawnshop,* and *The Gold Rush* in the historical context of "1913—the year that Henry Ford inaugurated the endless-chain conveyor for final assembly of the Model T. Treating people as human machines, Ford required workers to execute the same series of actions again and again at a pace determined by the speed of the line. At the same time, Frederick Taylor and others were proselytizing methods of industrial management that appropriated the knowledge of skilled workers and eliminated their functional autonomy" (37). Musser further notes that "The film industry was being subjected to the same sort of rationalization" (37). Musser is arguing that Chaplin's success emerged out of the response of viewers to the forms of rationalization and standardization taking place in the economy. Jack Zipes makes a similar argument in his "Towards a Theory of the Fairy-tale Film: The Case of *Pinocchio*" *The Lion and the Unicorn* 20 (1996): 1–24. There, Zipes argues that the standardization taking place in the economy and the film industry during the 1930s and 1940s led to the standardization and commodification of fairy 154tale adaptations such as *Pinocchio.*

[2]There are two ways of thinking about the relationship between technology and children's cinema and film. There is the technology that produces the films and the representation of technology within the films. With regards the latter, there are several issues worth raising. First, technology is generally represented as either good or bad depending on who is in control. In this sense, the representation of technology is never neutral in children's films. How could it? Today's youngsters are tomorrow's users and consumers of goods produced by technology. Second, technology in children's films is often engendered. Girls and boys are associated with technology in different ways: think here of films such as *WarGames* or *Jurassic Park.*

[3]See Peter Hollindale, "Ideology and the Children's Book," *Literature for Children: Contemporary Criticism,* Ed. Peter Hunt, New York: Routledge, 1992: 19–40.

[4]Here again, note the emphasis on enclosed spaces: Frank's treehouse and shoebox, Brad's bedroom, the locked safe in Brad's bedrooms where his meagre savings are kept, the dustbins where Frank dumps his prized possessions when the prostitute Vee accuses him of lying to his father about her "oldest" profession, the wetlands Frank's dad is trying desperately to save from becoming part of a nearby suburban subdivision, and so forth. Of course, each children's film presents its enclosed spaces differently, even though the enclosed space is a characteristic feature of all children's films.

PART FIVE

Pedagogy

Cineliteracy is long overdue in American education, and not just on the college level.

—GIANNETTI XI

Media literacy . . . is primarily critical. It teaches how to read film and television, revealing [films] as constructions with particular purposes and points of view which do not represent truth or reality.

—DAVENPORT 195

We understand pedagogy not commonsensically, as classroom practices or instructional methods as such, but as the act of producing and disseminating knowledges in culture . . . The goal of the dominant pedagogical practices is to situate people at posts of intelligibility from which the reigning economic, political, and ideological social arrangements are deemed to be uncontestably true. [In short] we conceive "pedagogy" to be a means . . . of constructing and maintaining subjectivities that are necessary for reproducing existing social arrangements.

—MORTON AND ZAVARZADEH VII

Disney . . . is not ignorant of history . . . reinventing it as a pedagogical . . . tool to secure its own interests, authority, and power . . . .[T]his intersection of the political and pedagogical . . . neccesitates making Disney's world of representations the object of critical analysis.

—GIROUX, "Beyond the Politics . . ." 80–88

TEACHING CHILDREN'S FILMS

As outlined in Part Two: Criticism, there exists a history of children's film criticism that includes a discussion of way in which films might be taught to teachers to prepare them to incorporate film instruction into the school curriculum. Part Five: Pedagogy, as the epigraphs suggest, continues that discussion by politicizing a pedagogy of film. I try to show how teachers might appropriate the language of literary and film theory to provide students with what David Whitley, in "Reality in Boxes: Children's Perception of Television Narratives" (1996), calls a "critical vocabulary" (50) for analyzing children's media in general and children's films in particular. Whitley borrows the word "modality" from linguistics to analyse the closing scenes of Walt Disney's *The Jungle Book,* arguing that because films such as *The Jungle Book* "have now begun to form a major strand of young children's viewing experience" (55), they should be taught seriously. Indeed, just as education students enrolled in Departments of Language and Literature are taught how to read and interpret children's literature using literary theories ranging from formalism to feminism, new historicism, and Marxist-informed cultural studies, in the name of what Louis Giannetti calls "Cineliteracy" (xi) and what Tom Davenport calls "Media literacy" (195), students also should be taught how to use those same literary theories (including those of linguistics) to critique children's films. Long overdue in all levels of American education, "visual literacy" (Stahl 6) provides teachers and students with a critical vocabulary for understanding how children's films produce meanings, which circulate within the text as well as within the economy, the effect Marsha Kinder calls a "supersystem: a network of interrelated narrative texts or media products" (quoted in Wartella, 40).

Children's films exist as textual practice and social practice, each of which is grounded in the material conditions of history (aspects of cinema studies largely ignored by UNESCO, Butler, and Tisch). To critique a film is to critique the society and history that made the film, the political function of media literacy, not just the analysis of film and television images but the institutions (Hollywood), economic systems (capitalism), and ideologies (bourgeois individualism) in whose interests those images are constantly reproduced. Cynthia Peters comments: "Almost no one . . . wants to look at key questions of who owns and controls the media. There is little attention to the profit-driven nature of our economy and how that gives rise to a commercially driven media" (25). Accordingly, Part Five: Pedagogy also discusses how "Pedagogy in the more critical sense illuminates the relationship among knowledge, authority and power" (Giroux, "Beyond the Politics" 85). The concluding essay in part five, for example, shows how in different historical periods like the Cold War and the post-Cold War children's films such as

MGM's *Kim* and Disney/Cap Cities' *Aladdin* are used to teach imperialist and colonialist versions of history and the "subjectivities that are necessary for reproducing existing social arrangements" (Morton vii), particularly as those "subjectivities" and "existing social arrangements" structure questions of race. Children's media in general and children's films in particular must be understood and taught as serious objects of "critical analysis" (Giroux, "Beyond the Politics" 88).

GENRE

What are the traditional elements of children's literature and film? What literary theories are used to discuss children's literature and film and how might those theories be used to discuss children's films? What "key concepts" or important terms might teachers use to show college students and others in "American education" (Giannetti xi) that the conventional lessons conventional children's films teach—the hero always wins, the villain always loses, winning means wealth, losing means poverty, wealth means the acquisition of private property and promotion to a middle-class position—are constructs designed to "situate [children] at posts of intelligibility from which the reigning economic, political, and ideological social arrangements are deemed to be uncontestably true" (Morton and Zavarzadeh vii)? What "critical vocabulary" will allow us to rethink not just the genres of children's films but the economic and ideological function children's film genres fulfill? How might we teach a liberating pedagogy of children's film, first by rethinking the issue of genre?

Rebecca Lukens's 1976 *A Critical Handbook of Children's Literature* lists "terms [that] are the critical tools and basic vocabulary we use to discuss and evaluate any piece of imaginative literature [though] writing for children presents some special concerns and problems . . ." (Preface). This litany of genre, character, plot, theme, setting, point of view, style, diction, and tone can be recited by any children's literature student. Picturebooks, Lukens adds, contain illustrative as well as literary elements. Nonfictional works raise questions of narrative form, style, illustration, tone, didacticism, and propaganda. To illustrate her ideas, Lukens uses E. B. White's 1952 *Charlotte's Web,* a canonical work of children's fantasy most famously adapted to the screen in 1973 as an animated musical voiced by Debbie Reynolds (Charlotte), Henry Gibson (Wilbur), Danny Bonaduce (Avery), and Agnes Moorehead (The Goose).

The traditional elements of film criticism are akin to the traditional elements of children's literature criticism: in one, we sense a relation to the other. Giannetti's chapter on "Literature" in *Understanding Movies* (1972), for example, also lists genre, motif, symbol, metaphor, allusion, and point of view as terms used to discuss film adaptations of literary works. Other terms used in film analysis would be mise-en-scène, for example. Giannetti's paradigmatic text is *Citizen Kane* (US, 1941), recently voted the best film of the twentieth century by the American Film Institute.[1] As he puts it: "The film, directed by Orson Welles (1915–85), is an ideal choice to demonstrate how [literary theories can] interact dynamically within a single text" (403). As a beginning, we might use some of these children's literature and filmic terms to construct a basic, working "critical vocabulary" (Whitley 50) that empowers concerned, politically conscious educators to "help students acquire the skills they need to manage in a media-saturated environment" (Hobbs 137).

Lukens says that "A genre is a kind or type of literature in which the members share a common set of characteristics" (13). According to Lukens, the main genres of children's literature are realism, fantasy, traditional literature, poetry, nonfiction, and picturebooks. These major genres consist of minor genres: problem realism, animal realism, historical realism, high fantasy, science fiction, and so forth. Minor genres can be further divided. A subset of realism, formula fiction stories, for example, contain mystery novels centered upon detective, crime, or espionage plots. Contemporary realistic fiction generally features round[2] rather than flat, fully developed rather than stereotyped, characters, because social issues realism usually shows the protagonist encountering a "problem engendered by society, like discrimination . . . race, gender, or social position" (Lukens 15). Complex social problems require complex young adult fictions such as Robert Cormier's *I Am the Cheese* or Nancy Garden's *Annie on My Mind,* books that Moss, borrowing from Barthes, calls "writerly" (45). Traditional literatures such as the folktale generally contain flat rather than round characters. Proppian-like, these characters fulfill specific narrative functions. Not all works of children's literature can be so easily classified, Lukens warns. Classic works of children's literature such as Carroll's *Alice's Adventures in Wonderland* use a full range of figurative devices as well as poetic, illustrative, and folkloric motifs, references, and allusions. Canonical texts, those that attract readers "from one generation to the next" (Lukens 28), are like all great works of art, classifiable even as they refuse classification.

Children's films can be similarly categorized according to genre, each of which has a "common set of characteristics." The major children's film genres are realism, fantasy, and animation as well as musicals, war, sports, literary adaptation, and so forth. The realist and fantasy traditions extend throughout the twentieth century. The realist tradition is said to have begun with the work of the Lumière Brothers[3] and continues through the twentieth century with films such as *Why?* and *Child Labor* in 1913 and 1912 respectively, *The Bicycle Thief* in 1948, *Salaam Bombay* in 1988, and *Searching for Bobby Fischer* in 1993. The fantasy tradition is said to have begun with Méliès[4] and extends from as early as *Barbe Bleue* (*Bluebeard*) in 1901 to *A Kid for Two Farthings* in 1955, *Jumanji* in 1995, and so forth. Animated films include *Gertie the Dinosaur* in 1909, *Pinocchio* in 1940, and *Antz* in 1998. Musicals include *The Wizard of Oz* in 1939, *Summer Holiday* in 1963, *A Hard Day's Night* in 1964, *Help!* in 1965, *Tommy* in 1975, and *Pink Floyd: The Wall* in 1982.[5] Let us examine some of these genres in more depth.

Fantasy

In "Movies Kids Like," Street notes that today's "six-to-ten-set prefers two kinds of films: highly visual, action-packed, super hero-inspired fantasy adventures like *Star Wars* and *Superman,* and the graphic, suspense-filled, terror-inducing blood films most aptly labeled by critics as "teen screams" (12). Street says that in both genres "the same characteristics emerge repeatedly" (12).

Action and adventure movies built around a superhero are as common today as they were in 1982, the year Street's article was published: one thinks of *The Power Rangers, The Saint, Star Kid, Star Wars Episode 1: The Phantom Menace*, and so forth. Current "teen screams" include *Scream, I Know What You Did Last Summer, I Still Know What You Did Last Summer, Carrie 2: The Rage*, and *Idle Hands.*

Musicals

For Harris, children's live-action musicals such as *The Wizard of Oz* (1939), *The 5000 Fingers of Dr. T* (1953), *Mary Poppins* (1964), *Pufnstuf* (1970), *Willy Wonka and the Chocolate Factory* (1971), and *Pete's Dragon* (1977) contain several characteristic features: a particular point of view, an imaginative appeal, the separation of reality from fantasy, an uncondescending tone, an absence of social commentary. According to

Harris, all of these characteristics are found in *The Wizard of Oz,* "the most famous and revered entry in the genre of children's musicals" (2).[6]

War

Films about World War I that star children would include *My Son, My Son* (1940) and *Lassie Come Home* (1943). Films about World War II would include *Shoeshine* (Italy, 1946), *The Search* (US, 1948), *Forbidden Games* (France, 1952), *Battle Hymn* (US, 1957), *The Diary of Anne Frank* (US, 1959), *Ivan's Childhood* (USSR, 1962), *Die Blechtrommel* (*The Tin Drum,* 1979), and *Sophie's Choice* (US, 1982). More recently, *Baxter* (France, 1991) uses a boy's relationship to his dog, Baxter, to comment upon the rise of Fascism during World War II. Films about nuclear war—World War III—in which children star or play supporting roles might include *The Road Warrior* (1981), *WarGames* (1983), and *Terminator 2: Judgment Day* (1991).

Classifying children's films by genre (war) is not a mere mechanical exercise for it teaches students to ask questions about film history and history itself. How are films about World Wars I, II, and III the same and yet different? How is war explained to children in war films from specific eras, if at all? Is war resolved by the decisive actions of an individual or the collective struggles of a group? Classifying war films starring children usefully engages young viewers with war and its historical and filmic contexts.

War films starring children contain common features or generic conventions. Most obviously, there is an overall loss of childhood innocence (a defining feature of all children's films) and an acquiring of adult experience. War films featuring children thus have an elegaic quality: appropriate lighting (low), dialog (dramatic, serious), and cinematography (close-ups of human faces opposite sweeping, panoramic shots of devasted world), suggests a lament for the passing of innocence. Children are often violently separated from friends and family, as in *Sophie's Choice* (US), or friends and family are killed, as in *Forbidden Games* (France). Despite, or because of, these often brutal moments of division, in war films, kids still play: children's play is a characteristic feature of war films, though not all the games the children play are the same. In *Forbidden Games,* Paulette (Brigitte Fossey) and eleven-year-old Michel (Georges Poujouly) play macabre games in the village cemetary as way of coping with the death of Paulette's mother, father, and dog due to an attack by Nazi airplanes. They steal crosses (half-broken to symbolize the children's half-broken spirit) and enact strange burial ceremonies.

Clearly audiences are meant to see that the innocence of childhood play and of childhood itself has gone. Through war and death, pain and suffering, Paulette and Michel have become little grown-ups, acculturated into the violent world of adults.

Forbidden Games powerfully exemplifies how war films centered upon children are often set not on the battlefield itself but in and around those institutions and buildings otherwise designed to protect children rather than expose them. *Au Revoir les Enfants* is set in a French boarding school. In the 1957 film *Battle Hymn,* the airman accidentally bombs not a military target full of adult soldiers but an orphanage full of innocent children. In the famous *The Diary of Anne Frank,* directed by George Stevens, who was one of the first American filmmakers "to witness and capture on film the concentration camps at Dachau" (Synard 37), Anne, her family, and friends hide in the rooms above a shop.

In war films starring children, the absence of battlefield bloodbaths does not diminish the ghastliness of war and its relation to children. Quite the contrary. The all-pervasive horror of war and its destructive effect on children is reinforced when shown as intruding on those places constructed for children's safety: the school, the orphanage, the local shop. Audiences are appalled that war effects not just innocent children but the innocent places children inhabit. If war is a disease, seeing it spread to the otherwise sanitary places children inhabit further sickens the audience.

In this regard, a characteristic feature of war films starring children is a director's use of a child (or children) in a specific scene to show the absolute horror of war (which ironically reinforces the idea of a lost childhood innocence). There is often a sequence of scenes edited together or a particular mise-en-scène arranged by the director (the metteur-en-scène) to stress war's horror and its affect on the child. James Cameron's *Terminator 2: Judgment Day* perfectly illustrates this point.

Whilst another characteristic feature of most war films starring children is the use of the child as a symbol of renewal and hope at the end, the image of the child is not simply one of innocence renewed. Spielberg's *Empire of the Sun* (1987), for example, shows how the moment of victory and gain is also the moment of surrender and loss. In *Empire of the Sun,* nine-year-old Jim Graham (played by Christian Bale) is physically untouched by the bulletts and bombs of war, but psychologically scarred by war's madness and cruelty. Alive on the outside, he has died on the inside.

With this, we stumble across the terrain of another characteristic feature of war films starring children: irony. Of the various kinds of irony available to directors, "dramatic irony" (Abrams 91) seems most relevant when discussing children in war films such as *Forbidden Games, Empire of the Sun,* and others. In dramatic irony, audiences share with the writer/director a knowledge of which the protagonist, often a naive hero, is usually unaware. In *Forbidden Games,* the irony is that audiences watch the peasants who are horrified by the children's death-games played inside the cemetary (the children here are the naive heroes) but not the adults' war-games waged outside the village. The villagers reject the former but accept the latter. The irony of *Empire of the Sun* is that Jim survives the nightmare of World War II only to wake up at the dawn of the nuclear age.[7]

Sports

The following list shows not just that there are sports movies starring children—there are—but that sports movies starring children can easily be divided by period and into those that concern particular sports: horse racing (*National Velvet*), ice hockey (*The Mighty Ducks*), baseball (*The Bad News Bears, Angels in the Outfield*), basketball (*Hoosiers, Space Jam*), football, martial arts (*The Karate Kid, 3 Ninjas*), and so forth.

Baseball:	1940s:	*It Happens Every Spring*
	1950s:	*Roogie's Bump, Damn Yankees, The Jackie Robinson Story, Angels in the Outfield* (1951)
	1970s:	*Bad News Bears* (1976), *The Bad News Bears in Breaking Training* (1977), *The Bad News Bears Go to Japan* (1978).
	1980s:	*Field of Dreams* (1989)
	1990s:	*Rookie of the Year, The Sandlot, Angels in the Outfield, Simon Birch* (1999)
Basketball:	1980s:	*Hoosiers*
	1990s:	*Space Jam*
Football:	1950s:	*Jim Thorpe: All American*
	1970s:	*Brian's Song*
	1980s:	*Lucas*
	1990s:	*Air Bud, Little Giants, Angels in the Endzone*
Hockey:	1990s:	*Mighty Ducks 1, 2, 3.*
Soccer:	1990s:	*The Big Green, Soccer Dog*
Horseracing:	1940s:	*National Velvet*
	1980s:	*Phar Lap*

Boxing:	1930s:	*The Champ*
	1970s:	*The Champ*
	1980s:	*The Chocolate War*
Martial Arts:	1980s:	*The Karate Kid 1, 2, 3.*
	1990s:	*3 Ninjas*

Here again, the classification of children's sports films in to specific sports raises question about sport and history. What's interesting about the 1950s film *The Jackie Robinson Story* is not the film itself, but the historical conditons of race to which the film alludes (but does not directly address). *Space Jam,* about African-American basketball player Michael Jordan (who plays himself), is arguably the legacy begun by *The Jackie Robinson Story* (Jackie Robinson plays himself also). Furthermore, the stylistic differences between *The Jackie Robinson Story* and *Space Jam*—black and white to color, drama to animation—perhaps illustrate some broader social and political developments in society from the 1950s to the 1990s: the coming of multiculturalism signified by the vibrant colors of picturebooks such as *The People Shall Continue* and *Tar Beach* and the rise of postmodernism and its refusal to treat even serious matters seriously.

Sports/Comedy/Literary Adpatation

Sometimes, recurring features exist in children's films from completely different major and minor genres. *The Champ* (sports), *Home Alone* (comedy), and *Harriet the Spy* (literary adaptation) all contain scenes—so defined as a number of connected shots united by a central point—of boys doing housework: *North* would be another example. Released in 1931, in *The Champ,* Jackie Cooper plays Dink, a young boy who cares for his father (Wallace Beery), a divorced, ex-heavyweight boxer given to bouts of excessive drinking rather than championship boxing. Set against the background of the Great Depression, *The Champ* treats Dink's housework seriously. Dink's housekeeping and general domestic labors are presented as integral to story, character development, and theme. By complete contrast, in 20th Century Fox's 1990 corporate extravaganza *Home Alone,* eight-year-old Kevin McCallister (Macaulay Culkin) survives alone in a wealthy Chicago suburban house when his family flies to Paris for a Christmas vacation. His parents in absentia, Kevin defends the home against two inept burglars but also does some of the housework. Accordingly, he shops at the local store and does some laundry. Set against the conservative background of Reaganomics and the family values ideology, in *Home Alone,* Kevin's domestic labors are not taken seriously at all in part because domestic labor is seen as women's work. Accordingly, household chores are the source of many comic gags: In *Home Alone,* housework gets cheap laughs, which in turn cheapens the the value of those who do housework. Indeed, in the film's closing scenes, after the family has all returned from France and been reunited with Kevin, the mother realizes that the house probably does not contain any food. Kevin chirps up that he has done all the shopping and the ironing and so forth. The father looks at him and says quizzically, "What a funny guy," as though boys doing housework is extraordinary, unnatural, a joke. In *Harriet the Spy,* housework is treated both comically but with a more serious edge. Because Harriet's father and mother have "high-pressure" jobs, they employ a nanny, Gully, to raise Harriet. Neither Harriet or Gully make great cooks. Gully burns her boyfriend's sausages in one scene. More seriously represented is the housework done by Sport (Gregory Smith) who takes care of the household chores for his father, "a struggling artist."

Often, the characteristic feature of a children's film relates more to a film's narrative structure than its thematic content. Films such as *How Green Was My Valley, Stand By Me,* and *The Night of the Shooting Stars* are quite different. John Ford's 1941 *How Green Was My Valley* is set in a Welsh mining village. Paolo and Vittorio Taviani's 1981 *The Night of the Shooting Stars* is set in a small town called San Miniato during the German Occupation of Italy in World War II. Rob Reiner's 1987 *Stand By Me* is set in Oregon in the 1950s. Despite the different content, nevertheless, these three films share the same narrative device or feature: the flashback.

A flashback is generally defined as a cinematic device used by filmmakers to allow characters to return to an earlier moment in their lives. The flashback is usually achieved either through a fade, a dissolve, a narrator's voice-over, or a combination of these cinematic elements.

Flashbacks are important aspects of children's cinema and film not just because the protagonists go back in time but because the time to which the protagonists return is often their childhood. The flashback is clearly more than a mere cinematic device directors use to explain a character's behavior. Directors use flashbacks to suggest that a character's behavior is determined by the conditions of his or her childhood experiences, particularly as those experiences are engendered by and through the oedipal journey, itself a characteristic feature of children's films. As such, flashbacks also suggest film's therapeutic function. To return with the hero or heroine to their childhood is to return to one's own past, one's own formative years. In watching the hero or heroine grow up, we relive the growing up process as we experienced it ourselves.

Finally, films starring children can often be found in the genres traditionally considered the preserve of adult cinema. Canonical westerns would likely include not just *High Noon* (US, 1952), directed by Fred Zinnemann and starring Gary Cooper (Will Kane) and Grace Kelley (Amy Kane), but also *Shane* (US, 1952), directed by George Stevens and starring Alan Ladd as Shane, Jean Arthur as Marion Starrett, Van Heflin as Joe Starrett, and Brandon de Wilde as Joey, the boy Shane reluctantly befriends. Howard Hawks' *Scarface* (US, 1932), with Paul Muni as Tony Camonte and Boris Karloff as Gaffney, might be classified as a gangster film but so might Alan Parker's *Bugsy Malone* (UK, 1976) starring child actress Jodie Foster as Tallulah. Horror movies include not just Alfred Hitchcock's *Psycho* (US, 1960), starring Anthony Perkins as the psychotic killer Norman Bates and Janet Leigh as Marion Crane, his victim, but also William Friedkin's adaptation of William Peter Blatty's bestseller *The Exorcist* (US, 1973), starring child actress Linda Blair. Buddy movies include not just *Easy Rider, Butch Cassidy and the Sundance Kid* (1969), *Thelma and Louise* (1991), and *Lethal Weapon,* but also *Stand By Me* (US, 1986), *Radio Flyer, Now and Then,* and *Toy Story* (1995). The four friends in *Stand By Me* are Gordie, Chris, Vern, and Teddy. The two friends in *Toy Story* are Woody and Buzz Lightyear.[8]

In sum: Overall, children's film genres include movies as historically, culturally, and aesthetically diverse as *Radio Flyer* and *I Am the Cheese* (social realism), *E.T.* (fantasy), *Toy Story* and *Beauty and the Beast* (animation), *The Wizard of Oz* and *Amadeus* (musical), *The Champ* and *Angels in the Outfield* (sports), *Empire of the Sun* and *Hope and Glory* (war), *To Sir With Love* and *The Breakfast Club* (school), *National Velvet* and *Dunston Checks In* (animal), *American Graffiti* and *Baby's Day Out* (comedy), *The Secret Garden* (historical and literary adaptation), *Salaam Bombay* and *Pixote* (foreign), *Los Olvidados* and *Kids* (avant-garde).

Louis Giannetti's definition of genre, that "A more precise method of classifying narrative structures is by genre, or story type" (268), is similar to that provided by Lukens but worth examining further anyway because it adds two points particularly relevant for teaching children's films: (1) that genres evolve over four stages, the primitive, the classical, the revisionist, and the parodic (271–2), and (2) that genres mirror changing socioeconomic and historical conditions. Discussing films like *Orphans of the Storm* (US, 1922) and *Heidi* (US, 1937), the former starring Lillian Gish and the latter Shirley Temple, Jean-Loup Bourget concurs. In "Social Implications in Hollywood Genres," he writes that "[T]he freedom of Hollywood directors is not measured by what they can openly do within the Hollywood system, but rather by what they can imply about American society in general and about the Hollywood system in particular" (473). The evolving concerns of society are mirrored in the evolving conventions of a genre. The history of the twentieth century is mirrored not just in film but in film genres.

Giannetti's first point is that genres evolve from the primitive to the parodic. For example, Alan Parker's *Bugsy Malone* (1976), a film starring Jodie Foster and dismissed by Mark Kermode as a "clumsy kiddie comedy" (599), revises the gangster genre, which began with primitive silent era films like Ince's *The Gangsters and the Girl* (1914) and then evolved into classical gangster sound films like *The Public Enemy* (1931), *Little Caesar* (1931), *Scarface* (1932), and *I Am a Fugitive from a Chain Gang* (1932). Films about homosexuality starring children or young adults such as *The Children's Hour* and *The Killing of Sister George* from the 1960s might be considered primitive, the *The Incredibly True Adventure of Two Girls in Love* from the 1990s classical.[9]

Giannetti's second point is that film genres reflect broad social trends and historical developments. This can be seen in the changing nature of the musical. Thus, in *101 Great Movies for Kids,* Jeffrey Lyons cites *Seven Brides for Seven Brothers* (1954), *Oklahoma* (1955), and *Carousel* (1956) as three 1950s musicals appropriate for children aged seven and older. Two popular 1960s children's musicals are *Mary Poppins* and *The Sound of Music.* What's important here is that these profamily-oriented musicals from the 1950s and 1960s, which emphasize traditional images of the child as obedient, respectful, and well-behaved, differ noticeably from antifamily musicals such as *Tommy* (UK, 1975) or *Pink Floyd: The Wall* (UK, 1982), which emphasize nontraditional images of the child as disobedient, disrespectful, and ill-behaved (the latter trait a common feature of recent children's films such as *Bad News Bears, Home Alone, Last Action Hero*). *Mary Poppins* and *Pink Floyd: The Wall* do contain a similar set of characteristics—special effects, musical numbers, children, dance routines, and so forth. But the social changes that have occurred within the family and childhood over the course of the twentieth century are surely there in the way, for example, *Pink Floyd: The Wall*'s representation of the family stresses con-

Figure 9. *Pink Floyd: The Wall.* Photo: The Museum of Modern Art/Film Stills Archive, New York. Courtesy of MGM.

frontation, confusion, dysfunctionality, and history, whereas *Mary Poppins* stresses precisely the opposite features: togetherness, clarity, the family unit as functional, timeless, universal (see Figures 9 and 10).

Perhaps surprisingly, sports genres, generally considered to be apolitical, in fact often reflect the conditions of particular historical periods and events. *The Champ* (US, 1931), a film about boxing, is set against the Great Depression. *Amazing Grace and Chuck* (US, 1987), a film about basketball, is set against the issue of nuclear war. *Angels in the Outfield,* both the 1951 and the 1994 version, is a film about the power of baseball but also the power of the state.[10]

Courtroom dramas starring children also reflect historical trends. Probably the most famous film from the 1960s set in a courtroom would be *To Kill a Mockingbird.* Movies like *To Kill a Mockingbird* (US, 1962), *The Client* (US, 1994), *A Time to Kill* (US, 1996), *Primal Fear,* and *Liar, Liar* (US, 1997) use the child in the courtroom motif to showcase important social issues current at the time. *To Kill a Mockingbird* and *A Time to Kill,* for example, both deal with questions of racial prejudice. *Primal Fear* deals with questions of child abuse, as does *The Boys of St. Vincent* (Canada, 1993).

Figure 10. *Mary Poppins*. Photo: The Museum of Modern Art/Film Stills Archive, New York. Courtesy of Walt Disney Productions.

To borrow from Thomas Elsaesser, these films also register in "more overtly metaphoric fashion" the way lawyers have become "stars." Warner Brothers/Joel Schumacher's 1996 action drama *A Time to Kill* begins with the brutal assault and rape of a black girl, ten-year-old Tonya Hailey (Rae'ven Kelly), by two foul-mouthed, drunken redneck white men as she innocently walks home alone down a deserted country road. The two men stop, taunt her, attack her, discard her body by the roadside when finished, and then drive to a bar to continue their drinking spree. Miraculously, Tonya survives the awful, horrible, degrading, and humiliating experience though inevitably her childbearing days are over. When her distraught, vengeful father, Carl Lee Hailey (Samuel L. Jackson) learns the time and the date the two white rapists are to appear before Judge Noose (Patrick McGoohan), he decides to appear also and, vigilante-style, murder them. Bailey is caught, imprisoned, and sentenced to death. But by the end of the story, we are as much concerned with the conflict between the two white lawyers, Matthew McConaughey as Jake Brigance and Kevin Spacey as Rufus Buckley, as we are with Tanya's horrible ordeal, which, ironically, becomes further and further buried beneath the emphasis on her father's trial and the moral/race issue of whether or not killing his daughter's rapists was justified. In other words, the movie ceases to be about Tonya, but about her father and her father's verbally sparring and warring defense and prosecuting lawyers—white lawyers at that. The movie ceases to be about the physical rape of a black girl and instead is about the intellectual skills of the white lawyers and whether or not they free or convict a black man. In the process, the courtroom becomes a place of spectacle rather than justice, of television entertainment rather than legal instruction as we head toward to the culminating courtroom scene. Of course, Carl Hailey is freed and then the movie is less about racial division than it is racial harmony—the plight of Tonya almost entirely forgotten.

Beyond the way in which children's film genres reflect broad social trends and historical developments, teachers might ask students to think about genre from perspectives such as ideology and economics. Contemporary film theorists and scholars like Thomas Elsaesser, Dudley Andrew, Fredric Jameson, and Linda Williams argue that film genres do not just passively reflect the social and historical conditions of any given period. That is, for Elsaesser, Andrew, and others, genres actively fulfill specific functions. "[G]enres are now to be thought of not as changeless structures. . . . They serve a precise function in the overall economy of cinema, an economy involving an industry, a social need for production of messages, a vast number of human subjects, a technology, and a set of signifying practices. . . . Genres are specific networks of formulas which deliver a certified product to the waiting customer. . . . In fact, genres construct the proper spectator for their own consumption" (Andrew 110). As Andrew later remarks: "Genre is a specific guise of ideology" (112). In other words, what's important is not so much how films fit generic contexts (textual matters) or how genres reflect social issues (historical matters) but how those generic contexts fit consumers (economic matters), how genres in Jameson's words are "essentially . . . *institutions,* or social contracts between a writer and a specific public, whose function is to specify the proper use of a particular cultural artifact" (106).

Teaching students how children's film genres function as institutions within the economy—the economics of children's film genres—is straightforward. For example, Street has noted how the conventions and characteristic features of the fantasy-adventure genre are all identical. If we see the corporate Hollywood studios like MGM, 20th Century Fox, Paramount, Pixar, DreamWorks SKG, and United Artists as analagous to corporations like Microsoft, Ford, or General Motors, the efficient production of the same product—films, computers, cars, toys—is unsurprising. Sameness (with minor variation) is precisely the point because fantasy-adventure movies such as *Warriors of Virtue,* those Louis Menand would call "spaceship movies" (6), are designed to fulfill a "precise function" (Andrew 110). All similar to one another, they are designed to circulate throughout the economy as affordable commodities child and adult consumers can acquire hoping (against all odds) to relive the experience of the movie: Tie-ins tie in the consumer both economically and emotionally.

In summary: Rethinking children's film genres from old and new, traditional (Lukens) and contemporary (Andrew), textual and contextual viewpoints provides a "critical vocabulary" for progressive-minded teachers interested in providing students a behind-the-scenes look at the politics of children's films. Cultural workers employed in the school system must know Lukens and Giannetti as well as Jameson and Andrew and Braudy and Williams so that students understand how genres generate textual and socioeconomic meanings.

In terms of the former (textual), students see that film texts and literary texts actively borrow from one another: they are intertextual. As Thomas Elsaesser points out: "[G]enres have always been perceived as instances of intertextual play: between different texts of the same genre and from genre to genre" (17). At the end of *Toy Story* (1995), a song from *The Lion King* (1994), "Hakuna Matata," is suddenly heard as Molly, Andy's baby sister, sees Buzz and Woody frantically trying to catch up to the moving van. *Beauty and the Beast* makes reference to other Disney films and also to Shakespeare. When villainous Gaston cries out "Screw your courage to the sticking place," Lady Macbeth's chilling exhortation to Macbeth surely comes to mind. Upon Macbeth's question, "If we should fail?" Lady Macbeth replies, "We fail / But screw your courage to the sticking-place, / And we'll not fail" (lines 60–64). Textually speaking, students are introduced to words like primitive, classical, revisionist, and parodic. Students see that directors *deliberately* work within the genre they revise and/or parody: think here questions of authorial intention. In terms of the latter (socioeconomic), students are introduced to the way genres arise out of general and specific historical conditions, including those of twentieth-century capitalism. Recall that corporate Hollywood refers to *Star Wars, Raiders of the Lost Ark, Superman, Free Willy, The Land Before Time,* and so forth as *franchises,* businesses that reproduce in microcosm the macro social and economic hierarchies of patriarchal capitalist democracies (CEO/director, workers/actors, higher-paid male stars/lower paid female stars, etc.).

CHARACTER

As with genre, students might see character in children's films from various textual, feminist, and Marxist/ideological viewpoints. Most obviously, one might simply discuss some characters from canonical children's films and decided whether or not those characters are "round" or "flat" (to use Forster's terms). As an extension of the classificatory practices that shape traditional genre studies, formalist discussions of character might also look at the type of child characters who appear in children's films: precocious imps, fix-it kids, good kids, bad kids, and so forth. More politically oriented approaches to character in children's films, such as feminism and Marxism, would focus on gender and class issues. That female child characters occupy contradictory positions in children's films—they are marginalized within the very narratives they dominate—should surprise no one familiar with feminist film theory in general and feminist children's film theory in particular. Neither should it surprise anyone familiar with children's studies that most male child characters in corporate films are white and middle class. These textual and political approaches to character might be combined. The function of a liberating pedagogy of children's films is not to privilege one critical methodology over another but to suggest, as Eagleton does in a different context, that all critical approaches "can be mobilized in a variety of different strategies for a variety of ends" (211).

Drawing on the terms used by Forster, Lukens notes that children's literature generally contains characters that are either flat or round. These characters statically and/or dynamically reveal themselves through their actions and words and the comments of others, including those of the author/narrator. To emphasize the importance of unity of action and character, Lukens quotes James's famous phrase: "What is character but the determination of incident? What is incident but the illustration of character?" (quoted in Lukens 41). Mostly, Lukens illustrates her ideas about character through reference to White's *Charlotte's Web* (1952).

Round and flat characters generally populate the world of children's films: They are a characteristic feature! Round characters, defined as "fully developed" (Lukens 45), exist in films as different as *Searching for Bobby Fischer* (1993), *The Secret of Roan Inish, Baxter,* and *The Incredibly True Adventure of Two Girls in Love* (noticeably independent production studios). The protagonists in these films demonstrate a "variety of [human] traits that make him or her believable" (43). By contrast, flat, or stock characters, those populating films from corporate Hollywood, hardly develop at all over the course of a film. Proppian-like, they remain static, playing supporting roles or fulfilling specific narrative functions. In *Aladdin,* Princess Jasmine's father, the Sultan, remains completely undeveloped and one-dimensional. A dimwitted, over-protective buffoon, the Sultan's primary narrative function is to make possible the marriage of Aladdin and Jasmine.[11]

Forster's terms, and their application to discussions of character in children's films, are useful but limited. Most characters in children's films are neither fully developed or fully undeveloped. Aladdin is a case in point. Aladdin is clearly meant to be a more rounded character than the Sultan, Jafar, Iago, Abu, or even Jasmine. Certainly, he has more on-screen time than the others, more dialog (with the exception of the Genie perhaps), more action sequences. He is seen singing, dancing, and escaping the Sultan's palace guards. As he falls in love with Jasmine, we see his dreamy, romantic, idealist side. When he defies Jasmine's potential suitors and later Jafar himself, we see his brave, realist, clever side. In a climatic sequence whereby all of the above features are combined, Aladdin rescues Jasmine, traps Jafar and Iago in the genie's lamp, and releases the genie from servitude. But for all his humanism, Aladdin remains curiously inhuman. He doesn't seek out starving children to redistribute the food he himself has stolen. He does not feed the two starving orphans out of grief-stricken consciousness, indignation, or the abhorrence of child poverty. He shares his stolen food with the foraging children, because he accidentally bumps into them. Taking from the rich and giving to the poor is merely a game. A character, Aladdin fills up the screen with everything but character!

Similarly Jasmine. Not unlike Belle, who, in *Beauty and the Beast,* consistently repells the unwanted advances of the handsome, conceited, and threatening Gaston, Jasmine rejects all her suitors, insisting to her stern, kind, but mostly mindless father that she be allowed to choose her own husband rather than have a husband chosen for her. Jasmine reiterates the idea of choice—"I choose, I choose you"—completely unaware apparently that as a beautiful young princess she has simply chosen to marry a handsome young prince! Thinking that she is exercising choice, she is merely walking in the shoes of countless other Disney heroines. Conceiving of herself as different, she remains nonetheless the same.

Kathy Merlock Jackson's *Images of Children in American Film: A Sociocultural Analysis* identifies a number of types of child characters: the child-as-monster, the precocious imp, the innocent child, the fix-it child, the good kid/bad kid opposition, and so forth.[12]

A recent example of the good kid/bad kid opposition in children's cinema can be found in *Toy Story* (1995). A generally responsible and respectful boy, Andy's friendly and caring disposition shows early when he cares for Molly, his baby sister. Mostly irresponsible and thoroughly disrespectful, Sid, no doubt an allusion to Sid Vicious of *The Sex Pistols* fame, is decidedly unfriendly and uncaring toward his sister, Hannah. Andy, along with Molly, is often seen with his mother. Sid's parents are in absentia, though once we hear Sid's mother cry out, "Sid, your Pop Tarts are ready," Pop Tarts (fast food) signifying a delinquent parent and the inevitable result—a delinquent child! Andy and Sid visit the same places but Andy does so in the company of his mother, whilst Sid does so in the company of no one: He is always alone, even when he is with others. At home, Andy sleeps comfortably in his bed wearing his pajamas. Sid sleeps awkwardly in his street clothes. Sid acts out vicious fantasies either as a demented, psychotic doctor. Andy simply behaves like a child, albeit a slightly spoiled child. We constantly see Andy playing with his toys. By comparison, we are repeatedly shown images of Sid destroying his toys and torturing those of his sister. When Andy's toys are broken or lost, as is the case with Woody and Buzz Lightyear, he is sad, even temporarily distraught. His toys are meaningful, worthy of care. Sid takes a perverse pleasure in breaking his own toys, blowing them up, executing them. Gleefully, he straps Buzz Lightyear to a rocket and prepares to launch him. Only a fortuitious downpour—a classic deus ex machina—saves Buzz from being blown to pieces high above Sid's backyard. Andy, a good kid, is reunited with his toys at the end of the film. By contrast, Sid, a bad kid, is friendless and toyless.

A recent work of children's literature criticism such as William

Moebius's "Introduction to Picturebook Codes" (1986) suggests how young readers learn to recognize characters as they come and go within a story. Drawing on theorists and critics like Susan Meyer, Barbara Bader, E. H. Gombrich, and Roland Barthes, Moebius argues, "What is presented in the text usually obeys certain conventions of recognizability and continuity" (134). Readers recognize the world in the text because of a "number of stable visual clues" (134), including those that relate to the text's characters. Young readers recognize, identify with, and follow "believable" characters through the story because of what Moebius calls "metonyms of personality" (135). An example of metonymy in *Where the Wild Things Are* is Max's wolfsuit. Another would be the symbols of power wielded by Max: the hammer, the fork, the crown, and scepter. The wolfsuit, the hammer, the fork, and so forth are "metonyms of personality, species, gender [or] character type [that] constitute elements of a semic code" (135). Metonyms of personality and conventions of "recognizability" allow children to recognize and identify specific characters as they appear and reappear throughout the story.

In *Toy Story,* Woody always wears cowboy clothes—a hat, badge, belt, gun, boots, spurs, and so forth. Buzz Lightyear always wears a spacesuit, a helmet, and boots. Though Little Bo Peep makes only a few appearances, she is nonetheless instantly recognizable by her bonnet, shawl, long dress, and staff (and she is the only toy to kiss Woody!). Mr. Potato Head, a well-known toy that can be taken apart and put back together (with body parts stuck in different holes), in fact constantly disassembles and reassembles himself. Slinky expands and contracts his silver rings. Children recognize, identify, and become familiar with the characters because of these various traits.

Produced by George Lucas and Stephen Spielberg and directed by Don Bluth, the animation box-office hit *The Land Before Time* contains several characters who appear and reappear throughout the narrative: the narrator, Littlefoot, Sharptooth, Sarah, Petrie, Ducky, Reuter, and so forth. Each of these characters is associated metonymically with a particular feature. Early in the film, a narrator's voice comments: "Once upon a time." Paternal, authorial, commanding, deep, and instantly recognizable, the narrator's voice comes and goes throughout the film. Never flustered, never angry, but always patient and understanding, the narrator's fatherly voice teaches us a history lesson, instructs us as to whose point of view we should take when a particular incident occurs, and generally guides us through the sometimes happy sometimes sad physical and emotional journey Littlefoot takes en route to the Great Valley.

The "metonyms of personality" (Moebius 135) just described do not merely identify certain characters but engender the roles such characters play. Littlefoot is established not just as a character but as the hero. Subsequent to his mother's death, Littlefoot is often seen on his own, set apart from the others in ways that mark him as different and therefore special. When the others decide to take an easier path to the Great Valley, Littlefoot heroically struggles up a harder path by himself. As the hero, he has insights not provided to his companions, Sarah, Ducky, and Petrie. Haunted by self-doubt, Littlefoot wanders away from his friends to seek communion with the spirit of his dead mother. Such cosmic communications reinforce Littlefoot's status as the film's hero.

Once Littlefoot has been identified as the hero, the other characters are inevitably forced into subordinate positions within the narrative. He becomes the leader, they the followers. For example, when Sarah, Ducky, Petrie, and so forth appear, they are marked as incapable: Ducky tries to make his tiny body as big as Littlefoot's, a futile exercise that merely reinforces his smallness. Ducky is also marked as helpless by the repetition of phrases such as "I'm all alone. I am. I am." Ducky's relative childishness in fact makes Littlefoot seem older, more mature, symbolically ready for adult (surrogate parental) responsibility. Unable to lead themselves—Sarah insists upon going the wrong way, Ducky is all alone, Petrie cannot fly—they must be lead, appropriately enough, by Littlefoot.

Sharptooth's huge presence is first announced by a dark shadow that casts itself over Littlefoot and Sarah who have wandered away from their respective parents to play. At other times, Sharptooth's evil presence is announced by a combination of shadow, glaring red eye, flared, snorting nostrils, and growls and hisses. Foreboding, solemn music also usually accompanies the appearance of Sharptooth, the combined effect of music, fiery eye, and flared nostril successfully working to inform young viewers that danger looms large for Littlefoot, Sarah, and Littlefoot's mother.

From a feminist point of view, it is important to study character. As Kuhn remarks in *Women's Pictures: Feminism and Cinema,* "The notion of character is in fact crucial to any consideration of the classic realist text, cinematic or otherwise" (31). For example, the narrative hierarchy established in the opening scenes of *The Land Before Time* is clearly based upon a sexual division. Littlefoot and Sarah, the film's most obviously heterosexual couple, function as surrogate parents, a common enough motif in children's films as different as *The Lion King* and *The*

Cement Garden. Littlefoot generally tells Sarah what to do. "You're going the wrong way," he tells Sarah first when they are fleeing Sharptooth in the beginning of the film, and, second, when Sarah tries to take Ducky and Petrie the short route to the Great Valley in the middle of the film. On another occasion, after having stumbled upon a dormant Sharptooth and barely escaping with her life, Sarah returns to the group and seizes the opportunity to make up a story about how she bravely and confidently (she was in fact terrified) confronted Sharptooth (she in fact fled). Littlefoot's response to Sarah's creative fabulism is dogmatic realism: "Don't be silly. Sharptooth's dead."

How might we examine character from Marxist/ideological viewpoints? This is not simply a question of identifying the social class to which most characters in children's films belong. Corporate children's films from Hollywood privilege middle-class values. Not unsurprisingly, the main characters in contemporary children's films are middle class. Rather, a discussion of character from Marxist viewpoints involves looking at how characters, their families, and their environments are represented in terms of social class. For example, are working-class children all portrayed stereotypically? Do particular films foreground or ellide class discussions? Are child characters allowed to understand their class position as a function of specific economic conditions or as the natural evolution of history? Which character and which social class in any given children's film controls the film's various discourses, its knowledge, its sense of reality? These and other similar questions must inform a discussion of character in children's films from Marxist/ideological viewpoints.

THEME

The traditional literary elements, so often the basis of orthodox approaches to children's literature, can provide alternative ways of seeing children's films. A particularly important term for teachers to discuss with students is theme. Lukens defines theme in children's literature as "the idea that holds the story together, such as a comment about society, human nature, or the human condition. It is the main idea or central meaning of a piece of writing" (87). Lukens argues that there are certain types of theme: explicit, implicit, multiple, and secondary. For Lukens, theme is presented through character: "A narrative with action and people but without theme is a story without meaning . . . (98).[13] Like most children's literature critics, Lukens acknowledges that mature themes such as fear, death, divorce, sexuality, premarital sex, drugs, child abandonment, and violence have become increasingly common in contemporary children's literature. M. Abrams argues that all works of literature "involve an implicit conceptual theme which is embodied and dramatized in the evolving meanings and imagery . . . (111). Theme is presented through characterization and imagery. Abrams adds that theme is closely linked to motif. A motif, or *leitmotif,* is defined as the frequent repetition of a "significant phrase, or set description, or complex of images, in a single work . . . (111). The repetition of either of these film elements produces the film's theme.

Children's films deal in sophisticated ways with what Lukens calls "mature themes" (98). Like classic works of children's literature such as Mildred Taylor's *Roll of Thunder, Hear My Cry,* classic films such as *To Kill a Mockingbird* and *Sounder* revolve around questions of race and gender. Films as different as *The Hunchback of Notre Dame* and *Radio Flyer* turn on the question of child abuse. *Walkabout* concerns itself with how race, class, and gender issues intersect in the wilderness rather than the city. *Pretty Baby* examines the relationship between art (photography) and pornography (child prostitution). *Lolita* is about child prostitution and pedophiles. Like young adult fictions such as Nancy Garden's *Annie on My Mind* and picturebooks such as *Heather Has Two Mommies,* films like *The Incredibly True Adventure of Two Girls in Love* deal with lesbian relationships. *Pixote* is about child poverty in South America.

Neil Synard's *Children in the Movies* explores the oft-quoted idea that "Childhood is the great universal theme" (7). Synard argues that "some of the greatest [directors] in the history of the cinema, from Bergman to Spielberg, from Tarkovsky to Charles Laughton, have focused on" (7) childhood issues. Synard points out that not all films thematize childhood in the same way, of course, despite childhood's "appeal to common experience" (7). Allen, Roeg, and Spielberg, for example, explore the lost innocence of childhood in films like *Radio Days, Track 29,* or *Empire of the Sun* respectively. Louis Malle considers childhood in films as different as *Zazie dans le metro, Au Revoir les Enfants,* and *Pretty Baby.* Given the autobiographical nature of *Au Revoir les Enfants,* the childhood explored is Malle's own but also that of society. For Malle, in other words, theme functions metaphorically. The lost childhood of the individual is the lost childhood of society. The artist reflecting upon his or her life, trying to understand the journey of the self from innocence to experience, childhood to adulthood, does so on behalf of society as a whole. True, this romantic and Freudian approach to childhood is problematic. It assumes an innocent child untouched by the experiences of history. Nonetheless, despite all the profound differences of race, class, and gender that separate people, the state of childhood is indeed a common experience.

SETTING

Lukens notes that "Both depiction of character and working out of plot and theme occur, of course, in time and place. These latter elements we call setting" (103). Setting is the place whereby character, theme, and so forth intersect. Lukens further distinguishes between types of setting—backdrop or integral—and the function of setting. Setting, she argues, "illuminates and clarifies a character's personality, acts as a character itself and enhances a story's mood and tone through the incorporation of symbols" (103–118). Abrams's definition of setting is similar to that of Lukens. Abrams writes, "The setting of a narrative or dramatic work is the general locale, historical time, and social circumstances in which its action occurs; the setting of an episode or scene within a work is the particular physical location in which it takes place" (175). Abrams is clearly in agreement with Lukens here. Settings involve the intersections between general and specific times and places and character, symbol, tone, and so forth.

Children's films are set in a variety of historical times and places. Rob Reiner's *The Princess Bride* (US, 1987) is set in medieval England. A Western, *Shane,* is set in the mythical days of the American Wild West. Clayton's *The Innocents* (US/UK, 1961) is set in Victorian England. Weir's *Picnic at Hanging Rock* (Australia, 1975) is set in an all-girls boarding school in Victoria, Australia at the turn of the twentieth century—St. Valentine's Day 1900. The action of Louis Malle's 1978 film about child prostitution, *Pretty Baby,* takes place against the backdrop of New Orleans 1917. Neame's *The Prime of Miss Jean Brodie* (UK, 1969) is set in a school in Edinburgh in 1932. The setting for *The Secret of Roan Inish,* directed by John Sayles, is Ireland in the 1940s. *Stand By Me* takes place in Oregon in the 1950s. *A World Apart* is set in Johannesburg in 1963 and, like *Cry Freedom,* confronts the politics of apartheid in the 1960s. Bombay in the 1980s is the setting for Mira Nair's Camera D'Or winner (at the 1988 Cannes Film Festival), *Salaam Bombay.* The film stars eleven-year-old Shafiq Syed as Krishna, a young boy who, abandoned by his family, buys a ticket to Bombay (Krishna is also known by the name Chaipau). In complete contrast, Chris Columbus's 1990 blockbuster hit *Home Alone* is set in a wealthy Chicago suburb, circa the

1990s. Steve Zaillian's 1993 *Searching for Bobby Fischer* is set in New York in the 1990s. Lasseter's 1995 *Toy Story* is set in cyberspace. Hamid Jebeli's *Son of Mary* is set in Azerbaijan.

Other films place children in futuristic settings or, rather, a combination of past, present, and future. Zemeckis's *Back to the Future* (US, 1985) has Marty McFly (Michael J. Fox) first travel back to 1955 and then back again to the 1980s. In *Back to the Future III,* McFly returns to the days of the Wild West before returning to the present.

Many films starring children or young adults are set in and around a school though not all school settings are the same. Consider, for example, the following films: *To Sir With Love, Au Revoir les Enfants, Milk Money, The Breakfast Club, Kindergarten Cop, Harriet the Spy, The Incredibly True Adventure of Two Girls in Love,* and *The Indian in the Cupboard.*

Children's films are often set on, in, and around small and/or enclosed spaces. In *Toy Story,* Andy's bed, for example, is important for two interconnected reasons. First, whomever sleeps on Andy's bed is considered the favorite toy. Everyone else is on the floor, under the bookshelves, or behind furniture. Second, whomever is the favorite toy not only sleeps on the bed (and thus looks down on everyone else) but is in charge of the other toys. In both instances, that toy is Sheriff Woody. Thus, in the opening scenes, after we see Andy playing affectionately with Woody, we see Woody placed on the bed, a symbol of his favored status with Andy and his position as fearless leader among the other toys. We then hear Woody announce to the other toys who are in hiding that Andy has left the bedroom—"Okay everybody. Coast is clear"—and, next, order a staff meeting to discuss the dreaded move and to pick a moving buddy. At the staff meeting, Woody (holding the microphone symbolizes his authority) tells the toys that Andy's party has been moved forward a day. Whilst the toys all fret in their own particular ways over being replaced by Andy's new birthday presents, Mr. Potato Head's sardonic comment—"Of course Woody's not worried [about being replaced]. He's been Andy's favorite since kindergarten"—confirms Woody's status as most favored toy.

As the leader, Woody's position at the top of the toy hierarchy makes all the other positions seem stable, real, worthwhile. Woody's presence as the surrogate father-figure (Little Bo Peep is the most obvious surrogate mother) guarantees the identities of the other toys, their subjectivities.

With the arrival of Buzz Lightyear, a present for Andy at his birthday party, Woody's governance is suddenly challenged: The old hierarchy that had served Woody well disappears. Completely mesmerized by

Buzz Lightyear, Andy discards Woody as though they had never been friends. Woody is thrown from the bed, demoted, deranked, made redundant. What was, up until Buzz's arrival, an established hierarchy among the toys that had obviously existed in "unaltered form" (Marx and Engels, *Manifesto* 87) for some time, is now decisively altered. As Marx and Engels put it, where once there was "Conservation" now there is "everlasting uncertainty and agitation . . . as . . . All that is solid melts into air" (87).

At this point, Andy's bed assumes an even greater significance in the narrative. No longer merely a balcony, or a pulpit, from which Woody, Andy's favorite, had previously dispensed the rules and regulations that had united the toys, the bed now becomes the place, or site, where the struggle over the rights of occupancy and ownership, for example, are fought.

However the bed might be regarded, it remains an important element in the development of the theme of friendship. Indeed, the conflict between Buzz and Woody that stems from the initial disruption—Buzz's arrival and Woody's departure—ends where it all began, in the bedroom on Andy's bed.

Is it possible to teach a sexual politics of setting? In this regard, one might consider the relation between setting and gender. Most obviously in *Toy Story,* Woody and Buzz go on what Lissa Paul calls "technicolor epic adventures" (151), whilst Little Bo Peep stays at home with the other toys and focuses on the "nuances of social relationships" (151). Woody and Buzz journey outside Andy's house. Little Bo Peep stays inside the house. Less obviously, even when Woody, Buzz, and Little Bo Peep are in one room together, mostly Andy's bedroom, the assumption is that the places they occupy are engendered. Early in the film, Woody orders Slinky to call a staff meeting. While waiting for the toys to gather, Bo Peep suddenly appears and coyly suggests to Woody that she'll "get someone else to watch the sheep tonight." She reminds him that she is "just a couple of blocks away." As Bo Peep moves out of the frame, Woody moves into the frame (she disappears, he appears) and takes control of the staff meeting by speaking into the microphone. Setting and gender are clearly connected in the most traditional of ways.

MISE-EN-SCÈNE

Abrams notes that: "When applied to a theatrical production, "setting" is synonymous with mise-en-scène" (175–76). Giannetti elaborates on the meaning of this term and its relevance to film analysis. Commenting that "In the best movies and stage productions, settings are not merely backdrops for the action, but symbolic extensions of the theme and characterization" (239), Giannetti's *Understanding Movies* defines mise-en-scène as the "arrangement of all the visual elements of a theatrical production within a given playing area-the stage . . . Mise-en-scène in the movies resembles the art of painting in that an image of formal patterns and shapes is presented on a flat surface and enclosed within a frame. But because of its theatrical heritage, cinematic mise-en-scène is also a fluid choreographing of visual elements that correspond to a dramatic idea, or complex of ideas" (34). Mise-en-scène is the arrangement of the "visual elements" on the screen in any given frame, said visual arrangement highly determined by lighting, costume, camera angles, the movement of the actors and actresses, and so forth.

POINT OF VIEW AND TONE

Point of view and tone has previously been discussed in relation to children's films.[14] In "Evaluating Attitude: Analyzing Point of View and Tone in Film Adaptations of Literature," Maureen Gaffney examines "several translations of literary works to film" (116) through point of view and tone. This formalist approach is necessary, Gaffney argues, because "In trying to develop a vocabulary for discussing and comparing different works" (116) existing terms are usually too "broad and too adult" (116). For Gaffney, discussing point of view and tone introduces students to a critical vocabulary that allows them to talk more rigorously about films and film representation. A critical vocabulary leads to a critical pedagogy.

Gaffney defines point of view as having to do with the telling of the story. That is, discussing point of view involves knowing who tells the story. Point of view relates to "who tells the story and how it is told" (116). Discussing point of view in relation to children's films also involves questions of voice, focus, and the study of values. A fourth aspect of point of view is "mode of expression" (116). Are the values of particular characters partisan or bipartisan? As Perry Nodelman states in a different context: "The point of view from which a story is told affects how we understand it" (69). Is the film's mode of expression naive, direct, didactic, etc.? Tone, Gaffney defines as "the emotional coloring, the feeling, that informs a given work. [Tone] can be charming, condescending, suspenseful, masochistic . . . serious and moralizing [or] light, reassuring, and slightly tongue-in-cheek" (117). Gaffney uses four films to illustrate more clearly what she means by point of view and tone: *Hansel and Gretel: An Appalachian Version, Whazzat, The Case of the Elevator Duck,* and *Zlateh the Goat.*

In her chapter on "Tone," Lukens notes that "Parody is usually a device for older readers, since it relies on the reader's memory of a known piece of writing or a way of talking. It retains the form of the original but changes the words and the tone for humorous effect. 'An hour of freedom is worth a barrel of slops' parodies 'An ounce of prevention is worth a pound of cure' " (163).

Children's films are often parodic. In *North,* for example, the Narrator (the Bruce Willis character) remarks to North that "A bird in the hand is always greener than the grass under the other other guy's bushes." This collapses and in the process parodies two more familiar sayings: "A bird in the hand is worth two in the bush" and "The grass is always greener on the other side." When in *Toy Story* Woody turns his head 360° to scare Sid out of his wits, he is mimicing, parodying, and of course alluding to, the famous scene in *The Exorcist* when Linda Blair, possessed by the devil, also turns her head 360°.

ALLUSIONS IN *THE LAND BEFORE TIME*

Noting in *Understanding Movies* the many similarities between literature and movies, the screenwriter of a film is like the author of a book, fades and dissolves are like scene changes and paragraph breaks, literary texts and films both contain metaphors, symbols, and so forth, Giannetti defines allusion as "an implied reference, usually to a well-known event, person, or work of art" (281). Similarly, Lukens defines an allusion as an "indirect reference to something or someone outside the literary work" (295). For Abrams an allusion is "a reference, explicit or indirect, to a person, place, or event, or to another literary work or passage" (8). Giannetti demonstrates the use of allusion in film through two examples. Howard Hawks's *Scarface,* Giannetti notes "was modeled on the gangster Al Capone . . . an allusion that wasn't lost on the audiences of the time" (281). Second, Giannetti argues that "the Christian myth of the Garden of Eden is used in such disparate works as . . . *Days of Heaven, How Green Was My Valley,* and *The Tree of the Wooden Clogs.* The films of Ingmar Bergman are also rich in Christian allusions" (281). According to Giannetti, directors pay homage to other important directors and influential films. Spielberg's films are often homages to Disney.

Allusions can be found in many children's television shows and films. A recent episode on the Disney Channel of *The Muppet Show Tonight* featured two skits called "Bay of Pig Watch" and "Seinfeld Babies," obvious allusions to *Baywatch* and *Seinfeld.* Another episode of *The Muppet Show Tonight* alluded to the *Jerry Springer Show,* at one time "the most popular late-afternoon TV program . . . among youngsters ages 6–17 in Metro Detroit" (Kiska 1). The allusion goes, "I know Jerry Springer and you ain't no Jerry Springer."

The Land Before Time contains many allusions to Christian mythology, including the mythology of the Garden of Eden. Indeed, watching *The Land Before Time* almost constitutes a lesson, or sermon, in religious iconography, the young viewer sat before the screen analagous to the young disciple sat before the preacher. Christian allusions appear throughout the film, interpellating young viewers into what Althusser calls "the religious ISA" (143).

In truth, *The Land Before Time* alludes to and thus teaches a combination of Christian, Protestant, and Calvinist beliefs and doctrines. For example, Littlefoot becomes the chosen one immediately he is born. The voice of a Godlike narrator (Pat Hingle) singles Littlefoot out as special: "One herd had only a single baby, their last hope for the future," the narrator solemly declares. Reading this prediction against the theological grain, as it were, of Christian/Calvanist belief, the omniscient narrator's comment informs the audience of the doctrine of recapitulation, whereby the fortunes of the race are inscribed and repeated in the fortunes of the individual, but also the idea of predestination and election. Albeit of the "herd" rather than "man," Littlefoot's predestined role as the chosen one is to lead himself and his followers—the elect—to salvation. Littlefoot's prophet, Christlike status is confirmed when a single, mouth-watering green leaf—a "tree-star"—attached to the branch of an otherwise barren tree, lands on his head. In the no doubt heartfelt minds of the audience, Littlefoot's symbolic annointment makes the allusion to his Christlike role as redeemer and savior clear.

Searching for meaning and direction in his life after his mother's tragic death, Littlefoot meets Sarah, Ducky, Petrie, and Spike, the elect whose souls, in Calvanist theology that is, will be saved only if Christ, that is, Littlefoot, is followed. Proudly displaying his tree-star to remind his followers of his chosen status, Littlefoot leads Sarah et al. in search of the Great Valley (for Christian in Bunyan's *The Pilgrim's Progress,* the journey is to the Celestial City). Urging his followers to resist temptation, Littlefoot leads them across various kinds of inhospitable terrain, joyfully expecting the Great Valley to reveal itself at any moment. However, tired and disillusioned, the elusive Promised Land nowhere in sight, Sarah and the others eventually part company from Littlefoot when they find themselves at the bottom of yet another mountain they must climb, the mountain here a metaphor for the hardship and struggle the true believer must endure before entering the Kingdom of Heaven. Petrie, begging forgiveness from Littlefoot even as he acknowledges his betrayal of Littlefoot, says: "Sarah's way is easier." Telling them that the easier way is "the wrong way," Littlefoot, desperately wanting rest himself, nonetheless struggles up the mountain, the emotional pain of self-doubt and betrayal as hurtful as the physical pain of exhaustion and fatigue.

Having gone the wrong way, of course, Sarah, Petrie, Ducky and Spike must learn their lesson-in this instance, a lesson in Christian theology. Now separated from Littlefoot, they find themselves in a place where volcanoes erupt and smoldering, red-hot lava spews forth all around them. In other words, having taken the easier path, having strayed from the true path to salvation, they find themselves in hell. Littlefoot valiantly descends into this hell, this Shadow of the Valley of Death to rescue his friends. Littlefoot's selfless bravery is not entirely altruistic, of course. Without followers there are no leaders, students no teachers, audiences, no films.

But the lesson in Christianity that is *The Land Before Time* has not finished. Sarah, refusing to accept that Littlefoot was right and that she was wrong, is publicly humiliated. The narrator informs the audience (the congregation really) that Sarah "was too proud to admit that she had gone the wrong way." The haughty, disdainful Sarah, her ego as pointed as her horns, has committed the ungodly sin of pride!

That *The Land Before Time* alludes generally to the Judaeo-Christian tradition, in particular the Christian belief in the Garden of Eden, is shown in the film's closing scenes. At the end of the film, a light shines down from heaven (the spirit of God) and reveals to Littlefoot and the others an edenic space. Appropriately awed by what is clearly a moment of divine revelation, Littlefoot and his friends descend from the mountain and enter the Kingdom of Heaven as it manifests itself on earth in the image of the Garden of Eden.

ALLUSIONS IN *STAND BY ME*

The various definitions by Lukens, Giannetti, and Abrams imply that allusions serve only a textual or filmic, master, that "in a closed circuit of illusion" (Lapsley and Westlake 9) allusions address audiences only about film matters. As Metz, discussing whether or not the cinema constitutes a language or a language system, remarks: "A sequence of film, like a spectacle from life, carries its meaning within itself" (43). Allusions enrich mise-en-scènes, giving them depth and texture. They develop character and complement theme. Allusions to famous people, events, places, or scenes, invite audiences into a film's world: The allusions to the Oscar ceremony in *In and Out* are instantly recognizable. Familiar allusions provide audiences with moments, or scenes, of recognition. Allusions create important visual links in a film narrative's otherwise verbal chain (a picture is worth a thousand words). Often with little compensation, allusions work hard, making films intelligible to audiences.

Whilst allusions speak about filmic matters, they also talk about extrafilmic matters. Allusions take audiences outside of the film. Allusions may generously invite viewers into the film, but they also forcibly eject audiences out into the real world, often with contradictory results. Rob Reiner's *Stand By Me* (US, 1986) uses famous songs to help audiences identify and identify with the film's central theme, the transcendent, timeless nature of human friendship, the way friendship overcomes the barriers of place and history and time itself. The soundtrack of *Stand By Me* accordingly includes songs like "Lollipop," performed by The Chordettes, "Great Balls of Fire," performed by Jerry Lee Lewis, "Everyday," performed by Buddy Holly, and, of course, "Stand By Me," performed by Ben E. King. These allusions reinforce the ideal of love's everlasting power and recreate the film's specific era—the 1950s. But as the musical allusions convey one image of 1950s America as small-town, idyllic, innocent, quaint, and peaceful, so we realize that there is a more violent image of 1950s America not being conveyed. Put another way, think here of what happened in the 1950s but is missing from a film about the 1950s: the detonation of the H-bomb, the pursuit and conviction of Communist sympathisers, the trial and execution of the Rosenbergs for selling atomic secrets to the Soviet Union, McCarthyism, the integration of schools in Arkansas and Kentucky, the Supreme Court's decision to strike down the long-standing doctrine of "separate but equal," Rosa Park's refusal to give up her seat to a white passenger, the death of Buddy Holly! This is not to argue that *Stand By Me* deliberately uses allusions to conceal the realities of a particular historical era. But then, *Stand By Me* was released in 1986, that point in history when the Thatcher and Reagan administrations were urging a return not to the turbulent 1960s but the tranquil 1950s—precisely the era in which *Stand By Me* is set. To understand and to teach a liberating pedagogy of children's films, teachers must inform students of the history a film's allusions reveal as well as the history a film's allusions conceal.

ADAPTATION

Dudley Andrew writes, "Frequently the most narrow and provincial area of film theory, discourse about adaptation is potentially as far-reaching as you like" (96). He says that there are generally two ways of considering questions of adaptation theory: aesthetically and historically. Aesthetic approaches look at how well a work of literature is adapted into a film, how well the film faithfully (or adulterously) reproduces the original text. The literary and filmic texts are usually canonical. But film adaptations also can be situated in general and specific historical contexts. Situating film adaptation historically is important. Not all periods in the twentieth century produce the same kind of film adaptation even though film adaptation, is a constant feature of the twentieth century.

Aesthetic and historical approaches are also discussed by Andrew in *Concepts in Film Theory.* In relation to the first, Andrew distinguishes between "borrowing," "intersecting," and "transforming" (98). Borrowing and intersecting involve the way art in general borrows and intersects with other works of art. Andrew cites "Medieval paintings featuring biblical iconography and miracle plays based on Bible stories . . ." (98) and films like Robert Bresson's *Diary of a Country Priest* (99) as art that borrows from and intersects with art from other genres.

About transforming, the third kind of adaptation, Andrew writes: "Unquestionably, the most frequent and most tiresome discussion of adaptation (and of film and literature relations as well) concerns fidelity and transformation. Here it is assumed that the task of adaptation is the reproduction in cinema of something essential about an original text" (100). According to Andrew, fidelity and transformation are considered tiresome, because reproducing the original literary text's "tone, values, imagery, and rhythm . . . is frankly impossible . . ." (100). It is impossible for a film faithfully to adapt the essence of a work of literature. Successful film adaptations are inevitably adulterous. That Andrew finds borrowing, intersecting, and transformation unsatisfactory is suggested by his declaration that "It is time for adaptation to take a sociological turn" (104), for adaptation issues to be historicized. Here, Andrew argues, quite rightly, that adaptation is an "instructive barometer for the age" (104) and that "The choices of the mode of adaptation . . . change from decade to decade" (104).

Critical essays that take both aesthetic/textual and sociological/historical approaches to children's film adaptation can be found in Douglas Street's *Children's Novels and the Movies* (1983). For example, Gene Hardy's "More Than a Magic Ring" emphasizes textual issues when it considers Arthur Ranken, Jr., and Jules Bass's 1977 animated film adaptation of Tolkien's 1937 *The Hobbit.* First, Hardy examines "*The Hobbit* both in itself and in the light of what the author thought about his own intention and success" (132). Hardy notes that Tolkein was "Aristotelian in his insistence on the primacy of narration, of plot" (132) and that there are "structural similarities" (134–35) between *The Hobbit* and other epics such as *The Iliad, The Odyssey, The Aeneid,* and *Beowulf* (135). Hardy also recognizes that the form and content of *The Hobbit* is not dissimilar to the canonical fairy tale: the former contains several elements of the latter. In the remainder of the essay, Hardy discusses how well the Rankin-Bass animated film adapts the plot and the character of Tolkien's original. In Hardy's judgment, the film "fails of greatness" (140) not because it eliminates several scenes from the original—"The truncation of the scenes of escape from imprisonment by the Elves need not be much regretted" (139)—but because it ignores what is central to the original: the inner journey of Bilbo Baggins. In short, Rankin-Bass are unable to reproduce in the film that which was "essential" (Andrew 100) to the literary original, clearly a reductive critical enterprise.

Other essays in Street's volume are less exclusively concerned with textual issues. Many discuss both textual and historical matters. Lucien L. Agosta's "Pride and Pugilism: The Film Versions of *Tom Brown,*" for example, argues that the various film versions of *Tom Brown's Schooldays* "reflect the political and social realities of their times and thus find their centers in the contemporary concerns of their audiences and directors" (3). Briefly, Agosta argues that the 1940 film version reflects the anxieties felt by wartime Anglo-American audiences. The 1950s version reflects not so much the "fascist agression" (5) of World War II but the general conditions of social class (9) in England of the time. Agosta notes, for example, that the casting of British actors for the 1950s version rather than the combined American and British actors used in the 1940s version "introduces into the film that feature so frequent in British cultural artifacts and so clearly missing from the 1940 Americanized version . . . the perennial social conflict between the artistocracy and the middle class" (9). The 1970s version differs again. It appears to reflect something of the "turbulent 1960s and early 1970s" (14). Echoing Andrew, Agosta says that each film version is a "product of its time . . ." (14).

In general, the essays in Douglas Street's *Children's Novels and the Movies* (1983) consider the adaptation of children's novels into films from mostly aesthetic/textual rather than sociological/historical points of view. The novels discussed are canonical. As Street says: "Since the infant days of the movies it has been repeatedly shown that the classic children's novel, judiciously adapted and perceptively filmed, can achieve new glory in the celluloid medium. The timelessness and imaginative richness of those truly great literary works attracts filmmakers decades apart" ("Introduction" xxi). The politics of canonicity aside, generally the essays in Street's edition focus on the metamorphosis of text into film by discussing the traditional elements of literature most often used by critics of children's literature: plot, character, setting, and so forth. Other visual and aural film criteria are considered. In his introduction, Douglas Street notes that whilst fiction and film are "distinct arts" (xvii) they are also similar in many respects. "For example, film has decided narrative qualities, and literature often freely borrows from film the equivalents of ellipsis, establishing and tracking shots, the long-shot and the close-up. These standard techniques are to be found in the work of several accomplished writers" (xvii). And Street recognizes that "The history of the cinematic adaptation of the children's novel is closely intertwined with the overall history of the movie industry . . ." (xix), and that therefore film adaptations emerge out of cinematic politics. Even so, for Street: "Ultimate success is dependent upon the perceptive preservation of original feeling and attraction in harmony with requirements necessitated by the new, cinematic setting" (xviii). Aesthetic issues are placed in the foreground. Historical issues are placed in the background.

AVANT-GARDE

What are the characteristics of the avant-garde? Avant-garde means in advance. In relation to the arts in general and film in particular, it means in advance of the traditions that preceed it. Avant-garde films in other words are in advance of mainstream films. Giannetti comments: "Since the 1970s, the term avant-garde has been applied to non-mainstream movies that are antiestablishment, subversive, or otherwise outrageous" (332). Giannetti also notes that "Film historians generally subdivide the avant-garde into four phases: (1) the Dadaist and Surrealist periods, roughly from 1920–1932, based primarily in Berlin and Paris; (2) the poetic and experimental period, roughly from 1940 to 1954, and centered mostly in the United States; (3) the Underground period, from 1954 to the late 1960s; and (4) the Structuralist cinema, which has dominated the avant-garde since then . . . Furthermore, while the most famous films tend to be produced in Paris, New York, and San Francisco, the avant-garde is essentially international" (338–39). Avant-garde films tend to be technically complex, intellectually difficult, and aimed at a minority rather than a majority of viewers. In part, this is because avant-garde movies tend to focus on taboo subjects. "Political and sexual themes abound, especially the latter, which have included overt homosexuality, lesbianism, voyeurism, fetishism, bestiality, masturbation, and sadomasochism, among others" (336). As well as dealing in depth with the kind of political and sexual issues mainstream movies treat superficially, precisely because they deal with so-called mature themes, avant-garde movies intentionally and unintentionally shock viewers. In Shlovsky's terms, avant-garde movies "estrange" or "defamiliarize" the spectator. Finally, avant-garde movies are often powerful autobiographical expressions of a director's repressed, deeply hidden self otherwise unable to find a creative outlet through the production of orthodox movies.

Among the films Giannetti discusses, four are particularly relevant to a discussion of the avant-garde in post–World War II children's cinema: Luis Bunuel's *Los Olvidados* (Mexico, 1950), Jean Cocteau's *Testament of Orpheus* (France, 1960), Stan Brakhage's series of films called *Dog Star Man* (US, 1959–64), and Alan Parker's *Pink Floyd: The Wall* (UK, 1982). For Giannetti, each movie defines an aspect of the avant-garde aesthetic. For example, influenced by Marx, Bunuel's films, particularly *Los Olvidados,* are politically uncompromising. The forerunner of politically avant-garde movies like Hector Babenco's *Pixote* (Brazil, 1981) and Miguel Littin's *Alsino and the Condor* (Costa Rica/Nicaragua, 1982), *Los Olvidados* portrays the stark realities of child poverty, of children left home alone.

More recent examples of avant-garde films starring children and young adults are *The Cement Garden, Kids,* and *The Incredibly True Adventure of Two Girls in Love. The Cement Garden* contains scenes of masturbation and sibling sexual relations. The sexual explicitness of *The Incredibly True Adventure of Two Girls in Love* takes place in the context of race and class.

These and other films are avant-garde not just because the politics of sexuality are graphically articulated within them, often in the added context of youth rebellion, race, class, and gender issues. Giannetti remarks that avant-garde films are often unscripted. Unlike mainstream films and television shows, avant-garde films "avoid the inflexibility of a preordained script" (336), preferring moments of unrehearsed rather than rehearsed spontaneity. Teachers might have older students compare the scripts of *Kids* and *The Lion King.*

A timeline of avant-garde films focusing on children might list the following:

1940–54: *Los Olvidados*

1954–60: *Testament of Orpheus, Dog Star Man*

1960s–80s: *Pink Floyd: The Wall, Pixote, Alsino and the Condor*

1990s: *The Cement Garden, Kids, The Incredibly True Adventure of Two Girls In Love, Welcome to the Dollhouse*

CHILDREN'S FILMS AS ETHNOGRAPHY: *SALAAM BOMBAY* AND *THE INDIAN IN THE CUPBOARD*

Halfway through *Toy Story,* Buzz says to Lizard and Slinky: "Say there, Lizard and Stretchy Dog. Let me show you something. It looks as though I've been accepted into your culture. Your chief Andy inscribed his name on me." This quote humorously points to what is in fact a serious subject, the degree to which children's films might be taught from the perspective of ethnography. Indeed, given that 1990s children's films like *Toy Story* self-consciously allude to ethnography suggests that the topic remains relevant and worth discussing further.

What is ethnography? What ethnographers do is observe and describe as many aspects of a particular culture as possible. They look at how specific groups feed, clothe, house, and reproduce themselves. They study the customs of a particular culture, such as birthing, rites-of-passage, marriage ceremonies, death rituals, religious beliefs,[15] the supernatural, the role of the family, and so forth. Ethnographers look at other aspects of a culture, its education, work habits, and art. To understand a culture, the ethnographer looks at that which the culture uses—art—to represent itself. As we saw in Part Two: Criticism, cultural anthropologist Margaret Mead in the 1950s and sociocultural critic Kathy Jackson in the 1980s both looked at and compared the image of the child in children's films from different cultures, Europe and America respectively, to understand the attitudes of those two cultures toward children. To see is to believe.

In "The Production of Third World Subjects for First World Consumption: *Salaam Bombay* and *Parama,*" Poonam Arora argues that whilst films such as *Salaam Bombay* function as indigenous ethnographies for Western audiences, they do so problematically in part because recent poststructuralist thinking about language and the use of representational codes has deconstructed the rather simplistic notion, grounded in a naive empiricism, that films showing other cultures do so accurately (293–94). Seeing is not necessarily believing.

Salaam Bombay, for example, appears real enough, heartbreakingly so at times. First, audiences see Bombay's drug trade, prostitution, child labor, and general squalor from the point of view of eleven-year-old Krishna/Chaipau who has arrived in Bombay alone after he has been abandoned by his family (they think he stole a bicycle) and tricked out of a job by the boss of the traveling circus (Chaipau is sent to get tobacco from a neighboring village and finds upon his return the circus gone). As the accompanying still shows, his friends and family are now Bombay's homeless, downtrodden, and orphaned kids (see Figure 7). Second, the film is directed by Mira Nair. Given Nair's insider status, the film carries with it the directorial stamp of cultural authenticity: how could, why would, someone (Nair) from a particular culture (India) depict their own culture inaccurately. Third, at the end of *Salaam Bombay,* a single credit informs the viewer that the film is dedicated to the street children of Bombay. Dedicating *Salaam Bombay* to actual street children reinforces for audiences the idea that what they have just seen on film is real.

Arora argues, however, that *Salaam Bombay*'s ethnography is problematic. *Salaam Bombay* appears real enough until we begin to realize that beneath the "veneer of documentary realism" (298), Bombay is merely a representative city and Chaipau a representative Third World child. Sweet Sixteen, the young girl brought from Nepal to Bombay to be traded for money, is torn from her actual cultural context. In other words, the city, Chaipau, and the girl serve as examples of what is "just another story of urbanization . . ." (295). Bombay is not necessarily representative of India as a whole, the plight of Chaipau and Sweet Sixteen not necessarily the plight of all Indian children. Ironically, *Salaam Bombay* perpetuates the problems it seeks to redress such as poverty, prostitution, drugs, and abandonment by making said images of deprivation so real and lifelike. The real on the reel is not real!

Poonam Arora's discussion of *Salaam Bombay* as a failed "indigenous ethnography" (294) has significant implications for teaching films like *The Indian in the Cupboard.* Adapted from the book by Lynne Reid Banks, *The Indian in the Cupboard* first allows audiences to observe and experience the social relations and customs and rituals of what appears to be a fairly typical white, middle-class, nuclear family. Director Frank Oz, whose other films include *The Dark Crystal, The Muppets Take Manhattan, Little Shop of Horrors, Housesitter,* and an appearance in *Star Wars*

Episode 1: The Phantom Menace as Yoda, shows Omri walking home from school with his mother, getting a surprise birthday party, and receiving the kind of gifts from his mother, father, brothers, and friends any boy might receive on his birthday—an action figure, a skateboard, a helmet, and so forth. As the family unit celebrates Omri's birthday, we are shown something of the relations between the family members. Omri is not allowed to go skateboarding until he has permission from his father. His mother adds that he must not go without someone: "Not alone," she commands. Omri therefore goes with his brothers (and his helmet). Omri is seen to belong to a family whose individual members obey both the mother and the father. These images reinforce for audiences the importance of traditional family relations in middle-class cultures.

These opening scenes are tremendously important from an ethnographical point of view, because they establish the dominant perspective from which the film is to be viewed: the archetypal, nuclear, white, middle-class family. From this vantage, neither home and school are seen as sites of struggle. Under the tutelage of parents and teacher, law and order prevails at home and at school. Parents are in charge of their children. Children occupy their proper place in the family hierarchy—near the bottom. Teachers are in charge of their students. Students occupy their appropriate place in the school hierarchy—near the bottom. They sit before the teacher and, in turn and when called upon, offer up examples from the history of great events—JFK's election, and so forth—the teacher praises (or not) and thus legitimates as historical knowledge. The nuclear family and the public school: two ideological state apparatuses, two solid foundations and institutions, the cornerstones of middle-class society past and present.

From this dominant, essentially conservative perspective, the film's other families, customs, and rituals can only be seen as challenges to middle-class society. Later scenes show what, for traditional middle-class families, is perhaps most opposed to home—the street. Unlike the home, where democracy reigns, the street is where anarchy rules. On one occasion, Omri, with his schoolfriend Patrick, skateboards under the expressway. On another occasion, Omri insists to his father that he is old enough to go to the local store and buy the nails his father needs to build a skylight. On the street, graffiti and loud music assault the senses. The graffiti and the music clearly symbolize that which middle-class cultures find unacceptable—slang, noise, impermanence, and excess—rather than that which middle-class cultures find acceptable: learning, quiet, permanence, and restraint, the stability of the home rather than the instability of the street. The dangers of the street are confirmed when Omri is mugged by a young punk.

In different ways, Oz, not so much a director but an ethnographer using film to study a cultural group, strives to reproduce for audiences Little Bear's Iroquois culture accurately. To emphasize language differences, Little Bear speaks Iroquois rather than English when he first appears and mistakes Omri for a "demon" or a "giant" and asks: "The great Spirit can be a child?" When Omri gives Little Bear a tepee, Little Bear, not recognizing the plastic out of which the tepee is produced, asks, "What's that?" Little Bear tells Omri about fighting the French on behalf of the English in 1761. When given the chance, Little Bear asks to see King George. Little Bear even differentiates himself from other Indian groups, telling Omri that the Iroquois always walk rather than ride. We see Little Bear hunting. When injured, Little Bear calls for corn husks rather than modern medicine. The film self-consciously attempts to portray Iroquois culture realistically.

But is the film a realistic portrayal of Native American culture in general and Iroquois culture in particular?[16] Or, as with *Salaam Bombay,* is the ethnography problematic? First, when Little Bear initially appears, he is certainly individualized by his dialect but eventually he speaks only standard American-English. Second, throughout *The Indian in the Cupboard,* Little Bear remains at the mercy of Omri. Their friendship develops but only in the ever-present context of the omniscient, Godlike power Omri wields through the key, the cupboard,[17] and the other toys he brings alive but then kills. This is most dramatically seen when Omri peers down at Little Bear through a magnifying lens (see Figure 11).

Though small, through the lens Little Bear appears huge. When the lens is removed, Little Bear seems small again. All the while, Omri, though a child, is presented as large. Third, for all the attention to detail the film provides about Native American culture, particularly that of the Iroquois Indians, noticeably absent from the scenes in which Omri takes Little Bear to school is an historical and political discussion about the fate of the Native Americans since 1761. The film champions the idea of tolerance for unfamiliar cultures—Native Americans—but provides no sustained historical and political explanation as to why Native American culture became unfamiliar in the first place. According to *The Indian in the Cupboard,* Native Americans in the nineteenth century faced only a few racist white cowboys[18] not a white racist government that, with the expansion of empire very much in view, systematically reduced the legal status of the Native American from human to ward of the court.[19]

Figure 11. *The Indian in the Cupboard*. Photo: The Museum of Modern Art/Film Stills Archive, New York. Courtesy of Columbia Pictures.

In this regard, the discussions in school in the film are crucial because of what they omit, because they make no mention of what in the following essay on *Kim* and *Aladdin* might be called a pedagogy of empire, although the omissions in *Indian in the Cupboard* amount to a lesson in imperial rule. In one of those curious sleights of hand only Hollywood can magically produce, *The Indian in the Cupboard* marginalizes that which it centers, blurs the reality of that upon which it focuses. *The Indian in the Cupboard* employed the technological skills and special effects wizardry of Industrial Light & Magic and Pacific Titles & Optical. However, as Marx put it: "Even the pure light of science seems unable to shine but on the dark background of ignorance" ("Speech" 134).

WHAT CHILDREN'S FILMS TEACH: THE PEDAGOGY OF EMPIRE IN *KIM* AND *ALADDIN*

"Telling Tales to Children: The Pedagogy of Empire in MGM's *Kim* and Disney's *Aladdin*"[20]

> *The mere story of their adventures, which to them were no adventures, on their road to and from school would have crisped a Western boy's hair. They were used to jogging-off alone through a hundred miles of jungle, where there was always the delightful chance*

> *of being delayed by tigers; but they would have no more bathed in the English Channel in an English August than their brothers across the ocean would have lain still while a leopard snuffed at their palanquin. . . . There was a boy who, he said, and none doubted, had helped his father to beat off with rifles from the veranda a rush of Akas, in the days when those head-hunters were bold against lonely plantations. And every tales was told in the even passionless voice of the native-born . . . Kim watched, listened, and approved. [The tales] . . . dealt with a life he knew and in part understood. The atmosphere suited him, and he throve by inches.*
>
> —KIPLING, *Kim* 172

On the historical terrain of the modern experience, two things stand out with striking clarity: the ongoing process of capital accumulation, and the ongoing process of centralizing bureaucratic power. Capital accumulation originates in the exploitation of labor and the control of material resources; bureaucratic power flows, in an ever-widening capillary network, from the massive edifice of the State. Statist bureaucracy and capital accumulation go hand in hand; the former makes possible the latter, and the latter gives rise to the former. Thus, in *The Communist Manifesto,* Karl Marx and Frederick Engels noted:

> [The bourgeoisie] . . . compels all nations, on pain of extinction, to adopt the bourgeois mode of production; it compels them to introduce what it calls civilization into their midst, i.e., to become bourgeois themselves. In one word, it creates the world after its own image . . . Just as it made the country dependent on the towns, so it has made the barbarian and semi-barbarian countries dependent on the civilized ones, nations of peasants on nations of bourgeois, East on West. . . . The necessary consequence of this was political centralization. Independent or but loosely connected provinces, with separate interests, laws, governments, and systems of taxation, become lumped together into one nation, with one government, one code of law, one national class interest, one frontier and one customs tariff (88).

The familiar name of "political centralization" (on the terms of "the bourgeois mode of production") is "empire," the colonial (and neocolonial) theater of capital accumulation, a racialized hierarchy, and bureaucratic (disciplinary) rule. Over the last three centuries, the intellectual servants of the bourgeois have labored mightily to convince the skeptics that empire is the preeminent vehicle for modernity. That is to say, the forced reduction of "nations of peasants" to "nations of bourgeois" must be seen as Progress, Development, Uplift, the benign "evolution" of human society toward "civilization." On occasion, however, the truth of the matter is frankly revealed to the light of day.

Thus, for example, the nineteenth-century British statesman Joseph Chamberlain observed that the administration of the colonies is not "the sole or main object that should interest us. It is our business in all these new countries to make smooth the paths for British commerce, British enterprise, the application of British capital" (quoted in Bennett 312). Chamberlain contended that "if we want our trade and industry to grow we must find new markets for it" (314). In the aftermath of World War II, the sun finally set on the main of the British Empire, as nation after nation gained independence. But as the sun rose on a new day, it also rose on a new empire. Michael Parenti writes:

> Today the United states is the foremost proponent of recolonization and leading antagonist of revolutionary change throughout the world. Emerging from World War II relatively unscathed and superior to all other industrial countries in wealth, productive capacity, and armed might, the United States became the prime purveyor and guardian of global capitalism. Judging by the size of its financial investments, and military force, judging by every standard, except direct colonization, the U.S. empire is the most formidable in history, greater than Great Britain in the nineteenth century. (*Against Empire* 36)

In U.S. political culture, if "class" is the great unmentionable five-letter word of the domestic social scene, then "empire" is its six-letter counterpart in foreign policy discourse, and its academic shadow. As Parenti puts it, "Of the various notions about imperialism circulating today in the United Stataes, the dominant one is that it no longer exists. Imperialism is not recognized as a legitimate concept, certainly not in regard to the United States. One may speak of "nineteenth century British imperialism . . . but not of U.S. imperialism (2–3). But it wasn't always this way.

Consider, for instance, the "honest" words of Woodrow Wilson in 1907:

> Since trade ignores national boundaries and the manufacturer insists on having the world as a market, the flag of his nation must follow him, and the doors of the nations which are closed against him must be bat-

> tered down. Concessions obtained by financiers must be safeguarded by ministers, even if the sovereignty of unwilling nations be outraged in the process. Colonies must be obtained or planted, in order that no useful corner of the world may be overlooked or left unused. (quoted in Parenti, *Against* 40)

Note the functional relationship outlined here between the manufacturers insistence "on having the world as a market" (the doctrine of so-called free-trade) and the military adventures of the imperial State. Wilson coolly recognizes that capital accumulation must proceed, if necessary, in the face of determined political resistance, that if "concessions obtained by financiers" come under threat, then the imperial State is obliged to conduct military intervention on the financier's behalf. One must attend to the fact that all this has nothing to do with human welfare, social justice, or even international law. The "right" of the manufacturer and the financier to reap profits (i.e., to "use" every "corner of the world" as a market) is superior to all other concerns. The problem that thus confronts the imperialist bourgeoisie, in their promotion of empire, is how to legitimate public support for the "defence" of what are essentially private interests. In other words, what is required to make citizens at home accept the necessaity of military intervention in a far-distant land, particularly when those same citizens are the ones who will be called upon to fight, kill, and perhaps die for goals not obviously their own?

Naturally, the answer lies in the realm of ideology, in what has been termed the "manufacture of consent" (Herman and Chomsky 1988). In the immediate aftermath of World War II, when the United States took on the task of compelling "all nations, on pain of extinction, to adopt the bourgeois mode of production" (88; i.e., to open their doors to manufacturers and financiers based in the imperial metropole), a hegemonic discourse of "civilization" and its blessings was devised and widely disseminated through printed word, airwave, and screen image; the discourse is familiarly known as "the anti-communist crusade" of the Cold War. The discourse of the Cold War invariably presented the United States in a defensive posture, even as the U.S. government routinely conducted military interventions throughout the world. The cornerstone of the Cold War propaganda was the doctrine of "containing" the "Soviet menace," "halting the spread of communism," making impossible the so-called domino effect. The architect of this doctrine was the distinguished statesman and historian George Kennan. Kennan believed that in the historical wake of the great European empires, the United States was duly obligated to undertake the "protection of raw materials" (notably, petroleum reserves in the Middle East). In a now infamous (originally top secret) State Department policy document (PPS23, February 1948), Kennan made clear his basic position:

> We have about 50 percent of the world's wealth, but only 6.3 percent of its population . . . In this situation, we cannot fail to be the object of envy and resentment. Our real task in the coming period is to devise a pattern of relationships which will permit us to maintain this position of disparity . . . We need not deceive ourselves that we can afford today the luxury of altruism and world-benefaction . . . We should cease to talk about vague and . . . unreal objectives such as human rights, the raising of living standards, and democratization. The day is not far off when we are going to have to deal in straight power concepts. The less we are hampered by idealistic slogans, the better. (quoted in Chomsky 318)

Of signal importance here is the call to *realpolitik,* the call to recognize that capital accumulation and bureaucratic power have an inherently brutal side that must needs be embraced, even further developed, if "we" would hold onto our grossly excessive share of "the world's wealth." Kennan concedes that "the day is not far off when we are going to have to deal in straight power concepts"; in this respect, he predicts what would become the National Security State, the State organized around military-industrial concerns, permanently primed for war. Kennan identifies "our real task" as keeping "the wretched of the earth" in their wretched state. "We need not deceive ourselves," he counsels with the chimerical "luxury of altruism and world-benefaction," what the nineteenth-century imperialist would have termed the work of "uplift." These shocking sentiments should be borne in mind by the reader, as we conduct her through our reading of the film adaptation of Rudyard Kipling's classic novel, *Kim* (1901), and, later, Clements's and Musker's *Aladdin* (1992).

The film version of *Kim,* directed by Victor Saville and released by MGM in 1950, is of considerable interest to the student of cultural hegemony, particularly as it affects the entertainment offered to children by corporate concerns, in the post-World War II context. For, with regard to the historical memory of the British empire in India (the so-called Jewel in the Crown), Saville's adaptation of Kipling's novel marshalls what Renato Rosaldo has termed "imperialist nostalgia," in the service of a nascent (silently stated) Cold War discourse of "containment."[21] Thus, the film eloquently bespeaks the vital role of popular culture in the ceaseless ideological struggle to uphold the imperial order. When Joseph

Chamberlain spoke of empire in the nineteenth century, the preeminent vehicle for propagating the sense of imperial mission was doubtless the printed word, principally the novel and the newspaper. But, by the mid-twentieth century, when George Kennan formulated his brutalist proposals, the daily newspaper was only one part of "the mass media," and the novel had already given way to the Hollywood film as the primary cultural diversion, for children and adults alike. Marshall Deutelbaum has noted that "it is difficult to determine precisely when the [film] industry chose to produce films specifically designed for children. To be sure, problems of censorship, or of threatened censorship, which resulted from children viewing films intended for adults, perpetually kept the industry aware of this group as a potential audience" (174). In August 1916, an article entitled "Motion Pictures for Children: Country Wide Movement by Prominent Women" appeared in *The Moving Picture World,* a leading trade journal of the time. The writer describes the pedagogical activities of Mrs. Edith Dunham Foster of the Community Motion Picture Bureau, in regard to a series of children's films presented in Boston:

> Mrs. Foster carefully selects pictures which she knows will satisfy the demand of the types of audiences she is supplying with programs. For the sophisticated children, and for a performance offered to rival the lurid and sensational drama of the poorer houses, she picks out thrillers of the western pioneer and Indian type, baseball, comedy, and anything that contains clean, legitimate action. For the children wh have not become movie fans she arranges programs of fairy tales, animal and nature studies, scenics and lighter dramas and comedies. (quoted in Deutelbaum 175)

One sees here the class and gender and racial concerns that informed the aesthetic and political values brought to bear on the development of an authentic children's cinema. For those already familiar with the film medium (i.e., "sophisticated children"), Mrs. Foster proposes "thrillers of the western pioneer and Indian type"; for "the children who have not become movie fans she arranges programs of . . . lighter dramas and comedies." The former category of audience perhaps corresponds to an imagined boy viewer, who is working class, European-American, athletically inclined; the latter perhaps corresponds to a middle-class European-American girl, who is contemplative, "romantic," sensitive. Note that films dealing with the colonial experience of the United States—the long, bloody conquest of the indigenous nations—are considered "clean, legitimate action," on par with sports programs.[22] This is the cultural and ideological context that we believe is relevant to Saville's *Kim,* as a covert discourse of the coming American empire.

In an insightful article on "the politics of innocence" in films produced by the Disney Corporation, Henry Giroux writes of "the importance of film as a central medium of popular culture, which must be addressed not simply as a pedagogical apparatus actively involved in diverse identity formations, but also for the crucial role it plays in the construction of national identities in the service of global expansionism and colonialism" ("Beyond" 101–102). As a primary instance of popular culture, the Hollywood film, in Althusserian terms, is a hailing or interpellation of "concrete individuals as concrete subjects" (Althusser 173). It is a distributive economy of cultural capital, an endowing of, say, racial identity, with specific prestige and meaning. The popular film is an institutionalization of (allegedly) "harmless pleasures" (ranging from narcissistic fantasy to carthartic mirth). And finally, it is a real social force that helps to establish the bounds on thinkable thought (concerning, for instance, cultural otherness or the responsibilities of the citizen). We believe that, contrary to what is oft asserted, visual media (from children's television to Hollywood cinema) are a highly effective means of indoctrination. Said media instruct children (not always successfully, we readily concede) about "how to place themselves in particular historical narratives, representations, and cultural practices" (Giroux, "Beyond" 84–85). Indeed, as Maria Elena Gutierrez has argued, "the media have perhaps the most powerful impact of children's attitudes toward the world and others in it" (86). Thus, in our reading of Saville's *Kim* we ponder the question of what the film reveals about the standing of U.S. children in the imperial polity, that is, the National Security State, which ever gained legitimacy behind the ideological shield of the Cold War.

Mrs. Foster recommended "clean, legitimate action" as the proper moral and aesthetic measure of cinema for boys. Viewed from within the province of colonial ideology, Saville's film certainly lives up to her prescription. (How could it fail with Errol Flynn, the prototypical "white hero," in the starring role?!) The film is all energy, noise, and "exotic color." Witness the opening statement to the film's narrative, voiced by a venerable, old Indian man ("a wise man of the East," as it were), who sits upon a cushion before a curtained screen—the screen upon which the film's action occurs. Thus, we are invited to *look through and past* Saville's camera lens, onto another stage of representation. The opening statement warrants quotation in full:

> This tale begins in the year 1885, when Alexander III was Tsar of Russia, and Victoria was Empress of India. India! Gateway to the East. Land of magnificent pageantry and exotic color. The jewel of the Orient. Land of mysticism and fantasy, whose history is filled with the romance and intrigue of the nineteenth century, which already belongs to a legendary past-the romantic domain of Rudyard Kipling, the days when the white man was called "Sahib." These were the days of turmoil and bloodshed: caste against caste, creed against creed. At this time all eyes were turned to the war-like hillmen who swept down the hills to battle. To prevent massacres, there was banded together a small group of men, some of whom were native-born, some of whom were British. Leading the Secret Service was a certain Colonel Creighton; he called their work "the Great Game," and the history books tell us that many died playing it.

In Kipling's novel the omniscient narrator is an ethnologically astute observer of the "hustling throng," all "the races of Upper India"; the narrator, like the eponymous hero of the text, is both of and not of India, thus making possible a perspective on the Indian scene that implies both intimate familiarity and ironic detachment. The complexities of the novel's double perspective are somewhat smoothed over by Saville's deployment of the old man as the film's narrator. To be sure, the old man's voice is a means of arriving at an "inside narrative" without the burden of self-reflection. The practical effect is to heighten the Orientalist tone of the film (witness the cinematic quotation of "exotic color"), and to lessen the distance between the camera and its cultural object. Thus the overworked literary phrases of popular Orientalism ("Gateway to the East," "Land of mysticism," etc.), and the claim that the camera eye is faithfully recovering a past historical moment: "This tale begins in the year 1885 . . . [In] the days of turmoil and bloodshed . . . [when] . . . all eyes were turned to the war-like hillmen who swept down the hills to battle." The device of an inside narrator should be seen as expressive of a will to enchant the child viewer, to draw him into "the romantic domain of Rudyard Kipling," made spectacularly visible on the screen within a screen. As the old man tells his tale, he draws aside the curtains and encourges us to match his words to the unfolding picture. In short, the eye is brought into harmony with the ear.

What, then, of the specific content of the preface? The key phrases, we suggest, are "Sahib," "the Great Game,' and "the history books tell us." As to the first, the inside narrative voice (the supposed voice of a colonized "native") is made to bespeak "the romance and intrigue" of nineteenth-century empire. The "white man," as "Sahib," is presented here as a benign and heroic subject, whose only concern is to teach caste to live with caste, creed with creed, in order "to prevent massacres." The hillmen sweeping down from the north are described as "war-like"; the British, having invaded an entire subcontinent, are not so described. This is imperialist apology in its purest form. The mundane reality of empire—"that an empire," as George Orwell observed, "is primarily a money-making concern" (126)—is nowhere entertained in the "tale" told by the film's narrator. In the film, as in the novel, the brutalities of capital accumulation are largely kept off the stage.[23] The child viewer learns from the inside narrator that Sahibs keep the peace, and they do so by playing "the Great game," the work of espionage, counterintelligence. Colonel Creighton's analogy for spying, "the Great Game," comes directly from Kipling's novel; it is thought that Kipling borrowed the phrase from Arthur Connolly's *Narrative of an Overland Journey to the North of India* (1838). Connolly was an officer in the Bengal cavalry. He was an avid chess player, and the game seemed to him the perfect metaphor for the political maneuverings of British and Russisan agents in their struggles over the colonized body-politic of India. As played by Robert Douglas, Colonel Creighton is portrayed in the film as the prototypical English gentleman in the colonies; stiff upper lip, waxed moustache, twirled at the ends, knee-high riding boots, tweeds or white uniform, pipe and pith helmet, "Oxbridge" accent. The film downplays Creighton's ethnological curiosity regarding the cultural splendor of India, so important a part of his standing in the novel. But what remains of Kipling's Creighton in Saville's film is his profound committment to colonial administration—surveillance, discipline, the strategic show of force, the cooptation of would-be resisters and all the other tactics of (statist) bureaucratic power. Thus, "the Great Game" is simply a euphemistic term for the real pacification of the colonial "other." In a brilliant essay on *Kim,* as a novel, Edward Said has commented:

> Creighton embodies the notion that you cannot govern India unless you know India, and to know India means understanding the way it operates. This immediately sets the governor apart from the ordinary human being, for whom questions of right and wrong, of virtue and harm are both emotionally involving and important. To the government personality, the main preprogative is not whether something is good or evil, and therefore must be changed or kept, but whether something works or not, whether it helps or hinders one in ruling what is in effect an alien entity. (34)

Reader, cast your mind back to George Kennan's policy directive that "we should cease talk about vague and unreal objectives such as human rights" and duly recognize that political rule is a matter of dealing in "straight power concepts." Nothing better demonstrates the fundamental continuity between British and American imperial statecraft than the disavowal of ethics as a measure of politics. We hold that Creighton's metaphor of "the Great Game" is only comprehended in the context of what Said calls "the government personality," or what Hannah Arendt has termed the "philosophy of the bureaucrat" (213). According to Arendt, the bureaucrat is one who will "obey the laws of the [bureaucratic] process, identity himself with anonymous forces that he is supposed to serve in order to keep the whole process in motion; he will think of himself as mere function, and eventually consider such functionality . . . his highest possible achievement" (215). The bureaucratization of the human mind (which Arendt identifies as one source of modern totalitarianism) is a key concern of *Kim,* as both a novel and a film.

In Saville's film, Kim (played by a young Dean Stockwell) is told by a British military officer that schooling will make "a white boy out of you." At a later point in the action, when Kim is undergoing training in the principles of espionage, the film effectively shows the pedagogy of the school flowing naturally into the pedagogy of the Colonial Secret Service, the intelligence wing of the imperial State. Thus, the nomadic ("romantic") libidinal energy brought into the world by Kim's shifting identity (from "Indian" to "English" and back again) is finally taken up and reduced to a mechanical "power concept" of knowing those whom one would rule. As Sara Suleri writes, "The figure of education in *Kim* . . . becomes synonymous with the tautology of the colonial encounter, in which the child who is already culturally fluent must be caught in order that he may learn the far more alienating idiom of cultural description. Where cultural authority was once disparate and as dialogical as Kim's delight in his various disguises, the very excesses of the Game render it localized within a colonizer's bureaucracy" (128). In the last analysis, the Great Game exists to keep the peace on the terms of the colonizer.

The film portrays a double threat to the British imperial order: the one emanating from within India in the form of "unruly natives," the other emanating from without in the form of "subversive activites" on the part of Russian agents. Note that throughout the film, the dissident native is presented as the stereotypical cruel and sensuous being of Orientalist lore.[24] At one point in the narrative, when Kim, now uncovered as "a white boy," is dangled over a cliff by the Indian ally of the Russian agents, in an attempt to force information out of him (no such event takes place in Kipling's novel), his torturer says to his sidekicks, "Leave him to me. We have our own way of loosening a tongue." As for the Russians, they call to mind the typical Hollywood portrayal of "cunning" German agents in World War II films. One notes that they are kept "other" to the film's imagined audience by the fact that theirs is the only speech in the film not translated into English. We are asked to suspend disbelief in regard to the "native" speech of the Indian characters (the use of archaic English—notably, "thee" and "thou"—signals the "reality" of the local vernacular). However, no such convention is employed to make known the speech of the Russians; the film thus encourages us to side with the British government, which regarded Russian infiltration of "its" territories as a deadly affair.

A crucial moment in the film is when Creighton briefs his superior officer as to the seriousness of the Russian threat. With a pointer in his hand, Creighton stands before a map of India and solemnly announces: "It looks like history is repeating itself. Russian influence again advances like a tide across Central Asia—another Afghan war, 1878." Creighton makes plain that it is agents of the Tsar who are organizing "war-like hillmen" to invade India. Notably absent in this convoluted "tale" of intraimperialist rivalry is the matter of the violent origins of the British imperial ascendancy; also missing is the reality of an Indian resistance that is not externally motivated, but organically arises from conditions within India. "The history books tell us that many died playing [the Great Game]." Kipling's novel implies as much. (Indeed, in the film adaptation, Huree Chunder, the man without a country, who yet faithfully serves the British, is found murdered by Kim.) The history books tells us who died and how they died, but they do not always tell us about *why* they died—or at least the "why" is often a misrepresentation, or even a deliberate distortion, of the facts. Significantly, George Orwell noted that "Kipling does not seem to realize that an empire is primarily a money-making concern. Imperialism as he sees it is a sort of forcible evangelizing. You turn a Gatling gun on a mob of unarmed 'natives,' and then you 'establish the Law,' which includes roads, railways and a court house. . . . He does not see that the map is painted red chiefly in order that the coolie may be exploited" (126–27). To the extent that Saville's film focuses on the intricacies of an allegedly benign bureaucratic power and not on the real brutalities of capital accumulation, it undertakes the same sleight of hand that mars the moral vision of Kipling's novel. This filmic duplication of what must be termed a disingenuous blindness is not without great significance for the Cold War discourse of "containment," which came into being in the late 1940s.

In a valuable article on "the politics of literature," Fred Inglis contends that "the novels [and films] which we recommend to our children represent the organization of history as we want children to see it. And 'history,' it is worth pointing out, 'may be servitude,' or 'history may be freedom,' but in either case it is not simply something which happended once upon a time, but is the action, the living inexorable principle of the past in the present" (161–62). This formulation is directly relevant to our concerns in this essay. How does the film adaptation of *Kim* organize history for children in a way that serves the present moment?

In our view, the film involves itself in Cold War ideology by propogating the (bureaucratic) narrative of empire as the advance of "civilization." The British presence in India is depicted as benign, just, necessary.[25] We are led to believe that the "days of turmoil and bloodshed" will come again if the British leave. The fact is the British did not intervene to halt wars of "caste against caste, creed agaisnt creed." Indeed, it is "increasingly clear," writes Nicholas Dirks, "that colonialism in India produced new forms of society that have been taken to be traditional, and that caste as we know it is not a residual survival of ancient India but a specifically colonial form of civil society" (59). According to Dirks, under colonial rule, caste was "appropriated and reconstructed" by the British to serve the demand of imperialist social control. Thus, the "tale" told by the inside narrator is not simply a distortion of history, it is a concerted falsification. The point of the tale, as we see it, is to legitimate the British presence in India vis-à-vis incursions from Imperial Russia. The parallels with Cold War propaganda are striking.

Consider the covert message of the film as regards the "moral" status of empire. Just as the British intervened overseas "to keep the peace," so the United States intervenes in country after country in order to "promote democracy." In both scenarios, Russian subversion of the realm is the ostensible pretext for large-scale military operations (in the case of the British Empire, the Tsarist State is the sworn enemy, while for the American Empire it is Bolshevism). By leave of the discourse of Colonel Creighton, the film expresses the central importance of the doctrine of "containment," and thus makes it easier for its contemporary audience to accept a similiar doctrine in their own day, lest history "repeat itself"! In Saville's film the work of maintaining empire is imagined as a "Great Game"; similarly, supposedly to prevent the "domino effect" (the "loss" of countries to "communism"), the National Security State gave rise to a massive bureaucratic culture of espionage—covert operations, overseas and at home, in the name of protecting the "interests" of the so-called Free World. In the last analysis, the ideological relegation of India to a peripheral status in the "Great Game" disguises the fact that intraimperialist rivalries are really *just that*—rivalries over the "right" to dominate and exploit. Thus, throughout the Cold War, the rhetoric of the Soviet threat justified military interventions here, there, and everywhere, and always the ground reality was the devastation of "Third World" lives, as revolutions were thwarted, progressive developments impeded, so that capital accumulation might proceed without significant resistance. In sum, as a being involved in the social world, Saville's film enacts a (covert) ideological translation of the pedagogy of the British Empire (that is, Kim's move from "bazaar and gutter" waif to Secret Service agent) into the emerging pedagogy of the National Security State, whose proper target is the open mind of the child viewer.

As distinct artistic forms, film and the novel have aesthetic concerns of their own. However, on the plane of narrative ideology, Saville's film shares with Kipling's novel an unabashed committment to what Hannah Arendt has called the "imperialst legend" (208). Arendt argues that although the legend has "little to do with the realities of British imperialism, it forced or deluded into its services the best sons of England" (209). Interestingly, the pedagogical value of the imperialist legend is made plain even within Kipling's novel. We refer to a key episode in Kim's late interpellation as a "Sahib" (a white man who "commands natives"), that is, when he listens to the "tales" of empire told by other English boys at St. Xavier's School. These are tales of adventure, courage, hardiness, self-sacrifice; tales of danger in "the jungle" and on "lonely plantations" in regions where "head-hunters" reside (see the epigram at the start of this section). Kipling tells us that Kim "throve by inches" listening to these tales.[26] Note, then, that as Kim becomes "white," he grows from a "boy" into a "man"—a man committed to the utility of "manly" action.

During the Cold War, the imperialist legend, as it played into a masculinist popular culture, perhaps went in two notable directions, both anticipated by Saville's film: On the one hand, the culture of espionage gave rise to the conventional motif of the freedom-fighter-in-disguise (Superman, Captain America, and the whole gallery of comic book "action heroes"); on the other hand, that same culture generated the paranoid spy thriller (the James Bond novel and film series, television programs like "The Man from U.N.C.L.E." and other examples of "clean, legitimate action"). The role of such popular forms in disseminating

Cold War propoganda is well documented and need not concern us here. What we have attempted to ponder is how the film adaptation of *Kim* prepares the imagined child viewer to accept entertainment that is heavily invested in the imperialist, militaristic, and racist values of the National Security State.

• • •

To what extent do recent Hollywood children's films appear to invest in National Security State ideology and the values of Empire? We have traced how MGM's *Kim* reproduces the covert and overt concerns of both late nineteenth-century British and mid-twentieth-century American imperialism. In both instances, the "Russian menace" functions as the principal reason for a state administered military-industrial complex which "contains" the unruly masses at home and abroad. What films today have replaced this Cold War, or "Old World Order" narrative, and suggest the New World Order of George Bush and Bill Clinton—one in which capital accumulation and bureaucratic centralization are linked to the manufacturing of consent around revisionist histories? One of the most successful businesses in corporate America today is the Disney Corporation, or, as it is often known, the Disney Empire. We ask to what extent do films produced by the Disney Corporation, such as *Aladdin* (1992), manufacture consent around U.S. policy in the Middle East. In short, because the expansion of the Disney "Empire" is coterminous with the expansion of the U.S. empire (the global reach of one reproduces the global reach of the other), we suggest that to understand Disney is to understand imperialism.

From this point of view, the similarities between Saville's *Kim* and Clements and Musker's *Aladdin* are striking examples of how empires commodify and reify culture and the cultural imaginary in ways that reproduce the *general* historical conditions of production and distribution that in turn produce *specific* periods of, in this instance, bourgeois hegemony and colonialism. Consider the example of the Persian Gulf "war" during which the Bush administration refused to see how U.S. intervention in the so-called Third World, Arab sovereignty and self-determination, OPEC's control and pricing of oil for U.S. consumption, and the withdrawal of U.S. troops from the Middle East might be linked. President Bush, Secretary of State George Baker, Commander-in-Chief of the Allied Forces Norman Schwarzkopf, and other members of what has been dubbed "Bush & Co" (Kopkind 112), declared that the Gulf War was not another "Vietnam War." Whilst this ploy effectively "contained" much opposition to the

Gulf War, nonetheless many commentators argued that "linkage" (between Israel in the Occupied Territories and Iraq in Kuwait, for example) as it became known, was precisely the issue. An editorial in *The Nation* entitled "The Wider War," for example, states that "Here, for all the differences, is the continuity between Vietnam and Iraq" (791). That is, the relation among, or "linkage" between, imperialist foreign and domestic policy and ruling class ideas do not just magically arise, like the Genie in *Aladdin,* but are manufactured and disseminated through specific cultural forms (the novel, films, and animated cartoons) during specific historical periods (late-monopoly capitalism) and with the consent of specific state, military, and capitalist institutions (UN, Washington, Pentagon, IMF, World Bank, Hollywood, etc.). In short, although *Kim* and *Aladdin* are separated by forty-two years and thus in some ways quite different (the special effects of the former seem positively ancient compared to the latter), they are nonetheless strikingly similar in their political significance. Both show how the bourgeoise compels other nations toward a world created "after its own image."

As noted, *Kim* opens with an old Indian man sitting cross-legged upon a cushion. Working with animation rather than live action, *Aladdin* deploys a similar narrative device: An old Middle Eastern merchant invites us to get close in order to listen to a tale ("perhaps you would like to hear it") about sultans, princesses, peasants, palace guards, and royal viziers. Like all cultural stereotypes, familiar yet strange, welcoming us in yet holding us at a distance, the voice (an "Anglicized" Arabic, as it were) sings the following song:

> Oh I come from a land, from a faraway place, where it's black and immense and the heat is intense. Its barbaric, but hey, its home! When the winds from the east and the suns from the west and the sand and the glass is bright, come on down, hop a carpet, fly to another Arabian Night. Arabian Nights. A fool off his guard could fall and fall hard out there on the dunes.

As the song, music, and credits end, the camera finishes by panning across the Arabian desert, stops at the edge of a bazaar and looks at a merchant. The merchant jumps down from a camel and invites the audience to "come on down," visit Agrabar, and inspect the quality of the goods for sale. Agrabar is not quite the "Land of mysticism and fantasy" evoked by the venerable old Indian man in *Kim,* but it is nonetheless a "city of mystery and enchantment [with] the finest merchandise this side of the River Jordan." The mystery in question is a tale that "begins on a dark night, where a dark man, waits with a dark purpose." Jafar, the dark man, seeks a "diamond in the rough." This turns out to be Aladdin, who we see leaping across the rooftops of Agrabar. Having stolen some bread, Aladdin is trying to evade the menacing palace guards. He is about to eat the bread when he sees out of the corner of his eye two hungry children rummaging through the garbage. In a gesture of benevolent goodwill and sympathy, reminiscent of the good deeds and services Kim regularly provides for his llama, Aladdin and his sidekick Abu give the children their loaf of bread. Grateful, the kids eat as Aladdin and Abu return once more to the "free" market and get caught up in other heroic deeds and action-packed adventures, the audience no doubt thoroughly entranced by their daring escapades. The remainder of the film conspires to make Aladdin meet and fall in love with Princess Jasmine (he rescues her in the market), release the Genie and defeat the evil Jafar and his sidekick Iago. Having won over the hearts and minds of all concerned, the film ends happily ever after (how else!). The Genie expels the evil Jafar, imprisoning him for "ten thousand years in the cave of wonders." The Sultan changes the law preventing commoners from marrying royalty. Aladdin uses his last wish to set the Genie free.

But *Aladdin,* and many of its more memorable scenes, are important as much for their "silence" as their "speech" (Macherey 85), as much for what they magically conjure up as for what they actually play down. In short, like *Kim, Aladdin* draws us inside and onto a second stage of representation where we see intraimperialist rivalries. This time, though, we are not in India but in the Middle East, looking not at the formal and overt mechanisms of a very public colonial rule but the informal and covert operations of a very private Empire.[27] No less than *Kim, Aladdin* manufactures consent around a certain kind of imperial history. In 1950, it was the Cold War. In 1992, it is the Gulf War.

Consider the last three decades of U.S. foreign policy, particularly, though not exclusively, in the Middle East. Note the relations between Britain, the United States, Soviet Union, and Iraq because if the function of corporate entertainment for the young is to make palatable for children and adults alike the kind of foreign and domestic policies that they might otherwise not stomach, our analysis of *Aladdin* as a vehicle for consolidating imperial hegemony over its dominions needs to be contextualized by history. Stephen Shalom's *Imperial Alibis: Rationalizing U.S. Intervention after The Cold War,* for example, discusses the unpalatable history noticeably missing from *Aladdin.* Shalom notes that Nixon and National Security Adviser Henry Kissinger began selling arms to

Iran in order that Iran might act as the "policeman of the Gulf" (Shalom 40), a role the United States has now assumed. Indeed, the United States sold "$21 billion worth of arms to Iran" (40). Not unsuprisingly, this fantastic arms extravaganza fueled Iraqi militancy. Shalom writes that "Between 1973 and 1980, Iraq's armed forces doubled in size and the number of armored and mechanized divisions grew four-fold" (41): One cannot but help think at this point of how the Genie grows and grows. As arms were being sold (accumulation) arms control negotiations (bureaucratic power) between the Soviet Union and America broke down. The "history" that followed is well known. The Iranian revolution took place in 1979. Iraq invaded Iran in 1980 and the Iraq–Iran war began. In 1989, Bush "signed top-secret National Security Directive NSD-26 [that permitted] $1 billion in dual-use technology" (43). Then, Shalom reports, "In September 1990, the Bush administration announced $20 billion in arms sale to Saudi Arabia . . . though Congress cut this to $7.5 billion. In March 1991, Secretary of Defense Dick Cheney declared that the United States would sell more not fewer weapons to the Middle East in the wake of the war" (43). All of this to preserve what Henry Pachter has called "a system of business" (quoted in Shalom 8). In short, U.S. policy in relation to the Middle East in general and the Gulf War in particular is characterized by a completely amoral politics. Control, profit, and the further destabilization of the area is achieved by selling arms to both sides. The U.S. mask of neutrality is merely that—a mask that barely conceals a reckless desire to proliferate, regardless of the human cost. The question, of course, is how you get domestic audiences to accept foreign policy. How do you manufacture consent around imperialism?

We can return to *Aladdin* for some answers. Most obviously, from an imagined child or adult point of view, the opening song about the "intense" desert heat, the dramatic warning that a fool could "fall hard" out there in the sand, and the aerial-like approach of the camera that zeros in on the merchant and then "lands" at the bazarre, are designed to establish setting, character conflict, mood, and tone (the humorous tone is particularly important in "containing" dissent as we shall see). The intoxicating mixture of color, music, words, and song could hardly fail to lull the audience into accepting the tale of intrigue, espionage, colonial heroism, and manly adventure about to unfold before them as they sit staring up at the screen. Bu the smooth and steady aerial-like movement of the camera perhaps sets the stage for another scene. The air to land trajectory might be seen as paralleling the "AirLand Battle" principles of war as they are set down in Army publication "Field Manual 100–5," a manual the U.S. military adapted to fight the Gulf War. This publication, which has its strategic roots in Cold War offensives against the Soviet Union, but is now seen as integral to future battle plans for World War III (Elmer-Dewitt 34), is taught to all military students and, significantly, is aimed at first defeating the "enemy's mind" (34) rather than body. In short, the way we see images is as important as the images we see. At any rate, the audience comfortably settling down to watch *Aladdin* on the big screen at the movie theater (just as they had settled comfortably down in 1991 to watch the Gulf War on the small screen at home) is metaphorically placed inside the "cockpit" (behind the camera) as it hones its sights on human beings (in Pentagon double-speak, "collateral damage"). Looking at the opening scenes of *Aladdin* from this dual-use perspective, whereby military offensives abroad are made entertainingly acceptable for those at home, becomes clearer when one knows that stills from *Top Gun* and pictures of Tom Cruise were the Disney animator's models for *Aladdin,* and that *Top Gun,* about U.S. fighter pilots killing Russian fighter pilots (the Cold War revisited), was financed by the Navy whose enlistments soared as a result of the film's success (Pallot 916). *Aladdin* similarly enlists its audience: Cheering on Aladdin, by analogy we cheer on the U.S. and American fighter pilots seeking out Saddam Hussein's ground forces.

Aladdin works in quite specific ways to enlist the audience to sanction U.S. foreign policy in general. For example, Aladdin's benevolent feeding of the children with a single loaf of bread (the religious overtones are clear) shows something of Aladdin's true nature, which is established as Aladdin humorously and heroically escapes the palace guards by walking across a bed of hot coal, hiding in a harem, and running through the bazaar. But, we argue, Aladdin's donation of food to these indigenous children also fulfills another function, inculcating sympathetic American audiences to receive images of starving (though *deserving*) children fed by sympathetic U.S. soldiers whilst on tours of military duty abroad (*undeserving* children and adults are left). This "benevolence" encourages a private response to poverty rather than a public call for the redistribution of wealth necessary to overcome the structural causes of impoverishment. Also, when audiences see on the big and small screens U.S. soldiers ("our troops") feeding starving children, or photographed at war with pictures of their own well-fed children pinned to their uniforms, it becomes harder to see U.S. soldiers as destroyers of civilian targets (napalming in Vietnam, bombing in Middle East). Of course, the "animated" starving children in *Aladdin* bear no resemblance to the "real" starving children of Somalia, Haiti, Panama, or any other place where U.S. troops have "intervened" in order to "contain" revolutionary or nationalist aspirations. In short, these ideal children that Aladdin feeds bear no resemblance to real children anywhere, particularly those slaughtered by the conflict in the Middle East.[28]

The Genie's strategic importance in the manufacturing of consent around U.S. policy in the Middle East cannot be underestimated. His role in the film is particularly instructive. Voiced by Robin Williams, the Genie first appears when inadvertently released from the lamp by Aladdin. Initially a tiny puff of smoke, the Genie suddenly mushrooms before Aladdin's eyes. Fantastic spectacle, the fall-out from the Genie's explosive appearance is a veritable deluge of impersonations and allusions drawn from the arts and from popular culture. Delivering joke after joke in rapid-fire succession just as he did in *Good Morning, Vietnam* (1987) and *Ferngully* (1992), Williams effectively parades (and parodies) before us twentieth-century popular culture, effectively reducing it to a series of one-liners. Charming rather than frightful, cuddly and lovable rather than alienating, friendly, amusing, witty, and charismatic it is hard to see the Genie's superhuman omnipotence as anything other than harmless innocence.

However, in an insightful chapter called "Trimming Uncle Remus's Tales," James Snead notes that "More than perhaps any other genre, animated cartoons encourage the rhetoric of harmlessness . . . Yet . . . this seeming harmlessness is far from the actual state of things" (84–85). Indeed, we argue that it is precisely this animated form and the Genie's innocent and harmless play that draws our attention to how the Genie steadily works to obfuscate the centralization and accumulation characteristic of empire building. From a bureaucratic point of view, the Genie organizes, administers, caters, and makes possible Aladdin's every wish, all of which, of course, are reduced (or "lumped together") to nothing more than the single-minded pursuit of Jasmine. From a military point of view, the Genie represents a weapon of almost unlimited power available for Aladdin to command at will. But, like capital itself, the Genie's power is unlimited because it is finally shown to bear no particular allegiance except to whomever is the most powerful master. That is, in one sense, weapons and capital know few national boundaries, as the Genie shifts sides from Aladdin, the Sultan, and the people of Agrabar to Jafar and back to Aladdin again. In a different sense, weapons and capital are politically bound: The United States must have "smart" bombs, whilst everyone else must have "dumb" bombs, just as capital must eventually have masters. An image of almost raw energy and power, the Genie surely calls to mind Kennan's point that the protection of oil in the Middle East would require "straight power concepts" (quoted in Chomsky 318) unhampered by idealism. But to understand the Genie we should recall not so much Kennan but Chamberlain who remarked that the function of government is to open the many paths of free trade so that finance capital might more safely tread around the world. That is, the Genie switches sides—"I work for senior psychopath now" he explains to Aladdin—not because there is a right or wrong side to the political struggles but because late-monopoly capitalism and "free trade" requires of capital no allegiance except to the accumulation of more capital. This is the deep and abiding contradiction in capital accumulation. It has no telos other than more capital accumulation and thus, like the Genie, twists and turns insanely on its own logic. We might now see why the ending of *Aladdin* and of most corporate films in general is crucial. Capitalist culture, which tends toward the nihilistic, must manufacture a purpose, even where there is none. In this day and age, "family values" is that ideological purpose which drives the engine of capitalism and fuels the consumption of commodities like oil. Thus, at the end of the film, the Genie (the so-called spirit of capitalism) finds a consuming body (Aladdin and Jasmine as one couple) and a protective body politic (a state palace modified for bourgeois use).

Watching the thoroughly bourgeois antics of Aladdin, the machiavellian politics of the Royal Vizier Jafar, the pathetic ravings of the Sultan, and the longings of Jasmine, it is hard to see the manic energy and shifting identity of the Genie as anything but unbridled and unfettered capitalism erasing history with every line and teaching audiences around the world to laugh at themselves and their neighbours. But then the structural function of humor in Disney—the Genie's improvisations, his inadvertent release from the lamp, Iago's wisecracks, Abu's funny faces, Aladdin's boyish charm and romantic mishaps—works to make the systematic and formal imposition of an empire on the world's peoples an insider's joke. If the Cold War logic of U.S. imperialism in the 1950s determines the form of *Kim,* the Gulf War logic of U.S. imperialism in the 1990s determines the form of *Aladdin.*[29]

MGM's *Kim* was not the first children's film to manufacture consent through National Security State propoganda, just as *Aladdin* will no doubt not be the last. *Aladdin* updates the Disney Corporation's work during the 1930s and 1940s. Before *Kim,* Disney was deeply involved in Third World politics and issues. Disney's global reach is insightfully discussed, for example, in Julianne Burton-Carvajal's " 'Surprise Package': Looking Southward with Disney," or Lisa Cartright and Brian Goldfarb's

"Cultural Contagion: On Disney's Health Education Films for Latin America." Burton-Carvajal's essay is particularly instructive here. It cleverly argues that Disney's *The Three Caballeros* "packages Latin America . . . as pure spectacle [and] "happens to be an allegory of First World colonialism par excellence [because] every story . . . is a narrative of conquest or of enslavement" (142). MGM's *Kim* in 1950 merely adapts or recapitulates Disney's 1944 *The Three Caballeros,* a film so described as a "must for all ages" (Pallot 898): different setting, different audience, same imperial politics. Animated films like *Aladdin* are not so much adaptations of timeless fairy tales, but adaptations of historically and culturally specific forms and genres for the dissemination of particular rather than universal bourgeois values. Metaphors of accumulation and centralization, heroic allegories of Third World colonialism, *Kim* and *Aladdin* work to inculcate individuals into the institutions of class society through the systematic revision of history and the construction of the racialized other. Old tales told in the language of a new empire, today's corporate entertainment for children and young viewers teaches the manufacturing of consent, a lesson that becomes quite clear if we set the film of *Aladdin* amid the corporate politics of the Middle East.

In this regard, it is worth pondering where U.S. forces have "intervened" in the name of "democracy" and where children's films are "set" in the name of "entertainment." A pattern emerges, one we might call the politics of entertainment for the unsuspecting young. U.S. troops have recently intervened in Lebanon, Grenada, Panama, Somalia, Iraq, Grenada, Haiti, and elsewhere around the world; the media sends back images of war few children will not have seen. Thus, two points become strikingly clear. First, we might understand these military interventions not as "tales" of defending democracy, but as the inevitable consequence of U.S. guardianship of the world capitalist system. Second, these tales of an allegedly benign and paternalistic interventionism are key to a resurgent neocolonialism made all the more possible by the collapse of the Soviet bloc. However we choose to respond to the military interventions of U.S. troops around the world, a look at where children's films are set suggests that, as in *Kim,* there is a hidden pedagogy of empire. Children's material culture in general and children's films in particular reflect how empires make palatable what children might not otherwise stomach. In the early 1930s, for example, Shirley Temple's *Kid in Africa* (1932) was set in Africa. As already noted, Disney's *The Three Caballeros* (1944) is set in Latin America (Brazil and Mexico). Disney's *The Jungle Book* is set in colonial India. *Aladdin* is set in the Middle East. *Pocahontas* (1995) is set in colonial Virginia. *Congo* (1995) is set in Africa. Paramount's *Raiders of the Lost Ark* (1981) is set in the Middle East. Disney's *The Lion King* (1995) is set in Africa. In short, where U.S. forces go on behalf of empire and the National Security State, U.S. corporate entertainment naturally follows. The celebrated innocence of the Disney Empire is merely the cultural ideology of an achieved neocolonialism. The infantile, narcissistic, and violent underside of Disney culture arises directly from the real world brutalities of capital accumulation.

In "Telling Tales," we have sought to analyze the subtle (though always powerful) influence of Cold War propaganda and National Security State ideology on the form and content of two children's films, namely Victor Saville's *Kim* and Musker's and Clements's *Aladdin.* Our readings turned on the way that each film deals with the discipline of the mind and the body and the human spirit, ultimately in the name of centralized bureaucratic power and capital accumulation. We have labored to suggest that far from being "innocuous" or "innocent," the two films in question represent the first lesson in the pedagogy of empire and war.

NOTES

[1]See Russell Watson and Corie Brown, "The 100 Best," *Newsweek Extra* Summer 1998: 17–20. This edition contains the AFI's list of one hundred best films and related articles.

[2]2.The words "flat" and "round" come from E. M. Forster's *Aspects of the Novel* (1927). According to Forster, "Flat characters were called 'humours' in the seventeenth century, and are sometimes called types, and sometimes caricatures. In their purest form, they are constructed around a single idea or quality; when there is more than one factor in them, we get the beginning of the curve towards the round. . . . The test of a round character is whether it is capable of surprising in a convincing way" (81).

[3]See Shipman, page 19.

[4]See Shipman, page 19.

[5]*Summer Holiday, A Hard Day's Night, Help, Tommy,* and *Pink Floyd: The Wall* are United Kingdom productions (Richard Lester, Ken Russell, etc.).

[6]Jane Feuer writes, "Within the musical film the most persistent subgenre has involved kids (or adults) "getting together and putting on a show" (486). Feuer refers here to the way that the cycles of musicals in the 1920s and 1930 always contained within them a parallel "backstage" (486) musical. Rather than the film within a film, audiences saw a musical within a musical, the love affairs of the latter eventually spilling over into the former. The paradigmatic text is, of course, *Singin' in the Rain.*

It's interesting to note that many children's films also contain a musical within a musical, or a play within a play, that has literal and symbolic import for those on the stage and those watching. The notion of self-reflexivity in children's films, not unlike the idea of metafilmicity I discussed in Part One: Introduction, can be found in films such as *Hook,* or, more recently, *Simon Birch.* In both, there is a play-within-a-play.

Overall, this aspect of children's cinema is explainable initially as a convenient narrative device directors employ as a way of maintaining multiple (or at least two) plot lines, both of which, like the "backstage" (486) musical, are usually resolved by the film's end. Yet, it is also part of that duality of children's films (which is also a characteristic feature of children's literature), the way in which children's films (unlike adult films) contain a dual voice: R-rated movies are for adults *not* kids, G-rated movies are for adults *and* kids. But this dual voice is part of a larger narrative framework. Here, I mean the way films starring children such as *Hook, Home Alone,* or even *Jumanji* are built along the more cosmic, metaphysical lines of reality and illusion, the present and the past, the present and the future.

Of course, we might marvel at the complexity previously hidden in children's films, wonder at the fact that what appears ordinary—a kid's film—is actually extraordinary—a kid's film. On the other hand, the actual and metaphorical duality I am suggesting structures children's films also points to a degree of duality in the viewer. This in turn deconstructs the notion of the innocent child within the film but also the innocent child within the audience. Far from being innocent, the child viewer is in fact an experienced viewer.

[7]The irony in *Jurassic Park, Terminator 2: Judgment Day,* and other corporate films for the young is less subtly presented than in *Forbidden Games* and *Empire of the Sun* but present nonetheless. In both, scientific invention and technological development produce life but also death. For example, in *Jurassic Park,* a robotic arm turns the dinosaur egg that produces the dinosaur that turns against its creator, the scientist. The electric fence—10,000 volts—designed to entrap the dinosaurs in the park is the same fence that nearly electrocutes the kids as they try to flee the dinosaurs. In *Terminator 2: Judgment Day,* the computer technology that runs the world is the computer technology that runs the world amok.

[8]Of course, the journeys of all these buddies are all quite different. Butch Cassidy (Paul Newman) and the Sundance Kid (Robert Redford) are train robbers for the most part running from the law (the opening sequence alludes to Edwin Porter's 1904 silent classic *The Great Train Robbery*) who wind up in South America where they are eventually shot to death. Ridley Scott's controversial 1991 film *Thelma and Louise* has Thelma (Geena Davies) and Louise (Susan Sarandon) as two housewives (rather than two train robbers) on the run from the law. In *Thelma and Louise,* the law is represented by the husbands, the rapist, the FBI, and patriarchal culture in general. Thelma and Louise also die at the end: rather than give themselves up to the law (literally and symbolically), they drive

off the edge of a cliff into thin air. In *Toy Story,* Woody and Buzz must escape the clutches of Sid and make their way back to Andy before he and his mother move to another neighborhood. Befitting a children's film from corporate Hollywood, Woody and Buzz do not die at the end of their journey. They become best friends.

[9]There are other examples of how film genres evolve from the primitive to the classical to the revisionist and the parodic. *Robin and Marian* (1976) and *Men in Tights* are comic parodies of the *Robin Hood* legend. De Sica's *The Bicycle Thief* is parodied by Mauricio Nichetti in his 1989 *The Icicle Thief. Pee-Wee's Big Adventure* (1985) might be seen as a parody of *The Icicle Thief.* Often, famous films like the *The Sound of Music* are parodied by television shows like *The Simpsons.*

[10]There are two versions of *Angels in the Outfield.* The first, directed by Clarence Brown, was made in 1951. The second, directed by William Dear, was made in 1994. The major difference is that in the 1951 version the prayers of a little girl, played by Donna Corcoran, bring the angel Gabriel and solve the team's dismal record. In the more recent version, the prayers of Roger (Joseph Gordon-Levitt) that brings the angels. Also of note: The 1951 version stars Janet Leigh as reporter Jennifer Paige who begins the investigation into the team's spirited successes. Janet Leigh, of course, would later star in Hitchcock's 1960 *Psycho,* itself the subject of numerous sequels, remakes, and revamps.

[11]Similarly, Iago, an allusion to Shakespeare's character in *Othello,* functions merely as a comic foil for Jafar. Abu, Aladdin's sidekick, functions the same way. In *The Lion King,* Zazu (voiced by Rowan Atkinson) acts as the comic relief to Mufasa (voiced by James Earl Jones) and Simba (voiced by Jonathan Taylor Thomas). An extended study of the sidekick, jester, or comic foil in children's films would be important, particulary when contextualized by questions of race, class, and gender.

[12]Some films starring children contain single protagonists who exhibit good and bad qualities. Think here of *The Good Son,* for example, starring Macaulay Culkin.

[13]Jill May and Donna Norton make similar points. Norton, for example, notes that "The theme of a story is the underlying idea that ties the plot, characters, and setting together into a meaningful whole. . . . A memorable book has a theme—or several themes—that children can understand because of their own needs" (98). Norton goes on to argue that theme is often revealed by changes in characters and/or through the nature of conflict. A central theme in children's books, according to Norton, is personal development: the theme of identity (99).

[14]See Cary Bazalgette and Terry Staples, "Unshrinking the Kids: Children's Cinema and the Family Film."

[15]From an ethnographical point of view, *The Land Before Time* is not so much a children's film as it is an expression of Western culture's religious beliefs and values.

[16]A similar point might be made in relation to *Harriet the Spy* and its representation of Asian-Chinese culture.

[17]A characteristic feature of children's films is that like children's literature, they each in their own way contain small, enclosed spaces. In *The Indian in the Cupboard,* the small, enclosed spaces are, for example, the cupboard itself, the tepee, Omri's pocket when he takes Little Bear and Boone to school, and so forth. In *James and the Giant Peach,* the enclosed space is the peach itself. In *Jurassic Park,* the kids Tim (Joseph Mazzello) and Lex (Ariana Richards) flee the rampaging dinosaurs by taking refuge inside the kitchen and then by hiding within the kitchen cabinets. Perhaps the most celebrated example of a child enclosed within a small space can be found in James Cameron's 1986 *Aliens,* starring Sigourney Weaver as the reborn Ripley and Carrie Henn as Newt, the feral-looking child whose parents were devoured by the aliens and who escaped by hiding in the spaceship's air vents and ducts. Cocooned inside her makeshift home, Newt has successfully survived the aliens because, not unlike Tim and Lex in *Jurassic Park,* she cannot be seen by them.

Set against these images of enclosure are images of openness. In *The Indian in the Cupboard,* the magical cupboard provides Omri instant access to the vast expanses of cultural and political history. Thus, to attend Little Bear's wounds, Omri, a perfect example of what Marx and Engels call "the sorcerer [unable] to control the powers of the nether world whom he has called up by his spells" (*Communist Manifesto* 89) conjures up from the past Tommy (Steve Coogan), a World War I medic who, after a little comic cultural exchange with Little Bear, sympathetically and attentively dresses his injuries. Similarly, the small hiding places Tim and Lex find to escape the dinosaurs (the car, the tree in which they fall asleep comforted by paleontologist Dr. Alan Grant (Sam Neill) are set against the vastness and interconnectedness of historical evolution. Thus, the dinosaurs (velociraptors, dilophosaurus, tyrannosaurus rex, and so forth) are recreated (brought back to life) by cloning miniscule fossilized DNA strands. Scientific experiments are conducted in laboratories on an otherwise deserted, edenic, paradisal island that clearly suggests the Garden of Eden. In other words, in characteristic fashion, Spielberg places images of protective safety, smallness, and enclosure against images of danger, hugeness, freedom, escape. Out of this dialectic emerges the film's central themes, allegorically the age-old conflict between history and christianity (scientific evolutionism and religious creationism) over the white, nuclear, bourgeois extended family (Dr. Alan Grant, Dr. Ellie Sattler, Tim, Lex, and John Hammond). Here, the extinction of the dinosaurs is brought up to date and represents the possible extinction of the nuclear family due to too much secularist thinking on the one hand or too much religious fundamentalist thinking on the other. Tyranosaurus rex represents evil that must be defeated by good—it is.

[18]*The Indian in the Cupboard*'s decision to portray Boone (David Keith) as a stereotypically loud-mouthed, politically incorrect but heart-of-gold Texan cowboy reiterates Robin Wood's point about the way in which 1980s films defuse the politics of the 1970s and 1960s. That is, the film's representation of Boone as a comic foil to Little Bear, a moronic white cowboy who nonetheless

realizes that Little Bear is not an enemy but a potential friend, and that he and Little Bear in fact have much in common, fulfills several functions. For one, Boone's racist language and the fact that he is sent back to the history from whence he came defuses the history of white racism toward Native Americans and suggests that whilst it existed in the past it has no place in the present. Put another way, the film uses the comic cowboy to play down the history of white racism toward minorities to such an extent that it begins ironically to defuse the history of white racism. White racism disappears as a thing of the past, the film oblivious to the fact that its liberal gestures toward multiculturalism—the film does focus on the relationship between a white boy and a Native American man—are the problem rather than the solution. *Indian in the Cupboard,* a supreme example of a corporate film desinged to inculcate young viewers into the mores of patriarchal, capitalist democracies, offers young audiences a fantasy that, to use Ward Churchill's words, is a "fantasy of the master race."

[19]See Walter L. Williams, "American Imperialism and the Indians," *Indians in American History,* ed. Frederick E. Hoxie (Arlington Heights, Illinois: Harlan Davidson, Inc., 1988) 231–49.

[20]The historian Michael A. Bernstein has observed that scholars "need to peel away the many layers of the history of Pax Americana of the past four decades. Understanding the intellectual and cultural impacts of the Cold War requires the study of a wide array of historical forces, ranging from political and economic to the social and ideological" (90). We situate our essay in the problematic outlined by Bernstein: Specifically, we seek to address the intellectual and cultural impact of popular cinema as a vehicle for the pedagogy of empire aimed at children.

[21]Rosaldo notes that in contemporary films like *Heat and Dust, A Passage to India, Out of Africa,* and *The Gods Must Be Crazy,* "white colonial societies" are portrayed as "decorous and orderly. . . . Hints of these societies' coming collapse only appear at the margins where they create not moral indignation but an elegaic mode of perception. Even politically progressive North American audiences have enjoyed the elegance of manners governing relations of dominance and subordination between the 'races.' Evidently, a mood of nostalgia makes racial domination appear innocent and pure" (68). The rhetoric of "nostalgia," to be sure, is a structural aspect of the filmic version of *Kim,* just as the rhetoric of "innocence" is a structural aspect of *Aladdin.* However, we contend that one's immediate response to the film is primarily determined by the rhetoric of "adventure," which stimulates heady excitement rather than poignant wistfulness. The difference between "nostalgia," "innocence," and "adventure" is perhaps the difference between empire on the wane and empire maintained.

[22]In this context, consider the telling observation made by the native American scholar M. Annette Jaimes, in her introduction to Ward Churchill's *Fantasies of the Master Race: Literature, Cinema and the Colonization of American Indians* (1992). Jaimes writes: "White [cultural] domination is so complete that even Indian children want to be cowboys. It's as if Jewish children wanted to play

nazis" (4). Note that in *The Indian in the Cupboard,* the fantasy of cultural domination is made spectacularly visible by the fact that the Indian is represented as a miniature plaything (see Figure 11).

[23]In Kipling's novel there is a brief, almost incidental reference to "the thousand cotton factory chimneys that ring Bombay" (213). But the novel refuses to say anything more about the economic aspect of empire—the hierarchical relations of superexploitation, the politics of labor resistance, the social demands of the factory owners and so forth. Saville's film totally avoids the political economy of colonialism. Indeed, we are typically shown familiar images of the markets and the bazaars, as if to imply that no greater economic organization exists within "British India."

[24]The trope of cruelty works to affirm the existential logic of Orientalist discourse, as pointed out by Edward Said, that "no matter how deep the specific exception [to the type], no matter how much a single Oriental can escape the fences placed around him [*sic*], he is *first* an Oriental, *second* a human being, and *last* again an Oriental" (Said 1985, 102).

[25]At this point we would like to remind the reader that it was Kipling who coined the extraordinary slogan, "the white man's burden."

[26]It seems that Kipling himself was reared on a diet of storytelling. As noted by William Walsh: "Kipling carried so much of India into so much of his work. His narrative style was influenced by the stories told to him in childhood by his Catholic Goan and his Hindu bearer, two of those closest to him and most loved by him. These stories were told in an idiom which mixed easy, intimate, everyday chat with ritual, symbol, and myth. It was an idiom developed by Kipling to be capable of considerable subtlety" (161).

[27]Shalom writes: "Of course, the United States never had a large, formal overseas empire as did Britain. Its overseas empire has been mostly an informal one: a neo-colonial rather than a colonial empire" (8). The neocolonialism is a function of the privatization of experience common to capitalist commodity production and consumption.

[28]A Harvard Study reported that as a result of the bombing and embargo on Iraq, "One hundred and seventy thousand additional children will die . . . from typhoid, cholera, malnutrition, and other health problems" (quoted in McCartan 4).

[29]This is most clearly seen in the way in which the two prefaces differ. In *Kim,* the camera maintains a certain distance from the venerable old Indian man, a distance that suggests a certain respect both for the old man, the Russians who are the pretext for the Cold War, and the viewer. By the time we get to 1992 and *Aladdin,* corporate Hollywood seems to us to have dropped any pretense at respect, either for the viewer or the object of the camera's focus. This is suggested by the fact that in *Aladdin* the camera smashes into the old Middle Eastern man's face when he invites us to come on down and listen to his tale. We are invited thus to "smash" the racialized other and to laugh at the violence committed on our behalf by the forces of technology. It is a telling moment in postmodernism.

Filmography

Abe Lincoln in Illinois. Dir. John Cromwell. RKO Radio, 1939.
Adventures of Huckleberry Finn, The. Dir. Richard Thorpe. MGM, 1939.
Air Bud. Dir. Charles Martin Smith. Walt Disney Productions, 1997.
Air Force One. Dir. Wolfgang Petersen. Columbia, Beacon, Radiant, 1997.
Ace Ventura: Pet Detective. Dir. Tom Shadyac. Ace Productions, Morgan Creek, 1994.
Ace Ventura: When Nature Calls. Dir. Steve Oedekerk. Warner Brothers, 1995.
Adventures of Dolly, The. Dir. D. W. Griffith. Perf. Gladys Egan. Biograph, 1908.
Adventures of Robin Hood, The. Dir. William Keighley. Warner Brothers, 1938.
Aladdin [*Aladin*]. Dir. Ferdinand Zecca. 1906.
Aladdin. Dir. John Musker and Ron Clements. Walt Disney Productions, 1992.
Ali Baba and the Forty Thieves [*Ali Baba et les 40 Voleurs*]. Dir. Ferdinand Zecca. 1902.
Alice in Wonderland. Dir. Cecil M. Hepworth. 1903.
Alice in Wonderland. Dir. Clyde Geronimi and Wilfred Jackson. Walt Disney Productions, 1951.
Alien Resurrection. Dir. Jean-Pierre Jeunet. 20th Century Fox, 1997.
Aliens. Dir. James Cameron. 20th Century Fox, Brandywine Prod., Concorde, 1986.
All Fall Down. Dir. John Frankenheimer. Perf. Brandon De Wilde. MGM, 1962.
All Dogs Go to Heaven. Dir. Don Bluth. United Artists, Goldcrest, Sullivan Bluth Studios, Ireland, 1989.
All the Way Home. Dir. Alex Segal. Paramount, 1963.
Alsino and the Condor [*Alsino y el Cóndor*]. Dir. Miguel Littin. Hernan Littin, 1982.
Amadeus. Dir. Milos Forman. AMLF, Tobis Filmkunst, Filmes Castello Lopes, Orion Pictures, 1984.

American Graffiti. Dir. George Lucas. Universal, Lucasfilm Ltd., Coppola Co., 1973.
American Tail, An. Dir. Don Bluth. Universal, 1986.
Amistad. Dir. Steven Spielberg. DreamWorks SKG, HBO, 1997.
Anastasia. Dir. Don Bluth. 20th Century Fox, 1997.
And Now Miguel. Dir. James B. Clark. Universal, 1966.
Angels in the Outfield. Dir. Clarence Brown. MGM, 1951.
Angels in the Outfield. Dir. William Dear. Walt Disney Productions, 1994.
Antz. Dir. Eric Darnell and Lawrence Guterman. DreamWorks SKG, Pacific Data Images, 1998.
Apple, The [*Sib*]. Dir. Samira Makhmalbaf. Makhmalbaf Productions, 1998.
Armageddon. Dir. Michael Bay. Touchstone Pictures, 1998.
Around the World in 80 Days. Dir. Michael Anderson and Kevin McClory. United Artists, 1956.
Au Revoir les Enfants. Dir. Louise Malle. Nouvelle Editions, MK2, Stella, 1987.
Austin Powers: International Man of Mystery. Dir. M. Jay Roach. Copella International, Juno Pix, Moving Pictures, New Line Cinema, 1997.
Austin Powers: The Spy Who Shagged Me. Dir. M. Jay Roach. Eric's Boy, Team Todd, Moving Pictures, 1999.
Avengers, The. Dir. Jeremiah S. Chechik. Warner Brothers, 1998.
Babe. Dir. George Miller. Kennedy Miller Productions, 1995.
Babe: Pig in the City. Dir. George Miller. Kennedy Miller Productions, 1998.
Baby Geniuses. Dir. Bob Clark III. Columbia, Triumph, Crystal Sky Comm., 1999.
Baby's Day Out. Dir. Patrick Read Johnson. 20th Century Fox, 1994.
Back to the Future. Dir. Robert Zemeckis. Amblin, Universal, 1985.
Bad Boys [*Furuyo Shonen*]. Dir. Susumu Hani. 1961.
Bad Company. Dir. Robert Benton. Paramount, 1972.
Bad Day at Black Rock. Dir. John Sturges. MGM, 1955.
Bad News Bears, The. Dir. Michael Ritchie. Paramount, 1976.
Bambi. Dir. David Hand. Walt Disney Productions, 1942.
Basic Instinct. Dir. Paul Verhoeven. TriStar, Le Studio Canal, Carolco, 1992.
Batman. Dir. Tim Burton. Warner Brothers, 1989.
Batman Forever. Dir. Joel Schumacher. Warner Brothers, 1989.
Battle at Elderbush Gulch, The. Dir. D. W. Griffith. Biograph, 1914.
Battle of Gettysburg, The. Dir. Thomas Ince. New York Motion Picture Co., 1913.
Battle Hymn. Dir. Douglas Sirk. Universal International Pictures, 1957.
Battleship Potemkin [*Bronenosets Potyomkin*]. Dir. Sergei Eisenstein and Grigori Aleksandrov. Goskino (USSR), 1925.
Baxter. Dir. Jerome Boivin. Christian Bourgois Prod., Aliceleo, Gerard Mital Prod., ISSA, MK2 Prod., Partner's Prod., 1988.
Beau Geste. Dir. Douglas Heyes. Universal, 1966.
Beauty and the Beast [*La Belle et la Bête*]. Dir. Jean Cocteau. Discina (Fr), 1946.

Beauty and the Beast. Dir. Kirk Wise and Gary Trousdale. Walt Disney Productions, Silver Screen Partners IV,1991.

Bedknobs and Broomsticks. Dir. Robert Stevenson. Walt Disney Productions, 1971.

Beetlejuice. Dir. Tim Burton. Warner Brothers, Geffen Pictures, 1988.

Ben-Hur. Dir. Fred Niblo. MGM, 1925.

Ben-Hur. Dir. William Wyler. MGM, 1959.

Benji. Dir. Joe Camp. Mulberry Square, 1974.

Bicycle Thief, The [*Ladri di Biciclette*]. Dir. Vittorio De Sica. Mayer, Burstyn, 1948.

Big. Dir. Penny Marshall. 20th Century Fox, 1988.

Big Jim McLain. Dir. Edward Ludwig. Wayne-Fellows Productions, 1952.

Birth Control. Dir. Margaret Sanger. The Message Photoplay Corp., B.S. Moss Motion Picture Company, 1917.

Birth of a Nation, The. Dir. D. W. Griffith. David W. Griffith Corp., Epoch Producing Corp., 1915.

Black Stallion, The. Dir. Carroll Ballard. United Artists, 1979.

Blank Check. Dir. Rupert Wainwright. Walt Disney Productions, 1994.

Blood of the Children, The. Dir. Henry MacRae. Universal Film Manufacturing Company, 1915.

Bluebeard [*Barbe Bleue*]. Dir. Georges Méliès. 1901.

Bon Voyage, Charlie Brown. Dir. Bill Melendez. Paramount, 1980.

Born Free. Dir. James Hill. Columbia, 1966.

Boys N the Hood. Dir. John Singleton. Columbia, 1996.

Boys Town. Dir. Norman Taurog. MGM, 1938.

Breakfast Club, The. Dir. John Hughes. Universal, 1985.

Breaking Away. Dir. Peter Yates. Fox, 1979.

Bridge Over the River Kwai, The. Dir. David Lean. Columbia, Horizon Films, 1957.

Brigadoon. Dir. Vincente Minnelli. MGM, 1954.

Bright Eyes. Dir. David Butler. Perf. Shirley Temple. Fox, 1934.

Brighton Rock. Dir. John Boulting. Boulting Brothers (UK), 1947.

Broken Blossoms. Dir. D. W. Griffith. D.W. Griffith Productions, 1919.

Browning Version, The. Dir. Anthony Asquith. Rank (UK), 1951.

Bug's Life, A. Dir. John Lasseter and Andrew Stanton. Walt Disney Prod., Pixar Animation Studios, 1998.

Bugsy Malone. Dir. Alan Parker. Paramount, 1976.

Burnt by the Sun [*Utomlyonnye Solntsem*]. Dir. Nikita Mikhalkov. Camera One, Sony Pictures Classics, Studio Trite, 1994.

Butch Cassidy and the Sundance Kid. Dir. George Roy Hill. 20th Century Fox, 1969.

Cabiria. Dir. Giovanni Pastrone. Italia Film, 1914.

Call of the Wild. Dir. William Wellman. 20th Century Pictures, 1935.

Can-Can. Dir. Walter Lang. 20th Century Fox, Suffolk-Cummings, 1960.

Captain January. Dir. David Butler. Perf. Shirley Temple. 20th Century Fox, 1936.

Captains Courageous. Dir. Victor Fleming. Perf. Freddie Bartholomew. MGM, 1937.

Carolina. Dir. Henry King. Perf. Shirley Temple. Fox Film Corporation, 1933.

Carousel. Dir. Henry King. 20th Century Fox, 1956.

Carrie. Dir. Brian De Palma. Perf. John Travolta. United Artists, 1976.

Carrie 2: The Rage. Katt Shea. United Artists, Red Bank Films, 1999.

Cement Garden, The. Dir. Andrew Birkin. Zweites Deutsches Fernsehen, Laurentic Film Productions, 1993.

Champ, The. Dir. King Vidor. Perf. Jackie Cooper. MGM, 1931.

Charlotte's Web. Dir. Charles A. Nichols & Iwao Takamoto. Paramount, 1973.

Charly Chan's Chance. Dir. John G. Blystone. Fox Film Corporation, 1932.

Child Is Waiting, A. Dir. John Cassavetes. United Artists, 1963.

Children Who Labor. Dir. Ashley Miller. Edison, 1912.

Children Pay, The. Dir. Lloyd Ingraham. Perf. Lillian Gish and Violet Wilkie. Fine Arts Film Co., 1916.

Children's Hour, The. Dir. William Wyler. United Artists, Mirisch Company, 1961.

Child's Play. Dir. Tom Holland. United Artists, 1988.

Chitty Chitty Bang Bang. Dir. Ken Hughes. 1968.

City of Lost Children [*Cité des Enfants Perdus, La*]. Dir. Marc Caro and Jean-Pierre Jeunet. Le Studio Canal, Lumière Pictures, 1995.

Children of Heaven [*Bacheha-Ye Aseman*]. Dir. Majid Majidi. Institute for the Intellectual Development of Children and Young Adults, Iran 1997.

Christmas Carol, A. Dir. Edward L. Marin. MGM, 1938.

Cinderella [*Cendrillon*]. Dir. Georges Méliès. Star, 1899.

Cinderella [*Cendrillon*]. Dir. Georges Méliès. 1912.

Cinderella. Dir. James Kirkwood. Perf. Mary Pickford. 1914. Famous Players Film Company, 1914.

Cinderella. Dir. Wilfred Jackson, Hamilton Luske, and Clyde Geronimi. Walt Disney Productions, 1950.

Cinema Paradiso [*Nuovo Cinema Paradiso*]. Dir. Giuseppe Tornatore. Perf. Salvatore Cascio. Ariane, Cristaldifilm, TFI, RAI-TRE, Forum (Italy/France), 1988.

Citizen Kane. Dir. Orson Welles. RKO Productions, 1941.

Clash of the Titans. Dir. Desmond Davis. MGM, Titan Productions, 1981.

Clash of the Wolves. Dir. Noel Smith. Warner Brothers, 1925.

Close Encounters of the Third Kind. Dir. Steven Spielberg. Columbia, EMI Films UK), 1977.

Closet Land. Dir. Radha Bharadwaj. Universal, 1991.

Color of God. (Rang-e Khoda). Dir. Majid Majidi. Varahonar Company, 1999.

Comin' Thro the Rye. Dir. Cecil M. Hepworth. Hepworth, 1922.

Congo. Dir. Frank Marshall. Paramount, Kennedy/Marshall, 1995.

Connecticut Yankee in King Arthur's Court, A. Dir. Tay Garnett. MCA, 1949.
Cowboys, The. Dir. Mark Rydell. Warner Brothers, 1972.
Cry Freedom. Dir. Richard Attenborough. Universal, 1987.
Cry of the Children. Dir. George Nichols. Perf. Marie Eline. Thanhouser Film Corp., 1912.
Curly Sue. Dir. John Hughes. Warner Brothers, 1991.
Dangerous Minds. Dir. John N. Smith. Via Rosa Prod., Buena Vista, Don Simpson-Jerry Bruckheimer Films, Hollywood Pictures, 1995.
Dark Crystal, The. Dir. Frank Oz & Jim Henson. Universal, Jim Henson Prod., 1982.
David Copperfield. Dir. David Selznick. MGM, 1935.
Dead Calm. Dir. Phillip Noyce. Kennedy Miller Productions, 1989.
Dead End. Dir. William Wyler. United Artists, 1937.
Deep, The. Dir. Peter Yates. Peter Guber and George Justin, 1977.
Deep Impact. Dir. Mimi Leder. Paramount, DreamWorks SKG, 1998.
Defiant Ones, The. Dir. Stanley Kramer. Lomitas Prod., Curtleigh Prod., 1958.
Dennis the Menace. Dir. Nick Castle. Warner Brothers, Hughes, 1993.
Diary of Anne Frank, The. Dir. George Stevens. 20th Century Fox, 1959.
Doctor Dolittle. Dir. Richard Fleischer. 20th Century Fox, 1967.
Doctor Dolittle. Dir. Betty Thomas. 20th Century Fox, Joseph M. Singer Ent., Davis Ent., 1998.
Dog Star Man. Dir. Stan Brakhage. Stan Brakhage, 1964.
Don't Look Now. Dir. Nicolas Roeg. Casey, Eldorado (UK/Italy), 1973.
Double Indemnity. Dir. Billy Wilder. Paramount, 1944.
Dresser, The. Dir. Peter Yates. World Film Services, Goldcrest Films, ltd., 1983.
Dumbo. Dir. Ben Sharpsteen, Norman Ferguson, Wilfred Jackson, Bill Roberts, Jack Kinney, and Sam Armstrong. Walt Disney Productions, 1941.
E.T. the Extra-Terrestrial. Dir. Steven Spielberg. Universal, 1982.
Easy Rider. Dir. Dennis Hopper. Columbia, Pando, Raybert Prod., 1969.
Edward Scissorhands. Dir. Tim Burton. 20th Century Fox, 1990.
Elephant Boy. Dir. Robert J. Flaherty and Zoltan Korda. Perf. Sabu. London Film Prod., 1937.
Empire of the Sun. Dir. Steven Spielberg. Warner Brothers, Amblin, 1987.
Empire Strikes Back, The. Dir. Irvin Kershner. Lucasfilm Ltd., 1980.
Encino Man. Dir. Les Mayfield. Encino Man Prod., Hollywood Pictures, 1992.
Enemy of the State. Dir. Tony Scott. Scott Free Prod., Jerry Bruckheimer Films, Touchstone Pictures, 1998.
Enoch Arden. Dir. Christy Cabanne. Majestic Motion Picture Company, 1915.
Ever After: A Cinderella Story. Dir. Andy Tennant. 20th Century Fox, 1998.
Every Sunday. Dir. Felix E. Feist. Perf. Deanna Durbin & Judy Garland. MGM, 1936.
Exorcist, The. Dir. William Friedkin. Warner Brothers, 1973.
Exploits of Elaine. Dir. Louis J. Gasnier & George B. Seitz. Wharton, Pathé, 1914.

Face-Off. Dir. John Woo. Perf. Dominique Swain. Douglas, Reuther Productions, Constellation Films, WCG, 1997.

Fallen Idol, The. Dir. Carol Reed. London Films (UK), 1948.

Fanny and Alexander. Dir. Ingmar Bergman. Svenska Film, Gaumont (UK), 1982.

Fantasia. Dir. Samuel Armstrong, James Algar, and Bill Roberts. Walt Disney Productions, 1940.

Fantomas. Dir. Louis Fevillade. 1913.

Fat Man and Little Boy. Dir. Roland Joffé. Paramount, 1989.

Ferngully: The Last Rainforest. Dir. Bill Kroyer. FAI Films, 1992.

Ferris Bueller's Day Off. Dir. John Hughes. Paramount, 1986.

Find Your Man. Dir. Malcolm St. Clair. Warner Brothers, 1924.

5,000 Fingers of Dr. T, The. Dir. Roy Rowland. Columbia, 1953.

Five Weeks in a Balloon. Dir. Irwin Allen. 20th Century Fox, 1962.

Flight of the Innocent [*Corsa dell'innocente, La*]. Carlo Carlei. Cristaldifilm, Fandango (It), 1992.

Fly Away Home. Dir. Carroll Ballard. Branti Film Prod., Sandollar Productions, 1996.

Forbidden Games [*Les Jeux Interdits*]. Dir. René Clément. Silver, (Fr), 1952.

Forrest Gump. Dir. Robert Zemeckis. Tisch Company, 1994.

Fox and the Hound, The. Dir. Ted Berman & Richard Rich. Walt Disney Prod., 1981.

400 Blows, The [*Quatre cents coups, Les*]. Dir. François Truffaut. Les Films du Carrosse, SEDIF, 1959.

Frankenstein. Dir. James Whale. Universal, 1931.

Fred Ott's Sneeze. Dir. William K.L. Dickson. Edison, 1894.

Free Willy. Dir. Simon Wincer. Donner-Shuler-Donner, Le Studio Canal Plus, 1993.

Freeway. Dir. Mathew Bright. Davis Films, Illusion Ent., Kushner-Locke Prod., 1996.

From Here to Eternity. Dir. Fred Zinneman. Columbia, 1953.

From the Mixed-Up Files of Mrs. Basil E. Frankweiler. Dir. Fielder Cook. Cinema 5, 1973. 1973.

Funny Girl. Dir. William Wyler. Columbia, 1968.

Germany Year Zero [Germania Anno Zero]. Dir. Roberto Rossellini. Tevere Film (It), Produzione Salvo D'Angelo (It), 1947.

Ghosts of Mississippi. Dir. Rob Reiner. Columbia, Castle Rock Entertainment, 1996.

Go-Between, The. Dir. Joseph Losey. EMI Films Ltd (UK), MGM, 1971.

Godless Girl, The. Dir. Cecil B. DeMille. Cecil B. DeMille Prod., 1929.

Gods Must Be Crazy, The. Dir. James Uys. Mimosa, 1980.

Godzilla. Dir. Roland Emmerich. TriStar, Fried Films, Centropolis, Independent, 1998.

GoldenEye. Dir. Martin Campbell. United Artists, Danjaq Prod., Eon, MGM, 1995.
Gone with the Wind. Dir. Victor Fleming. Selznick International Pictures, 1939.
Good Son, The. Dir. Joseph Rubin. Perf. Macaulay Culkin & Elijah Wood. 20th Century Fox, 1993.
Goonies, The. Dir. Richard Donner. Warner, Amblin, 1985.
Great Dictator, The. Dir. Charles Chaplin. United Artists, 1940.
Great Muppet Caper, The. Dir. Jim Henson. UA., Henson Ass., ITC (UK), 1981.
Great Train Robbery, The. Dir. Edwin S. Porter. Edison Manufacturing Co., 1903.
Gremlins, The. Dir. Joe Dante. Amblin Entertainment, Warner Brothers, 1984.
Guess Who's Coming to Dinner. Dir. Stanley Kramer. Columbia Pictures, 1967.
Gulliver's Travels [*Novil Gulliver*]. Dir. Alexander Prushko. 1935.
Gulliver's Travels. Dir. Willard Bowsky and Orestes Calpini. Fleischer Studios, 1939.
Gunga Din. Dir. George Stevens. RKO Radio Pictures, 1939.
Hamlet. Dir. Laurence Olivier. Two Cities Films Ltd., Pilgrim Pictures, 1948.
Hand That Rocks the Cradle, The. Dir. Phillip Smalley and Lois Weber. Universal Manufacturing Company, Universal Pictures, 1917.
Hansel and Gretel: An Appalachian Version. Dir. Tom Davenport. Davenport Films, 1975.
Hard Day's Night, A. Dir. Richard Lester. United Artists, 1964.
Harriet the Spy. Dir. Bronwen Hughes. Paramount, 1996.
Heart is a Lonely Hunter, The. Dir. Robert Ellis Miller. Warner Brothers, 1968.
Heat and Dust. Dir. James Ivory. Merchant-Ivory Productions, 1982.
Heidi. Dir. Allan Dwan. 20th Century Fox, 1937.
Heidi. Dir. Luigi Comencini. United Artists, Schweizer Fernsehen, 1952.
Heidi. Dir. Werner Jacobs. Warners–7 Arts, 1968.
Help! Dir. Richard Lester. Walter Shenson Films, Subafilms, 1965.
Hercules. Dir. Ron Clements and John Musker. Walt Disney Productions, 1997.
Hero Ain't Nothing but a Sandwich, A. Dir. Ralph Nelson. 1978.
High Noon. Dir. Fred Zinneman. Stanley Kramer Productions, 1952.
His Last Twelve Hours [É piu facile che un cammello]. Dir. Luigi Zampa. Pathé Cinéma, 1950.
Hitler's Children. Dir. Dir. Edward Dmytryk. RKO Radio Pictures, 1942.
Hobbit, The. Dir. Jules Bass and Arthur Rankin Jr. Rankin-Bass Prod., 1978.
Home Alone. Dir. Chris Columbus. 20th Century Fox, 1990.
Home Alone 2: Lost in New York. Dir. Chris Columbus. 20th Century Fox, 1992.
Honey, I Shrunk the Kids. Dir. Joe Johnston. Walt Disney Productions, 1989.
Hook. Dir. Steven Spielberg. Hook Productions, Amblin, 1991.
Hope and Glory. Dir. John Boorman. Columbia, Goldcrest Film, Nelson Ent., 1987.
HouseSitter. Dir. Frank Oz. Universal Pictures, Imagine Films Entertainment, 1992.

How Green Was My Valley. Dir. John Ford. Fox, 1941.
Hud. Dir. Martin Ritt. Paramount, 1963.
Hunchback of Notre Dame, The. Dir. Wallace Worsley. Universal, 1923.
Hunchback of Notre Dame, The. Dir. William Dieterle. RKO Radio Pictures Inc., 1939.
Hunchback of Notre Dame, The. Dir. Gary Trousdale and Kirk Wise. Walt Disney Productions, 1996.
I Am the Cheese. Dr. Robert Jiras. Almi Films, 1983.
I Still Know What You Did Last Summer. Dir. Danny Cannon. Mandalay Entertainment, 1998.
Icicle Thief, The [*Ladri di Saponette*]. Dir. Maurizio Nichetti. Reteitalia, Bambu, 1989.
Idle Hands. Dir. Rodman Flender. TriStar Pictures, Columbia Pictures, 1999.
If. . . Dir. Lindsay Anderson. Memorial (UK), 1968.
I'm Gonna Git You Sucker. Dir. Keenen Ivory Wayans. MGM, Ivory Way Prod., 1988.
Impossible Years, The. Dir. Michael Gordon. Marten, MGM, 1968.
In and Out. Dir. Frank Oz. Paramount Pic., Scott Rudin Prod., Spelling Films, 1997.
In Search of the Castaways. Dir. Robert Stevenson. Perf. Hayley Mills. Walt Disney Productions, 1962.
Incredibly True Adventures of Two Girls in Love, The. Dir. Maria Maggenti. Fineline Features, Smash Pictures, 1995.
Indiana Jones and the Temple of Doom. Dir. Steven Spielberg. Lucasfilm Ltd., Paramount, 1984.
Indian in the Cupboard, The. Dir. Frank Oz. Scholastic Productions, Kennedy Marshall, Reliable, Columbia, Paramount, 1995.
Innocents, The. Dir. Jack Clayton. Fox/Achilles (US/UK), 1961.
Intolerance. Dir. D. W. Griffith. Triangle Prod., Wark Producing Co., 1916.
Invisible Man, The. Dir. Carl Laemmle Jr. Universal, 1933.
Island of the Blue Dolphins. Dir. James B. Clark. Universal, 1964.
It Happens Every Spring. Dir. Lloyd Bacon. 20th Century Fox, 1949.
Ivanhoe. Dir. Richard Thorpe. MGM (UK), 1952.
Ivan's Childhood [*Ivanovo Detstvo*]. Dir. Andrei Tarkovsky. Mosfilm (USSR), 1962.
Jacob's Ladder. Dir. Adrian Lyne. Carolco (US), 1990.
Jack. Dir. Francis Coppola. Great Oaks, American Zoetrope, Hollywood Pictures, 1996.
Jackie Robinson Story, The. Dir. Alfred E. Green. MGM, 1950.
Jacquot. Dir. Agnes Varda. Cine-Tamaris, 1991.
James and the Giant Peach. Dir. Henry Selick. Walt Disney Productions, 1996.
Jazz Singer, The. Dir. Alan Crosland. Warner Brothers, 1927.
Jim Thorpe: All American. Dir. Michael Curtiz. Warner Brothers, 1951.
Jory. Dir. Jorge Fons. Cinematografica Marco Polo, Minsky-Kirschner, 1972.
Jumanji. Dir. Joe Johnston. Interscope Communications, Tristar, 1995.

Jungle Book, The. Dir. Wolfgang Reitherman. Walt Disney Productions, 1967.
Jurassic Park. Dir. Steven Spielberg. Universal, Amblin, 1993.
Just Pals. Dir. John Ford. Fox Film Corporation, 1920.
Karate Kid, The. Dir. John Avildsen. Columbia, 1984.
Kid, The. Dir. Charlie Chaplin. First National, 1921.
Kid for Two Farthings, A. Dir. Carol Reed. London Film Productions, 1955.
Kid From Left Field, The. Dir. Harmon Jones. 20th Century Fox, 1953.
Kid in Africa. Dir. Jack Hays. Educational Pictures, 1932.
Kids. Dir. Larry Clark. 1995. Independent Pictures, The Guys Upstairs, 1995.
Killing of Sister George, The. Dir. Robert Aldrich. Palomar Pictures, 1968.
Kim. Dir. Victor Saville. MGM, 1950.
Kindergarten Cop. Dir. Ivan Reitman. Universal, Imagine Ent., 1990.
Kingdom of the Fairies [Royaume des Fées, Le]. Dir. George Méliès. 1903.
King Kong. Dir. Merian C. Cooper and Ernest B. Schoedsack. Radio Pictures, 1933.
Kiss for Corliss, A. Dir. Richard Wallace. United Artists, 1949.
Land Before Time, The. Dir. Don Bluth. Sullivan-Bluth, Amblin, 1988.
Lassie Come Home. Dir. Fred M. Wilcox. MGM, 1943.
Last Action Hero. Dir. John McTiernan. Steve Roth Productions, Columbia, 1993.
Lawrence of Arabia. Dir. David Lean. Columbia, Horizon Pictures, 1962.
Learning Tree, The. Dir. Gordon Parks. Warners-7 Arts, 1969.
Lethal Weapon. Dir. Richard Donner. Warner Brothers, 1987.
Liar, Liar. Dir. Tom Shadyac. Perf. Justin Cooper. Imagine Entertainment, 1997.
Life is Beautiful. Dir. Roberto Benigni. Melampo Cinematografica (It), 1997.
Life of an American Fireman, The. Dir. Edwin S. Porter. Edison, 1903.
Life of Brian, The. Dir. Terry Jones. Handmade Films Ltd, 1979.
Lion, the Witch, and the Wardrobe, The. Dir. Bill Melendez. Bill Melendez Productions, 1979.
Lion King, The. Dir. Roger Allers and Rob Minkoff. Walt Disney Productions. 1994.
Little Colonel, The. Dir. David Butler. Perf. Shirley Temple. Fox, 1934.
Little Golden Key, The. Dir. Alexander Prushko. Amkino Corporation, 1939.
Little Lord Fauntleroy. Dir. Alfred E. Green and Jack Pickford, Mary Pickford Company, 1921.
Little Mermaid, The. Dir. John Musker and Ron Clements. Walt Disney Productions, Silver Screen Partners IV, 1989.
Little Rascals, The. Dir. Penelope Spheeris. Universal, Amblin, 1994.
Little Red Riding Hood [*Le Petit Chaperon Rouge*]. Dir. George Méliès. Star Film, 1901.
Little Robinson Crusoe. Dr. Edward F. Cline. MGM, Jackie Coogan Productions, 1924.
Little Shop of Horrors. Dir. Frank Oz. The Geffen Company, 1986.
Lolita. Dir. Adrian Lyne. Guild, Pathé, 1997.

Loneliness of the Long Distance Runner. Dir. Tony Richardson. British Lion, 1962.

Lonely Villa, The. Dir. D. W. Griffith. Biograph, 1909.

Longest Day, The. Dir. Ken Annakin and Andrew Marton. 20th Century Fox, 1962.

Look Back in Anger. Dir. Tony Richardson. Warner Brothers, 1958.

Lord of the Flies. Dir. Peter Brook. Two Arts Ltd., 1963.

Los Olvidados. Dir. Luis Bunuel. Tepeyac (Mex), 1950.

Lost Child, The. Dir. Wallace McCutcheon. Lubin Manufacturing Company, 1905.

Madeline. Dir. Daisy von Scherler Mayer. TriStar, Jaffilms, Madeline Films, 1998.

Mad Max. Dir. George Miller. Kennedy Miller Prod., 1979.

Maltese Falcon, The. John Huston. First National, Warner Brothers, 1941.

Man for all Seasons, A. Dir. Fred Zinneman. Alma-Kino-Filmverleih, 1966.

Manhattan Project, The. Dir. Marshall Brickman. Weintraub Ent., Gladden Ent., 1986.

Mary Poppins. Dir. Robert Stevenson. Walt Disney Productions, 1964.

Mask, The. Dir. Chuck Russell. New Line, Dark Horse Ent., 1994.

Matilda. Dir. Danny DeVito. TriStar, Jersey Films, 1996.

Matrix, The. Dir. Andy and Larry Wachowski. Village Roadshow, Groucho II Film Partnership, Silver Pictures, 1999.

Me and Mama Mia [*Mig og Mama Mia*]. Dir. Erik Clausen. Danish Film Inst., 1989.

Mighty Ducks, the Movie: The First Face Off. Dir. Joe Barruso and Doug Murphy. Walt Disney Productions, 1997.

Mighty Joe Young. Dir. Ron Underwood. Walt Disney Productions, RKO Radio, 1998.

Milk Money. Dir. Richard Benjamin. Paramount, Kennedy/Marshall Co., 1994.

Mimic. Dir. Guillermo del Toro. Dimension Films, 1997.

Miracle Worker, The. Dir. Arthur Penn. United Artists, 1962.

Mission Impossible. Dir. Brian De Palma. CW Productions, Paramount (UK), 1996.

Mist in the Valley. Dir. Cecil M. Hepworth, Hepworth, 1922.

Money Train. Dir. Joseph Ruben. Columbia, Peters Ent., 1995.

Mouchette. Dir. Robert Bresson. Argos Films, Parc Film (Fr), 1966.

Mouse Hunt. Dir. Gore Verbinski. DreamWorks SKG, 1997.

Mr. Smith Goes to Washington. Dir. Frank Capra. Columbia, 1939.

Mrs. Miniver. Dir. William Wyler. MGM, 1942.

Mrs. Wiggs of the Cabbage Patch. Dir. Norman Taurog. Universal, Paramount, 1934.

Mulan. Dir. Tony Bancroft and Barry Cook. Walt Disney Productions, 1998.

Muppet Movie, The. Dir. James Frowley. Henson Ass., ITC (UK), 1979.

Muppet Treasure Island. Dir. Brian Henson. Jim Henson Prod., Walt Disney Pr., 1996.
Muppets Take Manhattan. Dir. Frank Oz. TriStar, 1984.
Murmur of the Heart. Dir. Louis Malle. Vides-Film (It), Franz Seitz, 1971.
Mutiny on the Bounty. Dir. Lewis Milestone. MGM, Arcola Pictures, 1962.
My Fair Lady. Dir. George Cukor. Warner Brothers, 1964.
My Life as a Dog [*Mitt Liv som Hund*]. Dir. Lasse Hallström. Film Teknik, Svensk Film, 1985.
My Son, My Son. Dir. Charles Vidor. United Artists, 1940.
Mysterious Island, The. Dir. Cy Endfield. Columbia, 1961.
Naked Gun, The. Dir. David Zucker. Paramount, 1988.
Naked Gun 2 1/2, The. Dir. David Zucker. Paramount, 1991.
National Velvet. Dir. Clarence Brown. MGM, 1944.
Natural Born Killers. Dir. Oliver Stone. Warner Bros., Ixtlan Prod., J. D. Prod., 1994.
Never Been Kissed. Dir. Raja Gosnell. Never Been Kissed Prod., Bushwood Pictures, Flower Films, 1999.
Neverending Story, The. Dir. Wolfgang Petersen. Warner Brothers, 1984.
Night of the Hunter. Dir. Charles Laughton. United Artists, 1955.
Night of the Living Dead. Dir. George Romero. Image Ten, 1968.
Night of the Shooting Stars [*Notte di San Lorenzo, La*]. Dir. Paolo Taviani and Vittorio Taviani. Ager Cinematografica, Radiotelevisione Italiana (RAI), 1982.
Nightmare Before Christmas, The. Dir. Henry Selick. Touchstone Pictures, 1993.
1900. Dir. Bernardo Bertolucci. Artemis Productions, 1976.
Norma Rae. Dir. Martin Ritt. 20th Century Fox, 1979.
North. Dir. Rob Reiner. Castle Rock Ent., Columbia, New Line Cinema, 1994.
Oliver! Dir. Carol Reed. Warwick, Romulus (UK), 1968.
Oliver Twist. Dir. Frank Lloyd. Associated First National Pictures, 1922.
On the Waterfront. Dir. Eli Kazan. Columbia, Horizon, 1954.
One Hundred and One Dalmations. Dir. Clyde Geronimi and Hamilton Luske. Walt Disney Productions, 1961.
One Hundred Men and a Girl. Dir. Henry Koster. Universal, 1937.
Open City [*Roma Città Aperta*]. Dir. Roberto Rossellini. Excelsa, 1945.
Orphans of the Storm. Dir. D.W. Griffith. D.W. Griffith Productions, 1921.
Ossessione. Dir. Luchino Visconti Industrie Cinematografiche Italiane, 1942.
Our Man in Havana. Dir. Carol Reed. Kingsmead (UK), 1959.
Out of Africa. Dir. Sydney Pollack. Universal Pictures, 1985.
Pagemaster, The. Dir. Maurice Hunt and Joe Johnston. 20th Century Fox, 1994.
Paisan [Paisà]. Dir. Roberto Rossellini. 1946.
Paper Moon. Dir. Peter Nogdanovich. Paramount, 1973.
Paths of Glory. Dir. Stanley Kubrick. United Artists, Bryna Prod., 1957.
Parent Trap, The. Dir. David Swift. Walt Disney Productions, 1961.

Parents. Dir. Bob Balaban. Vestron, Great American Films, 1989.
Passage to India, A. Dir. David Lean. EMI (UK), HBO, 1984.
Pather Panchali. Dir. Satyajit Ray. Government of West Bengal, 1955.
Patriot Games. Dir. Phillip Noyce. Perf. Thora Birch. Paramount, 1992.
Paulie. Dir. John Roberts. DreamWorks SKG, Mutual, 1998.
Pee-Wee's Big Adventure. Dir. Tim Burton. Aspen, Shapiro, 1985.
Pelle the Conqueror. [*Pelle Erobreren*]. Dir. Bille August. Svensk (SFI), Det Danske Film., Svenske Film (SF), 1987.
Peppermint Soda. Dir. Diane Kurys. Alma, Alexandre, Gaumont (Fr), 1977.
Peter Pan. Dir. Hamilton Luske, Clyde Geronimi, and Wilfred Jackson. Walt Disney Productions, 1953.
Pete's Dragon. Dir. Don Chaffey. Walt Disney Productions, 1977.
Phantom Tollbooth, The. Dir. Chuck Jones and Dave Monaham. MGM, 1969.
Piano, The. Dir. Jane Campion. Jane Campion Productions. (NZ), 1993.
Picnic at Hanging Rock. Dir. Peter Weir. Australian Film Co., South Australian Film Corp., Picnic Productions Pty Ltd., 1975.
Pink Floyd: The Wall. Dir. Alan Parker and Gerald Scarfe. Goldcrest Films Ltd, MGM, Tin Blue, 1982.
Pinocchio. Dir. Cesare Antamaro. 1911.
Pinocchio. Dir. Ben Sharpsteen and Hamilton Luske. Walt Disney Productions, 1940.
Pippi Longstocking. Dir. Bill Giggie and Michael Schaack. Trickompany, BetaFilm GmbH, Nelvana Ltd., Iduna Films, Svensk, Telefilm Canada, 1997.
Pixote. Dir. Hector Babenco. Perf. Fernando Ramos da Silva. Embrafilm, 1981.
Pocahontas. Dir. Mike Gabriel and Eric Goldberg. Walt Disney Productions, 1995.
Polish Wedding. Dir. Theresa Connelly. Addis Wechsler Pictures, Lakeshore Ent., 1998.
Pollyanna. Dir. Paul Powell. Perf. Mary Picford. United Artists, Mary Pickford Co., 1920.
Pollyanna. Dir. David Swift. Perf. Hayley Mills. Walt Disney Productions, 1960.
Ponette. Dir. Jacques Doillon. Les Films Alain Sarde, Rhone-Alpes Cinema, BAC Films, 1996.
Pound. Dir. Robert Downey Sr. United Artists, 1970.
Power and the Glory, The. Dir. William K. Howard. Fox Film Corporation, 1933.
Pretty Baby. Dir. Louis Malle. Perf. Brooke Shields. Paramount, 1978.
Pretty in Pink. Dir. Howard Deutch. Paramount, 1986.
Prime of Miss Jean Brodie, The. Dir. Ronald Neame. 20th Century Fox, 1969.
Prince of Egypt. Brenda Chapman and Steve Hickner. DreamWorks SKG, 1998.
Princess Bride, The. Dir. Rob Reiner. The Princess Bride Ltd., Buttercup Films Ltd., Act III Comm., 1987.
Prisoner of Zenda, The. Dir. John Cromwell. United Artists, 1937.
Psycho. Dir. Alfred Hitchcock. Shamley Prod., 1960.

Pufnstuf. Dir. Hollingsworth Morse. Universal Pictures, 1970.
Purple Rose of Cairo, The. Dir. Woody Allen. Orion, 1985.
Puss 'n Boots. Dir. Ferdinand Zecca. 1903.
Quiet American, The. Dir. Joseph L. Mankiewicz. Figaro Films, 1958.
Quo Vadis. Dir. Enrico Guazzoni. Kleine-cines, 1912.
Radio Days. Dir. Woody Allen. Orion, 1987.
Radio Flyer. Dir. Richard Donner. Columbia, 1992.
Rafferty and the Gold Dust Twins. Dir. Dick Richards. 1975.
Raiders of the Lost Ark, The. Dir. Steven Spielberg. Lucasfilm Ltd., Paramount, 1981.
Railway Children, The. Dir. Lionel Jeffries. Universal, 1970.
Rambo. Dir. Max Moswitzer. Carolco, 1987.
Ransom. Dir. Ron Howard. Ransom Prod., Segue Prod., Imagine Ent., Touchstone Pictures, 1996.
Red Balloon, The. Dir. Albert Lamorisse. Columbia, 1956.
Red Desert, The. [Deserto rosso, Il]. Dir. Michelangelo Antonioni. Film Due Mila, 1964.
Reivers, The. Dir. Mark Rydell. National General, 1969.
Relic, The. Dir. Peter Hyams. BBC (UK), Universal, Pacific, Paramount, 1997.
Repossessed. Dir. Bob Logan. 1990.
Rescued by Rover. Dir. Lewin Fitzhamon and Cecil M. Hepworth. Cecil M. Hepworth, 1905.
Retreat Hell. Dir. Joseph Lewis. Warner Brothers, 1952.
Return of the Jedi. Dir. Richard Marquand. Lucasfilm Ltd., 1983.
Rice/Irwin Kiss, The. Dir. Edison, Thomas. Edison, S. Lubin, 1896.
Richie Rich. Dir. Donald Petrie. Warner Brothers, Davis Ent., Silver, 1994.
River's Edge. Dir. Tim Hunter. Hemdale (U.S), 1987.
Robin and Marian. Dir. Richard Lester. Columbia, 1976.
Robocop. Dir. Paul Verhoeven. Orion, 1987.
Romeo and Juliet. Dir. George Cukor. MGM, 1936.
Romeo and Juliet. Dir. Franco Zeffirelli, Paramount, 1968.
Rugrats Movie, The. Dir. Igor Koralyov and Norton Virgien. Nickelodeon, Paramount, Klasky-Csupo, 1998.
Rosemary's Baby. Dir. Roman Polanski. Paramount, 1968.
Rumble Fish. Dir. Francis Ford Coppola. Zoetrope Studios, Hotweather Films, 1983.
Rush Hour. Dir. Brett Ratner. New Line Cinema, 1998.
Salaam Bombay. Dir. Mira Nair. Perf. Shafiq Syed. Mirabai (India), 1988.
Saludos Amigos. Dir. Norman Ferguson and Wilfred Jackson. Walt Disney Productions, 1943.
Saturday Night Fever. Dir. John Badham. RSO, Paramount, 1977.
Scarface. Dir. Howard Hawks and Richard Rosson. United Artists, 1932.
Scream. Dir. Wes Craven. Woods Ent., Dimension Films, 1996.
Scrooge. Dir. Walter R. Booth. R. W. Paul, 1901.

Search, The. Dir. Fred Zinnemann. Prasens (US), 1948.

Searching for Bobby Fischer. Dir. Steven Zaillian. Paramount, Mirage Prod., 1993.

Secret Garden, The. Dir. Fred M. Wilcox. MGM, 1949.

Secret Garden, The. Dir. Agnieszka Holland. Warner Brothers, 1993.

Secret Kingdom, The. Dir. David Schmoeller. Kusher-Locke Productions, 1998.

Secret of NIMH, The. Dir. Don Bluth. Mrs. Brisby Ltd., 1982.

Secret of Roan Inish, The. Dir. John Sayles. Skerry Movies Corp., Peter Newman Productions, 1995.

Seven Deadly Sins, The. [*Sept Péchés Capitaux, Les*]. Dr. Yves Allegret and Claude Autant-Lara. Arlan, 1952.

Seventh Seal, The. Dir. Ingmar Bergman. Svensk, 1957.

Shaft. Dir. Gordon Parks. Shaft Productions, MGM, 1971.

Shane. Dir. George Stevens. Paramount, 1953.

She. Dir. Robert Day. MGM, 1965.

She's All That. Dir. Robert Iscove. Film Colony, All that Productions, Miramax, 1999.

Shoeshine [*Sciuscia*]. Dir. Vittoria De Sica. Societa Cooperativa, 1946.

Six Weeks. Skippy. Dir. Norman Taurog. Perf. Jackie Cooper. Paramount, 1931.

Silkwood. Dir. Mike Nicols. 20th Century Fox, ABC Motion Pictures, 1983.

Small Change [*L'Argent de Poche*]. Dir. Francois Truffaut. Carrosse, Artistes, 1976.

Small Soldiers. Dir. Joe Dante. United Pictures, DreamWorks SKG, 1998.

Smilla's Sense of Snow. Dir. Bille August. Greenland Film Prod., Smilla Films A-S, Constantin Film Prod., 1997.

Snow White and the Seven Dwarfs. Dir. David Hand. Walt Disney Productions, 1937.

So Dear to My Heart. Dir. Harold D. Schuster. Walt Disney Productions, 1949.

Something Wicked This Way Comes. Dir. Jack Clayton. Walt Disney Productions, 1983.

Son of Mary. Dir. Hamid Jebeli. 1999.

Song of the South. Dir. Harve Foster and Wilfred Jackson. Perf. Bobby Driscoll. Walt Disney Productions, 1946.

Sooky. Dir. Norman Taurog. Paramount, 1931.

Sophie's Choice. Dir. Alan Pakula. Incorporated Television Company (ITC), 1982.

Sound of Trumpets, The. Dir. Ermanno Olmi. Titanus Produzione, 24 Horses, Titanus, 1961.

Sounder. Dir. Martin Ritt. Radnitz, Mattel, 1972.

Sounder Part 2. Dir. William A. Graham. 1976.

South Park: Bigger, Longer, and Uncut. Dir. Trey Parker. Comedy Partners, Celluloid Studios, Comedy Central, 1999.

Sooky. Dir. Norman Taurog. Paramount, 1931.

Space Jam. Dir. Tony Cervone and Joe Pytka. Warner Bros., Courtside Prod., Northern Lights Ent., 1996.

Sparrows. Dir. William Beaudine. Pickford Corporation, 1926.

Spawn. Dir. Mark A. Z. Dippe. Todd McFarlane Ent., Juno Pix, New Line Cinema, 1997.

Spirit of the Beehive. [*El Espiritu de la Colmena*]. Dir. Victor Erice. Ellas Querejeta (Sp.), 1973.

Stagecoach. Dir. John Ford. Walter Wanger Productions, Inc. 1939.

Stand By Me. Dir. Rob Reiner. Columbia, 1986.

Stand Up and Cheer. Dir. Hamilton MacFadden. Fox Film Corporation, 1934.

Stakeout. Dir. John Badham. Cinderella, Silver Screen Partners, Touchstone, 1987.

Starship Troopers. Dir. Paul Verhoeven. TriStar, Touchstone, Big Bug Pictures, 1997.

Star Wars. Dir. George Lucas. 20th Century Fox, 1977.

Star Wars Episode 1: The Phantom Menace. Dir. George Lucas. Lucasfilm Ltd, 1997.

Steel Helmet, The. Dir. Samuel Fuller. Lippert Pictures Inc., 1951.

Storm Boy. Dir. Henry Safran. South Australian Film Corporation, 1977.

Street Kid [*Gossenkind*]. Dir. Peter Kern. Corazon Film, 1991.

Superfly. Dir. Gordon Parks Jr. Warner Brothers, 1972.

Superman. Dir. Richard Donner. Alexander Salkind, Int. Film Prod., Film Export A.G., 1978.

Swan Princess II: Escape from Castle Mountain, The. Dir. Richard Rich. Animation Studios, Nest Ent., 1997.

Tale of Two Cities, A. Dir. Jack Conway. MGM, 1935.

Tarzan. Dir. Chris Buck II and Kevin Lima. Walt Disney Productions, 1999.

Tarzan the Ape Man. Dir. W. S. Van-Dyke. MGM, 1932.

Taxi Driver. Dir. Martin Scorsese. Bill/Phillips, Columbia, Sony, 1976.

'Teddy' Bears, The. Dir. Edwin S. Porter, 1907.

Teenage Mutant Ninja Turtles. Dir. Steve Barron. Golden Harvest Prod., New Line Cinema, 1990.

Terminator 2: Judgment Day. Dir. James Cameron. Pacific Western, Le Studio Canal Plus, Carolco, 1991.

That Darn Cat. Dir. Robert Stevenson. Walt Disney Productions, 1965.

That Hagen Girl. Dir. Peter Godfrey. Perf. Shirley Temple and Ronald Reagan. Warner Brothers, 1947.

Thelma and Louise. Dir. Ridley Scott. United International Pictures, MGM, Pathé Ent., 1991.

Thief, The [*Vor*]. Dir. Pavel Chukhraj. Stratosphere, 1997.

Third Man, The. Dir. Carol Reed. London Films (UK), 1949.

Three Caballeros, The. Dir. Norman Ferguson, Clyde Geronimi, and Jack Kinney. Walt Disney Productions, 1944.

Three Smart Girls. Dir. Henry Koster. Perf. Deanna Durbin. Universal Pictures, 1936.

Three Worlds of Gulliver, The. Dir. Jack Sher. Columbia, 1960.

Tiller's Six Diamonds. Dir. Cecil M. Hepworth.

Tilly and the Fire Engines. Dir. Cecil M. Hepworth. 1911.

Tilly the Tomboy Goes Boating. Dir. Cecil M. Hepworth. 1910.

Trip to the Moon, A. [*Voyage dans la Lune, Le*]. Dir. Georges Méliès. Star Films, 1902.

Time to Kill, A. Dir. Joel Schumacher. Warner Brothers, 1998.

Tin Drum, The [*Blechtrommel, Die*]. Bioskop Film, Franz Seitz Filmprod., Hallelujah Films, Argos Films, Artemis Productions, 1979.

To Kill a Mockingbird. Dir. Robert Mulligan. Universal, 1962.

To Sir With Love. Dir. James Clavell. Columbia, 1967.

Tom Brown's Schooldays. Dir. Gordon Parry. Brian Desmond Hurst, 1951.

Tom Sawyer. Dir. John Cromwell. Paramount Public Corporation, 1930.

Tommy. Dir. Ken Russell. Hemdale (UK), 1975.

Tomorrow Never Dies. Dir. Roger Spottiswoode. United Artists, Danjaq, Eon, 1997.

Top Gun. Dir. Tony Scott. Paramount, 1986.

Top Hat. Dir. Mark Sandrich. RKO Radio Pictures, 1935.

Toy Soldiers. Dir. Daniel Petrie, Jr. TriStar Pictures, 1991.

Toy Story. Dir. John Lasseter. Walt Disney Productions, Pixar, 1995.

Tramp, The. Dir. Charlie Chaplin. The Essanay Film Manufacturing Company, 1915.

Trip to the Moon, A. Dir. George Méliès. Star, 1902.

Treasure Island. Dir. Victor Fleming. Perf. Jackie Cooper. MGM, 1934.

Treasure Island. Dir. Byron Haskin. Walt Disney Productions, 1950.

Truman Show, The. Dir. Peter Weir. Paramount, 1998.

Tuck Everlasting. Dir. Frederick King Keller. Howard Kling, 1980.

20,000 Leagues Under the Sea. Dir. Richard Fleischer. Walt Disney Productions, 1954.

Two Loves. 1961. Dir. Charles Walters. MGM, 1961.

2001: A Space Odyssey. Dir. Stanley Kubrick. MGM, 1968.

Up the Down Staircase. Dir. Robert Mulligan. Warners-7 Arts, 1967

Victory Through Air Power. Dir. James Algar and Clyde Geronimi. Walt Disney Productions, 1943.

Village of the Damned. Dir. Wolf Rilla. MGM, 1960.

Virtuosity. Dir. Brett Leonard. Paramount, 1995.

Walkabout. Dir. Nicolas Roeg. 20th Century Fox, 1971.

WarGames. Dir. John Badham. MGM, 1983.

Warriors of Virtue. Dir. Ronny Yu. Law Bros., Ent., China Film Co Prod., Corp, 1997.

Watering the Gardener. [Arroseur arrosé, L']. Dir. Louis Lumière. Gaumont, 1895.

Wee Willie Winkie. Dir. John Ford. 20th Century Fox, 1937.
Welcome to the Dollhouse. Dir. Todd Solondz. Suburban Pictures, 1996.
West Side Story. Dir. Jerome Robbins and Robert Wise. United Artists, Beta Prod., Mirisch Films, Seven Arts Prod (UK), 1961.
What Dreams May Come. Dir. Vincent Ward. Metafilmics, Interscope, PolyGram Filmed Ent., 1998.
What's Eating Gilbert Grape? Dir. Lasse Hallström. J & M Ent., Paramount, 1993.
When Harry Met Sally. Dir. Rob Reiner. Castle Rock, Columbia, Nelson Ent., 1989.
Where Are My Children? Dir. Lois Weber. Universal, 1916.
Where Is My Friend's Home? [*Khane ye Doust Kodjast?*]. Dir. Abbas Kiarostami. Farabi Cinema Foundation, 1987.
Where the North Begins. Dir. Chester M. Franklin. Warner Brothers, 1923.
White Dog. Dir. Samuel Fuller. Edgar J. Scherick, 1982.
White Line, The [Cuori senza frontiere]. Dir. Luigi Zampa. Lux Film, 1949.
Why? Eclair Prod., 1913.
Wild Boys of the Road. Dir. William A. Wellman. Warner Brothers, 1933.
Wild Child, The [L'enfant Sauvage]. Dir. François Truffaut. Carrosse, Artistes, 1969.
Willy Wonka and the Chocolate Factory. Dir. Mel Stuart. Warner Bros., Quaker Oats Co., 1971.
Window, The. Dir. Ted Tetzlaff. RKO Radio Pictures Inc., 1949.
Without Pity. Dir. Alberto Lattuada. Lux Film, 1948.
Wizard of Oz, The. Dir. Victor Fleming. Perf. Judy Garland. MGM, 1939.
Woman in the Window, The. Dir. Fritz Lang. International Pictures, 1945.
World Apart, A. Dir. Chris Menges. Working Title Films, British Screen (UK), Hippo Films Zimbabwe, 1988.
World of Apu, The [Apur Sansar]. Dir. Satyajit Ray. Satyajit Ray Prod., 1959.
Wuthering Heights. Dir. William Wyler. MGM, 1939.
Yearling, The. Dir. Clarence Brown. MGM, 1946.
You Lucky Dog. Dir. Paul Schneider. Walt Disney Productions, 1998.
Young Mr. Lincoln. Dir. John Ford. Fox, 1939.
Zazie [Zazie dans le metro]. Dir. Louis Malle. Nouvelle Editions de Films (Fr), 1960.

Works Cited

Abrams, M. H. *A Glossary of Literary Terms.* 4th ed. New York: Holt, Rinehart and Winston, 1981.

Abramowitz, Rachel. "How do you solve a problem like *Lolita?*" *Premiere* Sept. 1997: 80+.

Addams, Jane. *The Spirit of Youth and the City Streets.* New York: Macmillan, 1909.

Agosta, Lucien L. "Pride and Pugilism: The Filmed Versions of *Tom Brown*." Street, *Children's Novels* 1983: 1–14.

Allan, Cynthia. "*Homeward Bound:* The Incredible Journey of Mass Culture." Rollin: 1993. 153–166.

Althusser, Louis. "Ideology and Ideological State Apparatuses (Notes Towards an Investigation January–April 1969)." *Lenin and Philosophy and Other Essays.* Trans. Ben Brewer. New York: Monthly Review, 1971. 127–186.

"America's Dirty Little Secret: We Hate Kids." Editorial. *Mother Jones* May/June 1991.

Andrew, Dudley. *Concepts in Film Theory.* Oxford: Oxford University Press, 1984.

Arendt, Hannah. *The Origins of Totalitarianism.* New York: Harcourt and Brace, 1951.

Armes, Roy. *A Critical History of the British Cinema.* New York: Oxford University Press, 1978.

Arora, Poonam. "The Production of Third World Subjects for First World Consumption." Carson and Dittmar: 1994. 293–304.

Arthur, Paul. "Film Noir as Primal Screen." *Film Comment* Sept.–Oct. 1996: 77–79.

Ash, Russell. *The Top 19 of Everything.* London: Houghton Miffin, 1996.

Baker, Christopher P. "Prostitution: Child Chattel Lure Tourists for Sex." *National Times* Aug.–Sept. 1995: 8–10.

Barrett, Michèle. *Women's Oppression Today: The Marxist/Feminist Encounter.* London: Verso, 1988.

Barthes, Roland. *S/Z.* Trans. Richard Howard. New York: Farrar, 1970.

Bazalgette, Cary, and David Buckingham. Eds. *In Front of the Children: Screen Entertainment for the Young.* London: BFI, 1995.

———. "The Invisible Audience." Bazalgette and Buckingham: 1995. 1–14.

Bazalgette, Cary, and Terry Staples. "Unshrinking the Kids: Children's Cinema and the Family Film." Bazalgette and Buckingham: 1995. 92–108.

Bazin, Andre. "Bicycle Thief." *What Is Cinema? Vol 2.* Trans. Hugh Gray. Berkeley: University of California Press, 1971. 47–60.

Benedict, Ruth. "Continuities and Discontinuities in Cultural Conditioning—1938." *Childhood in Contemporary Cultures.* Eds. Margaret Mead and Martha Wolfenstein. Chicago: University of Chicago Press, 1955: 21–30.

Bennett, George. *The Concept of Empire: From Burke to Atlee, 1747–1947.* London: Adams & Charles Black, 1962.

Bernstein, Michael A. "American Economics and the National Security State, 1941–1953." *Radical History Review* 63 (1995): 8–26.

Bixler, Phyllis. "Continuity and Change in Popular Entertainment." Street, *Children's Novels:* 69–80.

Black, Gregory. *Hollywood Censored: Morality Codes, Catholics, and the Movies.* New York: University of Cambridge Press, 1994.

Black, Shirley Temple. *Child Star: An Autobiography.* New York: Warner, 1989.

Boroughs, Don L., Dan McGraw, and Kevin Whitelaw. "Disney's All Smiles." *U.S. News and World Report* 14 Aug. 1995: 32–46.

Bourget, Jean-Loup. "Social Implications in the Hollywood Genres." *Film Theory and Criticism: Introductory Readings.* Eds. Gerald Mast, Marshall Cohen, and Leo Braudy. 4th ed. New York: Oxford University Press, 1992. 467–474.

Boyden, Jo. *Children of the Cities.* London: Zed Books Ltd., 1991.

Bradley, Ruth. Introduction. By Ruth Bradley. "Children and Film." *Wide Angle: A Quarterly Journal of Film History, Theory, Criticism, and Practice* 166.4 (1994): 1–3.

Bronski, Michael. "Reel Politick: Zeitgeist Peewee." *Z Magazine* Sept. 1991: 64–67.

Brooks, Peter. "Toward Supreme Fictions." *The Child's Part.* Boston: Beacon Press, 1972: 5–14.

Brownlow, Kevin. *Behind the Mask of Innocence. Sex, Violence, Prejudice, Crime: Films of Social Conscience in the Silent Era.* Berkeley: University of California Press, 1990.

Burton-Carvajal, Julianne. "'Surprise Package': Looking Southward With Disney." Smoodin: 131–47.

Butler, Francelia, Bernard Queenan, and Phillip J. Sleeman. Ed. *200 Selected Film Classics For Children Of All Ages.* Springfield, Illinois: Charles C. Thomas, 1984.

Cahiers Du Cinema. Editors. "John Ford's *Young Mr. Lincoln.*" *Cahiers Du Cinema* no. 223 (1970). Rpt. in *Movies and Methods: An Anthology.* Ed. Bill Nichols. Berkeley: University of California Press, 1976: 493–529.

Campbell, Joseph. *The Hero with a Thousand Faces.* 2nd ed. Bolingen Ser. XVII. Princeton, NJ: Princeton University Press, 1968.

Cannon, Damian. Rev. of *Kids,* dir. Larry Clark. *Movie Reviews UK* 1997. <http://www.film.u-net.com/Movies/Reviews/Kids/.html> Online 1 Feb. 2000.

Carson, Diane, Linda Dittmar, and Janice R. Welsch. Introduction. Ed. *Multiple Voices in Feminist Film Criticism.* Minneapolis: University of Minnesota Press, 1994: 1–23.

Case, Christopher. *The Ultimate Movie Thesaurus.* New York: Henry Holt and Co., 1996.

Cawley, Janet. "The Barrymore Curse: Can Drew Beat It?" *Biography* Apr. 1998: 32–37.

Chandler, Suzanne. *Children of Babylon: The Untold Stories of Hollywood's Youngest and Brightest Stars.* Stamford, CT: Longmeadow Press, 1993.

Chase, Donald. "Romancing the Stones: Jack Clayton's *The Innocents.*" *Film Comment* Jan.–Feb. 1998: 68–73.

Chaston, Joel D. "The 'Ozification' of American Children's Fantasy Films." *Beyond the Written Word: Children's Media of the Twentieth Century.* Spec. issue of *Children's Literature Association Quarterly* 22.1 (1997): 13–21.

Chatterjee, Pratap. "Economic Intelligence: Spying for Uncle Sam." *Covert Action Quarterly* Winter 1995–96: 41+.

Chetwynd, Josh, and Andy Seiler. "Top 10 'toons." *USA Today* 20 Nov. 1998: 8E.

Chomsky, Noam, and Edward S. Herman. *Manufacturing Consent: The Political Economy of the Mass Media.* New York: Pantheon, 1988.

Chomsky, Noam. "Intervention in Vietnam and Central America: Parallels and Differences." *The Chomsky Reader.* Ed. James Peck. New York: Pantheon, 1987: 315–38.

Churchill, Ward. *Fantasies of the Master Race: Literature, Cinema, and the Colonization of American Indians.* Boulder, CO: Common Courage Press, 1992.

Cohen, Warren, and Katia Hetter. "Tomorrow's Media Today." *U.S. News and World Report.* 14 Aug. 1995: 47–49.

Comolli, Jean-Luc, and Jean Narboni. "Cinema, Ideology, Criticism." 1969. Rpt. in *Film Theory and Criticism.* Eds. Gerald Most, Marshall Cohen, and Leo Brandy. 4th ed. New York: Oxford University Press, 1992. 682–689.

Coontz, Stephanie. *The Way We Never Were: American Families and the Nostalgia Trap.* New York: Basic Books, 1992.

Corliss, Richard. "The Kids Are Alright." *Time* 15 Mar. 1999: 85.
———. "Queen of the Movies." *Film Comment* Mar.–Apr. 1998: 53–62.
Cox, Carole. "Children's Preferences for Film Form and Technique." *Language Arts* 59.3 (1982): 231–238.
Dassin, Jules. "I'll Always Be an American." Interview with Patrick McGilligan. *Film Comment* 32.6 (1996): 34–48.
Davenport, Tom. "Media Literacy for the Future." Rollin: 195–203.
Dawes, Amy. "Comic Book Heroes Hottest New Stars." *Ann Arbor News* 17 Aug. 1997: E7.
deMause, Lloyd. "The Evolution of Childhood." *The History of Childhood.* Ed. Lloyd deMause. New York: The Psychohistory Press, 1974: 1–73.
Dirks, Nicholas. "Castes of Mind." *Representations* 37 (1992): 56–78.
Deutelbaum, Marshall. "Film Archives: Unexplored Territory," in *Society and Children's Literature: Papers Presented on Research, Social History, and Children's Literature at a Symposium Sponsored by the School of Library Science, Simmons College,* 1976. Ed. James Fraser. Boston: David Godine and ALA, 1978: 169–179.
"Do We Care about Our Kids?" Editorial. *Time* 8 October 1990.
Doane, Mary Ann. "Ideology and the Practice of Sound Editing." *Questions of Cinema.* Ed. Stephen Heath. London: Macmillan, 1981. 47–48.
Eagleton, Terry. *Criticism and Ideology: A Study in Marxist Literary Theory.* London: Verso, NLB, 1976.
———. *Literary Theory: An Introduction.* Minneapolis: University of Minnesota Press, 1983.
Editorial. *Sight and Sound* 5 1936: 18.
Eisenstein, Sergei. "Dickens, Griffith, and the Film Today." 1944. Rpt. in *Film Theory and Criticism: Introductory Readings.* Eds. Gerald Mast, Marshall Cohen, and Leo Brandy. 4th ed. Oxford: Oxford University Press, 1992: 395–402.
Eliot, Marc. *Walt Disney, Hollywood's Dark Prince: A Biography.* Secaucus, NJ: Carol/Birch Lane P, 1993.
Elmer-Dewitt, Philip. "Fighting a Battle by the Book." *Time* 25 Feb. 1991: 34–35.
Elsaesser, Thomas. "Film History as Social History: The Dieterle/Warner Brothers Bio-pic." *Wide Angle: A Film Quarterly of Theory, Criticism, and Practice* 8.2 (1986): 15–31.
Engels, Frederick. *The Origin of the Family, Private Property, and the State.* 1884. New York: Pathfinder Press, 1972.
Erens, Patricia. "A Childhood at the Cinema: Latent Fantasies, the Family Romance, and Juvenile Spectatorship." *Wide Angle* 16:4 (1994): 24–56.
Feuer, Jane. "The Self-Reflexive Musical and the Myth of Entertainment." *Film Theory and Criticism: Introductory Readings.* Eds. Gerald Mast, Marshall Cohen, & Leo Braudy. 4th ed. Oxford: Oxford University Press, 1992: 486–97.

Forman, Henry James. *Our Movie Made Children.* New York: Macmillan, 1935.
Forster, E. M. *Aspects of the Novel.* 1927. Ed. Oliver Stallybrass. Harmondsworth: Penguin, 1979.
Freidman, Steven. "Taking Action Against Disney." *Rethinking Schools* 11:4 (1997): 18–19.
French, Sean. "Diary." *New Statesman & Society* 6 Nov. (1992): 8.
Frye, Northrop. *Anatomy of Criticism: Four Essays.* New Jersey: Princeton University Press, 1957.
Gaffney, Maureen. "Evaluating Attitude: Analyzing Point of View and Tone in Film Adaptations of Literature." *Children's Literature* 9 (1981): 116–125.
Giannetti, Louis. *Understanding Movies.* 4th ed. New Jersey: Prentice Hall, 1987.
Giannetti, Louis, and Scott Eyman. *Flashback: A Brief History of Film.* 2nd ed. New Jersey: Prentice Hall, 1991.
Giroux, Henry. "Disney, Southern Baptists, and Children's Culture: The Magic Kingdom as Sodom and Gomorrah?" *Z Magazine* Sept. 1997: 47–51.
———. "Beyond the Politics of Innocence: Memory and Pedagogy in the Wonderful World of Disney." *Socialist Review* 23:2 (1993): 79–107.
———. "Race, Pedagogy, and Whiteness in *Dangerous Minds.*" *Cinéaste* 22:4 1997: 46–49.
Gledhill, Christine. "Image and Voice: Approaches to Marxist-Feminist Criticism." Carson and Dittmar 1994: 109–123.
Goldstein, Ruth M., and Edith Zornow. *The Screen Image of Youth: Movies about Children and Adolescents.* Metuchen, NJ: Scarecrow Press, 1980.
Gomery, Douglas. "Towards an Economic History of the Cinema: The Coming of Sound to Hollywood." *Questions of Cinema.* Ed. Stephen Heath. London: Macmillan, 1981.
———. "Disney's Business History: A Reinterpretation." Smoodin: 71–86.
Greene, Graham. "*Wee Willie Winkie/The Life of Emile Zola.*" 1937. Rev. of *Wee Willie Winkie,* dir. John Ford. Perf. Shirley Temple. *The Graham Greene Reader: Reviews, Essays, Interviews & Film Stories.* Ed. David Parkinson. New York: Theatre Book Publishers, 1995: 233–35.
———. "*Under Two Flags/Captain January.*"1936. Rev. of *Captain January,* dir. David Butler. Perf. Shirley Temple. *Grahame Greene on Film: Collected Film Criticism 1935–1940.* Ed. John Russell Taylor. New York: Simon, 1972: 127–128.
"Growing Up Scared." Editorial. *Newsweek* 10 Jan. 1994.
Gutierrez, Maria Elena. "Children Like Me—Where Do We Fit In?" *Media Studies Journal* 8.4 (1994): 85–9.
Haas, Susan D. "'Snow White' poisons kids' self-esteem." *Detroit News* 18 July 1993: 1B+.
Hardy, Gene. "More Than a Magic Ring." Street, *Children's Novels:* 1983. 131–40.

Harris, Thomas J. *Children's Live-Action Musical Films.* Jefferson, N.C.: McFarland, 1989.

Hart, John. "'Aliens' arrives in nearly plural-perfect condition." *www.film.com/film-review* 23 Sept. 1986: 1–3. Online. 1 Apr. 1999.

Hartmann, Heidi. "The Unhappy Marriage of Marxism and Feminism: Toward a More Progressive Union." *Women and Revolution: A Discussion of the Unhappy Marriage of Marxism and Feminism.* Ed. Lydia Sargent. Boston: South End Press, 1981: 2–41.

Hastings, Waller A. "Moral Simplification in Disney's *The Little Mermaid.*" *The Lion and the Unicorn* 17 (1993): 83–92.

Hayward, Susan. *Key Concepts in Cinema Studies.* New York: Routledge, 1996.

Healey, Michelle. "Digital Flicks." *USA Today* 10 June. 1999: D1.

Healey, William. *The Individual Delinquent.* Boston: Little, Brown, 1915.

Herman, Edward S. "Low Intensity Class War." *Z Magazine* April 1996: 9–12.

Hiaasen, Carl. *Team Rodent: How Disney Devours the World.* New York: Ballantine, 1998.

Hobbs, Renee. "Teaching Media Literacy-Yo! Are You Hip to This." *Media Studies Journal* 8:4 (1994): 135–45.

Hollindale, Peter. "Ideology and the Children's Book." 1988. *Literature for Children: Contemporary Criticism.* Ed. Peter Hunt. London: Routledge, 1992: 19–40.

Industrial Worker. "Disney contractor fires 4 unionists." July 1997: 9.

Inglis, Fred. "Reading Children's Novels: Notes on the Politics of Literature." *Writers, Critics, and Children: Articles from Children's Literature in Education.* Ed. Geoff Fox et al., New York: Agathon, 1976: 157–73.

"Italian neo-realism." Hayward: 191–4.

Jackson, Kathy Merlock. *Images of Children in American Film: A Sociocultural Analysis.* London: Scarecrow Press, 1986.

Jameson, Fredric. "The Politics of Theory: Ideological Positions in the Postmodern Debate." *Modern Criticism and Theory: A Reader.* Ed. David Lodge. London: Longman, 1988: 373–83.

———. "Metacommentary." *The Ideologies of Theory: Vol 1 Situations of Theory.* Theory and History of Literature, Vol. 48. Minneapolis: University of Minnesota Press, 1988: 3–16.

———. "Periodizing the 60s." *The Ideologies of Theory: Vol 2 Syntax of History.* Theory and History of Literature, Vol. 49. Minneapolis: University of Minnesota Press, 1988: 178–208.

———. "Marxism and Historicism." *The Ideologies of Theory: Vol 2 Syntax:*148–77.

Johnson, William. "Message Movies: Do They Deliver." *Film Comment* 31.3 (1995): 39–45.

Jowett, Garth S., et al. *Children and the Movies: Media Influence and the Payne Fund Controversy.* Cambridge: Cambridge University Press, 1996.

"Jumanji." *Movie Guide:* 337.

Katz, Ephraim. *Film Encyclopedia.* 2nd ed. New York: Harper Collins, 1994.

Kermode, Mark. "Lucifer Rising." *Sight and Sound* July 1998: 6–11.

———. "1980s." *1930–1990: Hollywood Sixty Great Years.* London: Prion-Multimedia Books Ltd., 1985: 560–636.

Kincaid, James R. *Child-Loving: The Erotic Child and Victorian Culture.* New York: Routledge, 1992.

Kincheloe, Joe L. "The New Childhood: Home Alone as a Way of Life." *The Children's Culture Reader.* Ed. Henry Jenkins. New York: New York University Press, 1998: 159–177.

Kipling, Rudyard. *Kim.* Introduction. Edward Said. Harmondsworth: Penguin, 1987.

Kiska, Tim. " 'Springer' rates No. 1 among kids." *Detroit News* 21 Mar. 1998: C1.

Kopkind, Andrew. "The Wider War." Editorial. *The Nation* 4 Feb. 1991: 110–13.

Koppes, Clayton R. and Gregory D. Black. *Hollywood Goes to War: How Politics, Profit, and Propaganda Shaped World War II Movies.* New York: Macmillan, 1987.

Kuhn, Annette. *Women's Pictures: Feminism and Cinema.* 1982. 2nd ed. London: Verso, 1994.

Lapsley, Robert, and Michael Westlake. *Film Theory: An Introduction.* New York: Manchester University Press, 1988.

Lawson, Terry. "Get out the hankies for Iran's sentimental '*Children of Heaven.*' " *Detroit Free Press* 9 Apr. 1999: 6D.

Lehman, Peter. *Defining Cinema.* Ed. New Brunswick: Rutgers University Press, 1997.

Lenin, Vladimir. "Liberal and Marxist Conceptions of the Class Struggle." Marx et al. *On Historical Materialism,*" 457–458.

Leuchtenburg, William. *Franklin D. Roosevelt and the New Deal: 1932–1940.* The New American Nation Ser. New York: Harper and Row, 1963.

Lieberman. David. "Hollywood fare fit for families." *USA Today* 18 Nov. 1997: 6B.

Lowry, Tom, and Thor Valdmanis. "$5.5B deal creates USA's No. 1 HMO." *USA Today* 29 May 1998: B1.

Lukens, Rebecca. *A Critical Handbook of Children's Literature.* 4th ed. New York: Harper Collins, 1990.

Lyons, Jeffrey. *101 Great Movies for Kids.* New York: Simon, 1996.

Macherey, Pierre. *A Theory of Literary Production.* Trans. Geoffrey Wall. New York: Routledge, 1978.

Magid, Ron. "Fruit of the Loons." *Cinescape* April 1996: 46–51.

Martin, Michelle. "Periods, Parody, and Polyphony: Fifty Years of Menstrual Education Through Fiction and Film." *Children's Literature Association Quarterly* 22:1 (1997): 21–29.

Marx, Karl, Frederick Engels, and V. Lenin. *On Historical Materialism: A Collection.* Progress Publishers. Moscow: Progress Publishers, 1972.

Marx, Karl, and Frederick Engels. *Manifesto of the Communist Party.* 1847–48. Marx et al. *On Historical Materialism:* 84–102.

———. *The German Ideology.* 1845–46. Marx et al. *On Historical Materialism* 14–76.

Marx, Karl. "Speech at the Anniversary of the *People's Paper.*" 1856. Marx et al. *On Historical Materialism:* 134–35.

———. *Das Capital.* Vol 1. Introduction. Ernest Mandel. Trans. Ben Fowkes. New York: Vintage Books, 1977.

———. *Theses on Feuebach.* 1888. Marx et al. *On Historical Materialism:* 11–13.

"Mary Poppins." *Movie Guide:* 426.

Mast, Gerald. *A Short History of the Movies.* 4th ed. London: Macmillan, 1986.

Matoian, John. "Book to Film: The Process Explained." May, "The Audio-Visual Arts," 17–19.

May, Jill. *Children's Literature and Critical Theory: Reading and Writing for Understanding.* Oxford: Oxford University Press, 1995.

———. "The Audio-Visual Arts and Children's Literature." *Children's Literature Association Quarterly.* 7 (1982): 2–5.

McCartan, Greg. "Disease, hunger stalk Iraq as result of U.S. war, embargo." *The Militant* 7 June. 1991: 1+.

McGill, Larry. "By the Numbers—What Kids Watch." *Media Studies Journal* 8:4 (1994): 95–104.

Mead, Margaret. "Theoretical Settings—1954." *Childhood in Contemporary Cultures.* Eds. Margaret Mead and Martha Wolfenstein. Chicago: University of Chicago Press, 1955: 3–20.

Mellen, Joan, "The Mae West Nobody Knows." *Film Theory and Criticism: Introductory Readings.* Eds. Gerald Mast, Marshall Cohen, and Leo Brandy. 4th ed. New York: Oxford University Press, 1992. 646–653.

Menand, Louis. "Hollywood's Trap." *New York Review of Books.* 19 Sept. 1996, 4+.

Mepham, John. "The Theory of Ideology in *Capital.*" *Ideology.* Ed. Terry Eagleton. Longman: London, 1994: 211–237.

Metz, Christian. *Film Language: A Semiotics of the Cinema.* Trans. Michael Taylor. Chicago: University of Chicago Press, 1974.

Miller, Mark Crispin. "Free the Media." *The Nation* 3 June 1996: 9–12.

Moebius, William. "Introduction to Picturebook Codes." 1986. *Children's Literature: The Development of Criticism.* Ed. Peter Hunt. London: Routledge, 1990: 131–47.

Moi, Toril. *Sexual/Textual Politics: Feminist Literary Theory.* London: Metheun, 1985.

Moley, Raymond A. *Are We Movie Made?* New York: Macy-Masius, 1938.

Morton, Donald, and Mas'ud Zavarzadeh. Preface. *Theory/Pedagogy/Politics: Texts for Change.* Eds. Donald Morton and Mas'ud Zavarzadeh. Chicago: University of Illinois Press, 1991: vii–x.

Mosley, Leonard. *Disney's World: A Biography.* Lanham, MD: Scarborough House, 1985.

Moss, Geoff. "Metafiction, Illustration, and the Poetics of Children's Literature." *Literature for Children: Contemporary Criticism.* Ed. Peter Hunt. Routledge, 1992: 44–65.

Movie Guide, The. Ed. James Pallot, et al. 3rd ed. New York: Pedigree-Penguin, 1998.

Mulvey, Laura. "Visual Pleasure and Narrative Cinema." 1975. *Film Theory and Criticism: Introductory Readings.* Eds. Mast Gerald, Marshall Cohen and Leo Braudy. 4th ed. New York: Oxford University Press, 1992. 746–57.

Munsterberg, Hugo. *The Photoplay: A Psychological Study.* New York: D. Appleton & Co., 1916.

Musser, Charles. "Work, Ideology, and Chaplin's Tramp." *Resisting Images: Essays on Cinema and History.* Ed. Robert Sklar and Charles Musser. Philadelphia: Temple University Press, 1990. 36–67.

———. *The Emergence of Cinema: the American Screen to 1907.* New York: Macmillan, 1990.

Muybridge, Eadweard. *Complete Human and Animal Locomotion.* 2 vols. New York: Dover, 1979. Rpt. of *Animal Locomotion.* 1887.

National Council of Public Morals. *The Cinema: Its Present Position and Future Possibilities Being the Report of and Chief Evidence Taken by the Cinema Commission of Inquiry Instituted by the National Council of Public Morals.* New York: Arno Press & New York Times, 1970.

National Entertainment State. Chart. *The Nation* 3 June 1996: 23–26.

Navasky, Victor. "The Costs of War." Editorial. *The Nation* Dec. 24, 1990.

Neupert, Richard. "Painting a Plausible World: Disney's Color Prototypes." Smoodin: 106–17.

Nodelman, Perry. *The Pleasures of Children's Literature.* New York: Longman, 1992.

Oak Ridger, The. "National Children's Film Festival has entry forms for kids." 12/11/98. The Oak Ridger Online. *www.oakridger.com/stories* 4/9/99.

Orwell, George. "Rudyard Kipling." *A Collection of Essays.* Garden City, New York: Doubleday, 1954.

Palmer, William J. *The Films of the Eighties: A Social History.* Carbondale and Edwardsville: Southern Illinois University Press, 1993.

Parenti, Michael. *Make-Believe Media: The Politics of Entertainment.* New York: St. Martin's, 1992.

———. *Against Empire.* San Francisco: City Limits, 1995.

Parkinson, David. *History of Film.* London: Thames and Hudson, 1996.

Paul, Lissa. "Enigma Variations: What Feminist Theory Knows About Children's Literature." *Children's Literature: The Development of Criticism.* Ed. Peter Hunt. London: Routledge, 1990: 148–65.

Pena, Richard. "Being There." *Film Comment* May-June 1999: 70–71.

Peters, Cynthia. "The Politics of Media Literacy." *Z Magazine* Feb. 1998: 25–30.

Peters, J. M. L. *Teaching About Film.* Press, Film, Radio and Television in the World Today. New York: Columbia University Press, 1961.

Petersen, Evelyn. "Parents get animated over Disney violence, sexism." *Detroit Free Press* 3 Feb. 1998: D1.

Pewewardy, Cornel. "Why One Can't Ignore *Pocahontas.*" *Rethinking Schools* 10:1 (1995): 19.

Phillips, Jerry, and Ian Wojcik-Andrews. "Telling Tales to Children: The Pedagogy of Empire in MGM's *Kim* and Disney's *Alladin.*" *The Lion and the Unicorn* 20 (1996): 66–90.

Puig, Claudia. "Little Girl Power in Hollywood." *USA Today* 29 July. (1998): D1–2.

Quart, Barbara. *Women Directors: The Emergence of a New Cinema.* New York: Praeger, 1988.

Quart, Leonard. "A Second Look." *Cineaste* XXI.3 (1995): 55–57.

Ray, Robert B. *A Certain Tendency of the Hollywood Cinema, 1930–1980.* New Jersey: Princeton University Press, 1985.

Rhodes, Anthony. *Propaganda: The Art of Persuasion in World War II.* Ed. Victor Margolin. Secaucus, NJ: The Wellfleet Press, 1987.

Rollin, Lucy. Ed. *The Antic Art: Enhancing Children's Literary Experiences Through Film and Video.* Fort Atkinson, Wisconsin: Highsmith Press, 1993.

Rosaldo, Renato. "Imperialist Nostalgia." *Culture and Truth: The Remaking of Social Analysis.* Boston: Beacon Press, 1989: 68–87.

Rose, Jacqueline. 1984. *The Case of* Peter Pan *or The Impossibility of Children's Fiction.* Philadelphia: University Pennsylvania Press, 1993.

Rushdie, Salman. *Haroun and the Sea of Stories.* London: Granta, 1990.

Sachs, Aaron. "The Last Commodity: Child Prostitution in the Developing World," *World Watch* July/Aug. 1994: 24–30.

Said, Edward. Introduction. Rudyard Kipling. *Kim.* Harmondsworth: Penguin, 1987. Macmillan 1901.

Sayers, Frances Clarke. "Walt Disney Accused." Interview with Charles M. Weisenberg. *The Horn Book Magazine.* XLI (1965): 602–11.

Schrader, Paul. "Notes on Film Noir." *Film Comment* sp. (1972). Rpt. in *Film Noir Reader.* Ed. Alain Silver and James Ursini. New York: Limelight, 1996. 53–64.

Schindel, Morton. "Working With Picture Book Artists in Adapting Their Work . . . From Page to Screen." May, "The Audio-Visual Arts," 23–25.

Scott, Sophfronia. "Alone Again?" *Time* 25 Feb. 1991: 79.

Seaman, Barrett, and Ron Stodghill II. "The Daimler-Chrysler Deal: Here Comes the Road Test." *Time* 18 May (1998): 66–69.

Seiter, Ellen. "Survival Tale and Feminist Parable." Street, *Children's Novels:* 182–191.

Shakespeare, William. *Macbeth. The Complete Signet Classic Shakespeare.* Ed. Sylvan Barnet. New York: Harcourt, 1972. 1233–1261.

———. *Othello. The Complete Signet Classic Shakespeare.* Ed. Sylvan Barnet. New York: Harcourt, 1972. 1096–1136.

Shalom, Stephen Rosskamm. *Imperial Alibis: Rationalizing U.S. Intervention After the Cold War.* Boston: South End Press, 1993.

Shipman, David. *The Story of Cinema: A Complete Narrative History from the Beginnings to the Present.* New York: St Martin's, 1982.

Silver, Alain. Introduction. *Film Noir: A Reader.* Ed. Alain Silver and James Ursini. New York: Limelight Editions, 1996. 3–16.

Sinyard, Neil. *Children in the Movies.* New York: St. Martin's, 1992.

Sklar, Holly. "Upsized CEOs." *Z Magazine* June 1996: 32–35.

———. "Boom Times for Billionaires." *Z Magazine* November 1997: 32–37.

Smoodin, Eric. Introduction. "How to Read Walt Disney." *Disney Discourse: Producing The Magic Kingdom.* New York: Routledge, 1994: 1–20.

Snead, James. *White Screens Black Images: Hollywood from the Dark Side.* Eds. Colin MacCabe and Cornel West. New York: Routledge, 1994.

Solomon, Charles. *The Disney That Never Was.* New York: Hyperion, 1995.

Stahl, J. D. "Media Adaptations of Children's Literature: The Brave New Genre." May, "The Audio-Visual Arts," 5–9.

Stark, Susan. "Australian's 'Truman Show' takes Carrey in new direction." *Detroit News* 30 May. 1998: C: 1–2.

Staples, Terry. *All Pals Together: The Story of Children's Cinema.* Edinburgh: Edinburgh University Press, 1997.

Stephens, Ben. "*Pee-Wee*'s Big Adventure." Rev. of *Pee-Wee's Big Adventure,* dir. Tim Burton. *www.imdb.com. www.eusa.ed.ac.uk.* 1996–97. Online. 6/18/99.

Storck, Henri. *The Entertainment Film for Juvenile Audiences.* Paris: UNESCO, 1950.

Strassel, Kimberley A. "If There's Something Rotten in Denmark, Mickey Denies All Guilt." *Wall Street Journal* 12 Jan. 1999: A8+.

Street, Douglas. Introduction. Ed. *Children's Novels and the Movies.* New York: Frederick Ungar Publishing Co, 1983. xiii–xxiv.

———. "Movies Kids Like: Current Trends in Juvenile Taste in Cinema." *Children's Literature Association Quarterly* 7 (1982): 12–14.

———. "An Overview of Commercial Filmic Adaptation of Children's Fiction." *Children's Literature Association Quarterly* 7 (1982): 13–17.

Streisand, Betsy. "Disney's Lion King." *U.S. News and World Report* 14 Aug. 1995: 46.

Studio Briefing #2. "Lucas: It's Just a Kids' Movie." *Internet Movie Data Base. www.imdb.com.* Online. 12 May 1999.

Suleri, Sara. *The Rhetoric of English India.* Chicago: University of Chicago Press, 1992.

Sun, Chyng Feng. "*Mulan*'s Mixed Messages.' *Rethinking Schools* 13:1 (1998): 18.

Taylor, John Russell. "1940s." *1930–1990. Hollywood: Sixty Great Years.* London: Prion, 1992: 122–230.

Temple, Michael. Rev. of *Ponette,* dir. Jacques Doillon. *Sight and Sound* July 1998: 51.

Thomas, Bob. *Disney's Art of Animation: From Mickey Mouse to Beauty and the Beast.* New York: Hyperion, 1991.

Turner, Adrian. "1950s." *1930–1990. Hollywood: Sixty Great Years.* London: Prion, 1992: 232–75.

Veeser, Aram H. Ed. *The New Historicism.* New York: Routledge, 1989.

Viacom. <http://ww.viacom.com.html>

Wallace, Amy. "Film Studios find PG-13 can be golden." *Ann Arbor News* 12 Oct. 1997: E2.

Walsh, William. *Indian Literature in English.* New York: Longman, 1990.

Wartella, Ellen. "Electronic Childhood." *Media Studies Journal* 8:4 (1994): 33–43.

Watkins, Tony. "Cultural Studies, New Historicism and Children's Literature." *Literature for Children: Contemporary Criticism.* Ed. Peter Hunt. New York: Routledge, 1992: 173–95.

Watson, Russell, and Corie Brown. "The 100 Best of 100 Years." *Newsweek Extra* (See ms 236.) Summer 1998: 17–20.

Watt, Ian. *The Rise of the Novel: Studies in Defoe, Richardson and Fielding.* Berkeley: University of California Press, 1957.

Watts, Steven. *The Magic Kingdom: Walt Disney and the American Way of Life.* New York: Houghton. Mifflin, 1997.

Welkos, Robert. "To Japan, 'Lion King' has a familiar ring." *Detroit Free Press* 3 Feb. 1997: D1.

White, Susan. "Split Skins: Female Agency and Bodily Mutilation in *The Little Mermaid.*" *Film Theory Goes to the Movies.* Ed. Collins, Jim, Hilary Radner, and Ava Preacher Collins. New York: Routledge, 1993: 182–95.

Whitley, David. "Reality in Boxes: Children's Perception of Television Narratives." *Potent Fictions: Children's Literacy and the Challenge of Popular Culture.* Ed. Mary Hilton. New York: Routledge, 1996: 47–67.

Williams, Linda. *Hard Core: Power, Pleasure, and the "Frenzy of the Visible."* Berkeley: University of California Press, 1989.

Williams, Raymond. *Marxism and Literature.* New York: Oxford University Press, 1977.

Williams, Walter L. "American Imperialism and the Indians." *Indians in American History.* Ed. Frederick E. Hoxie. Arlington Heights, Illinois: Harlan Davidson, Inc: 231–49.

Wojcik-Andrews, Ian. "The Politics of Children's Films." Rollin: 217–29.

Wolf, Virginia L. "Psychology and Magic: Evocative Blend or a Melodramatic Patchwork." Street, *Children's Novels:* 121–31.

Wolfenstein, Martha. "The Image of the Child in Contemporary Films." Eds. Margaret Mead and Martha Wolfenstein. *Childhood in Contemporary Cultures.* Chicago: University of Chicago Press, 1955: 277–93.

Wondra, Janet. "A Gaze Unbecoming: Schooling the Child for Femininity in *Days of Heaven.*" *Wide Angle* 16.4 (1994): 4–23.

Wood, Robin. *Personal Views: Explorations in Film.* London: Gordon Fraser, 1976.

———. "*Hollywood From Vietnam to Reagan.*" New York: Columbia University Press, 1986.

Wollen, Peter. "Cinema and Technology: An Historical Overview." *Questions of Cinema.* Ed. Stephen Heath. London: Macmillan, 1981: 16–17.

Zierold, Norman. *The Child Stars.* New York: Coward-McCann, Inc., 1965.

Zipes, Jack. *Breaking the Magic Spell: Radical Theories of Folk and Fairy Tales.* New York: Metheun, 1979.

———. "Towards a Theory of the Fairy-Tale Film: The Case of *Pinocchio.*" *The Lion and the Unicorn* 20 (1996): 1–24.

———. "Taking Political Stock: New Theoretical and Critical Approaches to Anglo-American Children's Literature in the 1980s." *The Lion and the Unicorn* 14 (1990): 7–22.

Zonn, Leo E., and Stuart C. Aitken. "Of Pelicans and Men: Symbolic Landscapes, Gender, and Australia's *Storm Boy.*" *Place, Power, Situation, and Spectacle: A Geography of Film.* Ed. Stuart C. Aitken and Leo E. Zonn. Maryland: Rowman and Littlefield Publishers, Inc., 1994: 137–159.

Index